T0648494

William Moore, Jr.

Lonnie H. Wagstaff

BLACK
EDUCATORS
IN WHITE
COLLEGES

Jossey-Bass Publishers
San Francisco • Washington • London • 1974

BLACK EDUCATORS IN WHITE COLLEGES
Progress and Prospects
by William Moore, Jr., and Lonnie H. Wagstaff

Copyright © 1974 by: Jossey-Bass, Inc., Publishers
615 Montgomery Street
San Francisco, California 94111
&
Jossey-Bass Limited
3 Henrietta Street
London WC2E 8LU

Library of Congress Catalogue Card Number LC 73-12066

International Standard Book Number ISBN 0-87589-206-X

Manufactured in the United States of America

JACKET DESIGN BY WILLI BAUM

FIRST EDITION

Code 7346

The Jossey-Bass
Series in Higher Education

JOHN E. ROUECHE, *University of Texas*
Special Advisor, Community and Junior Colleges

PREFACE

*I*n the last few years we have seen a flood-tide of professional writing on two related subjects: the entry of women into higher education as faculty members and administrators, and the new activism of black students. Hundreds of books, articles, monographs, and reports, as well as various symposiums and workshops, have publicized the demands of women petitioning for professional access to colleges and universities, and for equal treatment within them. The same sources have publicized the demands of black students for open admissions, Black Studies, increased relevance in the curriculum, financial assistance, and identification models from their own ethnic group —all legitimate demands that cut against the grain of tradition in higher education. But while the concerns of these two groups have been widely publicized, little has been said in print about the recruitment, selection, hiring, and professional activities of black educators in predominantly white colleges and universities. (By *predominantly white institutions,* we mean postsecondary schools in which the student, faculty, and administrative populations are each over 50 percent Caucasian.)

Very little is known about the black faculty member or administrator. The academic community does not know, for example, if black faculty members and administrators differ significantly from white ones on predominantly white campuses. While it is true that we have some hard statistical data on discipline, age, advanced degrees, and socioeconomic classification, there has been no systematic information on the perceptions and behavior of black faculty members and administrators in white colleges. Perhaps this is because their behavior has not been as militant, nor their situation as well publicized, as that of other groups seeking professional entry into colleges and universities. Perhaps it is benign neglect. Perhaps because their concerns have not hardened into "nonnegotiable" demands or resulted in confrontation, scholars have not deemed them worthy of investigation.

The presence of black educators in predominantly white colleges and universities can be seen as an immense problem or an unprecedented opportunity; from either point of view, it raises some significant questions. For example, how do you locate and recruit black faculty members and administrators? Which type of institution has attracted the most black professionals—community colleges or senior institutions? What can a college expect when black educators join the staff? What unique contributions can black scholars make? Are black administrators effective? What about black women in the community of scholars? What do black professors think about research and publication? How do they feel about their white colleagues? Are credentials important to them? Do they demand more from white students than they do from black students? How do they feel about Black Studies? What can a black considering higher education as a career expect when he petitions the academic community? Are blacks in a seller's market, as some reports indicate? How are black educators treated in predominantly white institutions? Are they consumed with hostility and seized with rage? Is their presence an indication of reverse discrimination? What do they think about affirmative action? And the question which is asked most of all: are they qualified? To seek the answers, we contacted six thousand black educators in two-year and four-year colleges across the nation. More than three thousand of them responded.

Some of the responses were startling and unexpected. Many

addressed themselves to speculations which they proceeded to validate as fact or to confirm as hearsay. For example, because of the recent visibility of black professionals in higher education, it has been speculated that truly significant progress has been made in the recruitment, selection, and hiring of blacks and the assigning of them to positions of responsibility commensurate with their education and training. Is this myth or reality? Our respondents (as well as the presidents of their colleges) gave us the answer.

Some people assume that the presence of black educators in predominantly white colleges is an idea whose time has come. If this is a valid assumption, the academic community faces a new challenge. A whole new set of responses may be necessary. Already the professoriate is beginning to be viewed from a new perspective. Its members are acting out a new role and projecting a new image. Black educators have also discovered many things about the academic community that are new to them, and this knowledge has caused them to respond in unique ways. The interaction of the white professoriate with the new black educators, if used creatively, could produce some profound new dimensions in higher education; if it is misused, it could cause wounds that will take generations to heal.

This book is discriminatory, biased, and prescriptive. It is discriminatory because it focuses primarily on black educators. It is biased because it reports and discusses only the perceptions of black faculty members and administrators in predominantly white colleges and universities. It is prescriptive, we hope, because it provides information and techniques that may be used by the academic community in attempting to relate to its newest members, black educators.

We believe that this book should be required reading for presidents, deans, department heads, and faculty members in predominantly white colleges and universities as they recruit and interact with black educators. It is not a guide for blacks or whites, but a compendium for both. Nor is it an inflexible prescription for change. Rather, it is an attempt to sensitize the reader to the problems and prospects of black educators as they petition for access and acceptance into the larger world of higher education; and it is an attempt to demonstrate how the academic community thus far has responded to that petition. We have no desire to stir up sound and fury, but the subject itself is a volatile one, and emotions will inevitably break through.

Every volume is born in debt, and this one is no exception. We are indebted to the Mershon Center for Education in National Security and the Research Committee of the College of Education, both of The Ohio State University, for providing us with financial support to carry out our investigation. The funds were provided without prescription. In the end, however, it is the work of people that makes an achievement possible. Although some of those who helped us had titles such as research associates, they really worked like laborers, handling boxes of questionnaires, stuffing envelopes, counting, sorting, and stamping; they often ate their lunches on the run, gave up their spare time, and left their families to work with us evenings, Saturdays, and Sundays. Their names are appropriate here: Elvalee Banks, William Cofield, Ethel Lineberger, Ronald McFadden, and Charles McNair. We are also particularly indebted to Jill Hake, Linda Irwin, Bonita Williams, and Ann Yurco, who worked as our typists and secretaries. Racially, our assistants were black, white, and "other." More important, they were good human beings. Finally, this book owes its greatest debt to the three thousand two hundred and twenty-eight black men and women who took time from their busy schedules to answer our questions and complete our questionnaire. To them we extend our profound thanks.

Columbus, Ohio   WILLIAM MOORE, JR.
January 1974   LONNIE H. WAGSTAFF

CONTENTS

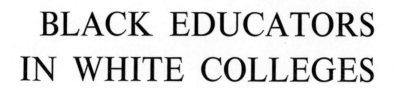

BLACK EDUCATORS IN WHITE COLLEGES

Progress and Prospects

Chapter One

•••••••••••••••••••••••
•••••••••••••••••••••••
•••••••••••••••••••••••

ALIEN IN THE
PROMISED LAND

•••••••••••••••••••••••
•••••••••••••••••••••••
•••••••••••••••••••••••

*M*ore than three thousand black educators, men and women, from hundreds of colleges in the United States, have been in contact with us.* Militants and moderates, traditionalists and innovators, separatists and integrationists have shared their opinions with us. We have found among them activists in Brooks Brothers suits, pacifists in dashikis, and persons of all ages, political persuasions, and economic backgrounds. We have heard from administrators, professors, counselors, and others on the campuses of two-year colleges and four-year colleges, some of them public, some of them private. Some of them have changed their surnames, or "slave names," from Smith, Jones, and Jackson to names of African origin.† Others have discarded their biblical

---

* The distribution by sex was 2136 men and 1073 women (19 respondents did not report sex); total respondents, 3228. Of the men, 604 were from two-year colleges and 1532 from four-year colleges. Of the women, 440 were from two-year colleges and 633 from four-year colleges.

† One's name has unique historical roots for blacks. The naming ceremony of certain African tribes, the Dogon for example, was a very important exercise which had lifelong significance for the individual. A member of that tribe could not become a part of the society if he had not taken part in the naming ceremony.

1

names of Andrew, James, and Sara for names from other religious traditions. These men and women indicated that they are of all faiths, and of no faith. When we asked them to report how they perceive themselves in predominantly white educational institutions, they did not respond simply and solely as long-suffering advocates of racial betterment. But in stating their perceptions they have done much to expose the deep intransigence, the massive resistance in the academic community concerning the recruitment, hiring, and promotion of black faculty members and administrators. And—if their perceptions are correct—they have dramatized two things. The first is discrimination, the extent to which the academic community will go to evade the crucial issue of providing equal opportunity employment to minorities and women. The second is racism, that great American tattoo that even the academicians, with all of their proclaimed scholarly objectivity, cannot remove.

Our respondents may not always perceive things the way things really are. In some cases conditions are worse than they are perceived to be, and in other cases they are better. To the pure researcher, the responses of our subjects may be taken as impersonal, mechanical, and problematic, but to those who must work with these educators daily, their answers should be taken personally, psychologically, and prescriptively.

In spite of the contrasts and contradictions in the answers we received, there is one perception in which we did not find any significant disagreement among our respondents, and it must be made explicitly clear from the outset: *A black educator in a predominantly white college or university perceives himself as an alien.* He is an alien first of all because he *is* black. To be black in any major institution in America is to be different. And when one looks different, he is looked upon differently.

Most black professionals who are now on white campuses have "paid their dues," "picked themselves up by their bootstraps," and made sure that they were *qualified* as demanded by their white colleagues. They sacrificed, attended college, studied hard, were appropriately penitent when accused of some minor infraction of the rules, and fulfilled all of the other prerequisites for entry into the academic community. Still they consider themselves aliens. They find themselves covertly sizing up their powerful white colleagues as real enemies, seeing in the eyes of their fellow aliens the same loneliness and obscurity they feel, and waiting, always waiting, for that inevitable moment when another white colleague will confirm the ancient suspicion of racism. In a sense, it is a tragedy to be so calibrated that one does not trust one's colleagues. But so ingrained is the suspicion and so real the past inequities that when a black does find a white who cares about him and respects him, it is a trauma for him. The skeptic must stand there, shocked, not knowing what to do with his stockpile of preconceived resentment.

To say that blacks feel themselves alien in a predominantly white institution is not an unsubstantiated claim. Kent Mommsen found (1972a) that 94 percent of the black faculty members in white colleges and universities believed that racial discrimination was existent with regard to their hiring. Our own findings support Mommsen's data: only 5.5 percent of our sample did not view discrimination as a problem in their hiring. If such a high percentage of blacks have this perception of discrimination and its implied racism in their institutions, it seems a reasonable assumption that these persons feel alienated and isolated in the institutions which they serve.

To many blacks, higher education was perceived as the promised land. In reality, they found it to be a fortress—almost impenetrable to all but Caucasian males. Publicly, some blacks continue to affirm their former perception, but in private they admit that higher education is different from what they thought it would be. They are aware that the practices of higher education do not fit with the image of it. They now know that they cannot fit easily into a structure largely based on their own exclusion. Or, as one respondent has said, "We find ourselves compelled to help maintain a structure that we weren't meant to share. So here I am—drinking to the system's health, while I lose my own." Some blacks are critical, even hostile, as they appraise higher education. Those who are most critical say that the academic community is decadent, its interests artificial, its standards meretricious, and its defenses palpably vulnerable. Some do not attack it but instead indicate that they regard its continued elitism and historical pretensions as discriminatory and anachronistic; they talk about its inevitable collapse with ironic detachment.

Such attitudes are understandable when we look into the present state of affairs of black educators in predominantly white institutions of higher education. It is more than coincidence that the number of black educators is small, they are awarded the lowest academic ranks (17 percent of our respondents held academic rank above the assistant professorship*), their positions are the most poorly defined, and their jobs are the least secure. This is true in both two-year and four-year colleges. Blacks are acutely aware of this situation and frequently petition for affirmative action and other means to change it.

Ironically, white faculty members and administrators often attack affirmative action plans as discriminatory. They maintain that such plans violate the rights of whites by establishing preferential treatment for the previously excluded blacks. Blacks, on the other hand, have an immediate response to this attack. They point out that white faculties and administrators have far too long enjoyed an advantage of their own. This advantage was based on the discriminatory exclusion of nonwhites. They postulate, therefore, that what is lost to the white academicians is not a right but an expectation of benefits coming from illegal practices, acts, and systems—benefits to which they were never entitled in the first place. They insist that what appears to be special treatment for blacks is not a preference but a remedial measure designed to ameliorate present inequities that have resulted from past discrimination.

In some ways, black educators encounter worse situations in community colleges than in four-year institutions. Of the 1111 two-year colleges listed in the *1972 Directory of Junior Colleges,* 34 are predominantly black. We sent questionnaires to the presidents of the 1077 predominantly white ones. Eighty-one percent of the college presidents responded to our survey. Of the 1300 four-year colleges and universities listed in the *Comparative Guide to American Colleges, 5th Edition,* 88 are predominantly black. We submitted our questionnaires to the presidents of the remaining 1212 predominantly white ones, and 74 percent of the presidents or their designees responded. The statistical results of these surveys are shown in Table 1.

Clearly, four-year institutions are hiring a significantly

---

* Considerably lower than the 51 percent found by ACE, August 1973.

Table 1.

NUMERICAL DISTRIBUTION OF BLACK FACULTY MEMBERS
AND ADMINISTRATORS IN TWO-YEAR AND FOUR-YEAR
PREDOMINANTLY WHITE COLLEGES AND UNIVERSITIES

Type of College	F/A	NF/NA	FO	AO	Total
Two-year	236	416	192	28	872
Four-year	439	273	137	43	892
Total	675	686	329	71	1764

F/A—black faculty members and administrators
NF/NA—no black faculty members and no black administrators
FO—black faculty members only
AO—black administrators only

greater percentage of black professionals than two-year colleges.
Almost half (48 percent) of the two-year colleges of this country
have no blacks on their faculties or in their administration. Community colleges are, in reality, the neighborhood schools of higher
education, and their administrators claim (and the society believes)
that the community college is the most democratic of all postsecondary institutions. Where black faculty members and administrators are concerned, however, these claims are false. John
Egerton, staff writer for the Race Relations Information Center in
Nashville, Tennessee, is even more explicit: "The often-repeated
claims of . . . junior colleges that they are 'open-door' institutions
are exaggerated. Exceptions can be found, of course, but on the
whole . . . junior colleges deserve no more pride of accomplishment in this regard than the public colleges and universities—which
is to say, not much at all" (Egerton, 1971).

While community college personnel claim that they enroll
one-third of all black high-school graduates, according to the
Chronicle of Higher Education, May 30, 1972, they have not hired
corresponding ratios of black faculty members and administrators.
We found community colleges located in communities which had as
large as a 40 percent black population with a 60 percent black
enrollment without a single black faculty member or administrator.
Perhaps this is because a disproportionate number of community

colleges are located in rural and suburban areas; urban areas are underserved (Corcoran, 1972, p. 32). Working as consultants to an Iowa community college, for example, we were asked why so few black students from their community attended the local two-year college. The answer seemed obvious to us: the college was located fifteen miles outside the city.

The *Directory of Junior Colleges* does not list the number of faculty and administrators by race (or sex). A designation by race, for example, would immediately show that 95 percent of the faculty members and administrators in two-year colleges are Caucasian (Gleazer, 1973, p. 27). Contrary to the claims of two-year college administrators that "significant progress" has been made in hiring black educators and assigning them to positions of responsibility commensurate with their training and experience, the lone black faculty member, counselor, or administrator is still very common. On eighty-nine of the community college campuses and 73 of the senior college campuses purported to have black faculty members or administrators, only one black person—a faculty member, an administrator, or a counselor—was employed on each of the campuses.

There are other surprises with regard to two-year colleges. While there are twice as many two-year institutions (including branches, vocational and technical institutes as well as private schools) in the State of New York as in the State of Florida (*1972 Junior College Directory*), our data show that for every black who reported working in community colleges in the State of New York, two reported serving as professionals in the State of Florida. In fact, there are almost as many blacks who reported working in the State of Florida (162) as in the states of New Jersey, New York, and Pennsylvania combined (176).

Our data further show that there are five times as many black educators who reported working in two-year colleges in the State of Florida as in all of the New England states combined (Connecticut, Maine, Massachusetts, New Hampshire, Rhode Island, and Vermont). Only the California colleges reported more black staff members than the Florida colleges. In only seven states did 50 or more black educators report working on college staffs (New York 83, Florida 162, North Carolina 55, Illinois 75, Michigan 51, California 196, Washington 52). This is not to say that there are not other states with more than fifty black educators working in postsecondary institutions or that the numbers cited include all blacks working in colleges in these states. The numbers represent the respondents.

Even more startling, more black professionals reported working in the state of California than in *all* the following states combined: the New England states (Connecticut, Maine, Massachusetts, New Hampshire, Rhode Island, and Vermont); the East South Central States (Alabama, Kentucky, Mississippi, Tennessee); the Mountain States (Arizona, Colorado, Idaho, Montana, Nevada, New Mexico, Utah, Wyoming); and the West North Central States (Iowa, Kansas, Minnesota, Missouri, Nebraska, North and South Dakota). This is half of the states (25).

Obviously we are speaking to our data. We do not suggest that we identified every black professional in these states and only slightly more than 50 percent of these we did identify in two-year colleges responded to our questionnaire. Even if we quadrupled the number of our 1054 respondents to 4216, that would only represent 3 percent of the total number of faculty members who work in community colleges.* In short, black educators are not doing too well in two-year colleges. And the picture does not look significantly better in four-year colleges.

The statistics may be dramatic, but they are not as dramatic as the quality and character of conditions for black faculty members and administrators in higher education. Figures and tables alone cannot demonstrate the conflicts and the moral significance of the struggle of black protagonists who were our respondents.

While attitude is the mainspring of racism, conflict is the flywheel. Arguments about the qualifications of black faculty members, about maintaining standards, about Black Studies, about the necessity for affirmative action plans, and about other heated issues in higher education are perceived by our respondents to be mainly arguments that stem from bigotry in the academy.

The comments and observations that we received on this subject compel us to record the general and collective conclusion that racism and discrimination in higher education are so self-

---

* The number 4216 is higher than any known estimate of the number of blacks who work in community colleges.

evident that one must be appalled at the intransigence of educators in denying the reality of these attitudes.

Understandably, conflict has arisen in the academy because the various forms of racism and discrimination in higher education continue to be perceived as the major forces underlying decisions to recruit, select, and hire blacks on previously all-white campuses. Campuses with black Americans exhibit a racial dualism—separate and unequal. Pressures and constraints are nothing new to blacks. But they are shocked to find that even in higher education there is no reprieve from the cultural and social structures that generate discriminatory practices and behavior.

Alienation takes many forms—obscurity, insulation, isolation, and racism with its accompanying inhumanity. Many blacks feel anonymous in predominantly white colleges; they are hidden in small numbers among vast numbers of whites, but mainly they are hidden because of administrative actions and manipulations.

Some administrators attempt to conceal the number of black faculty members and adminstrators they have on their campuses because so few blacks are on their staffs, contrary to the affirmative action guidelines of the federal government with regard to hiring blacks and other minorities, including women. In some cases, identities and numbers are concealed in a grouping of black part-time instructors, personnel on funded projects, and maintenance and cafeteria workers, along with the regularly appointed black professionals (Rafky, 1972). To distinguish between the part-time and support personnel and the professionals would often reveal that there are many more blacks among the former than among the latter. Many of the semiskilled workers have long tenure, while the few faculty members and administrators may be of recent vintage.

Some administrators attempt to hide the presence of blacks on their campuses because they do not want to be accused of recruiting black faculty members and administrators away from predominantly black colleges and universities (Conyers, 1968; Jencks and Riesman, 1968; Poinsett, 1970; Mommsen, 1970). In some cases, to pacify black students, administrators have hired black educators in what the students call *showcase positions*. Students maintain that this strategy, the *politics of imagery*, is the easiest way to buy off their movement, whether it is done consciously or unwittingly. But such symbolic affectations as placing blacks in a front office here and there, and on powerless committees do not appease the students, who see the discrimination and exclusionary tactics in the institutions still reflecting the social realities of society. The students know and resent that some blacks are hidden away in offices and facilities out of the sight of powerful alumni members and other influential white citizens who may be opposed to black professionals and the perceived liberal attitude of white administrators.

We searched nationwide for black faculty members and administrators in predominantly white institutions. The search was a monumental undertaking in itself. The American Council on Education, the American Association of Higher Education, the American Personnel and Guidance Association, and even the black associations we contacted do not maintain such lists, certainly not complete ones. The U. S. Office of Education did not answer our letters.

Some administrators maintain that they do not know of, or are not acquainted with, blacks on their campus; some insist that there is no way to determine this information. This is simply not true. Administrators *always* know the blacks on their campuses. Even if they are not personally acquainted with the blacks, administrators know how many there are, which departments they are in, and how long they have been there. If blacks are on their campuses and they do not know it, then they are irresponsible. With the exception of women, no educator is chosen more carefully, has his performance watched more closely, sees his presence evoke more comment, has his competency under such scrutiny, and has to prove himself more consistently than does the black faculty member or administrator. A California respondent sums up these observations, "Man, from the day we're hired until the day we're retired we are on probation!"

When blacks come onto a college campus too many individual and institutional adjustments are set into motion for administrators to be unaware of their presence. When blacks are around, certain statements become taboo, a different language must often be used in conversation, ethnic jokes must be told only to a selected audience within certain cliques, the popular restauranteur in town must sometimes be alerted, staffs must be briefed, and so on. Routine matters for all new faculty members, such as office space, parking, identification cards, orientation, and housing must be attended to. And it is difficult to see how a faculty member could even be interviewed and sign a contract without the administrators knowing about his race.

Aside from the individual adjustment, institutions have had to establish offices and designate officers to deal with affirmative action procedures. Programs such as Black Studies have often required special administrative actions. Administrators must be apprised of the court cases which have been instituted with regard to hiring and remuneration; they must make adjustments in order to respond when charges have been brought against them. Administrators would be remiss not to be aware of these things and not to take actions and make adjustments in the institution to successfully meet these problems.

It is also common for a black who is touring a campus as a visitor, working as a consultant, invited as a speaker, or applying for a job to be asked if he is acquainted with a specific black on the same campus. If the response is negative—and it usually is—he is likely to be taken to meet that specific black. Visiting blacks are frequently escorted into the kitchen to meet the black cafeteria help and to the custodial quarters to meet the janitorial employees. The typical perfunctory compliments follow: "This is the most important person on the campus," "This place would fold without Chester," and so on. Sheila Rush and Chris Clark have described this phenomenon (1972, p. 35): "When the black . . . speaker at a gathering is a prominent person, whites . . . have found it extremely difficult to resist sharing the eminence of such a great man with all who might benefit from his aura. It has happened, consequently, that house servants, faithful and true hotel employees, and other blacks who serve whites have been summoned forth on such occasions to shake hands and exchange greetings with the famous guest."

Many administrators who do this kind of thing do not understand that sometimes both the visitor and the worker may resent it. During a coffee break at a recent conference, one old matron said to us: "They always parading our people through the kitchen to show how many colored folks they got working here. We proud o' you; but they didn't bring that [Clark] Kerr fellow to the kitchen when he came here t' speak. They ain't got but one person here who ain't in the kitchen and the only one of us who ever stands on the floor of the administration office is the one that's sweeping it. They know what they doin' I guess, they brought you where they got us."

Rush and Clark (1972, p. 35) suggest, "For all of the democratically inclined, let it be noted that there is nothing objectionable or racially offensive about such a practice per se. What is objectionable is its exclusive application to situations where the prominent guest is black."

When you are brought face-to-face with college personnel they do everything possible to make sure that you *are* aware that blacks are working at the college. The same information in writing, however, is more difficult to obtain. Nonetheless, with the aid of many letters, telephone calls, and personal contacts, we were able to gather the elusive data. Some administrators and faculty members attempted to distract us by asking if we identify Arabs and other such persons of dark skin as black when we asked them if they have *blacks* (Afro-Americans, Negroes) on their campuses. When we asked a black administrator, faculty member, student, or clerk for the identical information, using the same means, that person knew immediately without further definition whom we were seeking to identify.

"It is illegal to keep such information," wrote one president who has set up illegal segregated dormitories on his campus to appease black student demands. Another wrote, "We don't want our people studied." Frequently administrators were defensive: "When we find some qualified Negroes, we will hire them." Other campus leaders—and we believe rightfully so—felt that they should get permission from the black educators before their names were released to us. For many two-year and four-year colleges, securing a roster of black professional personnel was not a problem at all. It was a source of pride. They boasted about it in the way a college would identify and boast of a Nobel Prize winner on the staff.

These institutions submitted their directories of black staff by return mail and simply requested a copy of our findings once our investigation was completed.

Some blacks themselves refused to help us identify other blacks on their campuses. Fortunately, we were able to depend upon students for assistance. The leaders of five hundred black student organizations helped us to identify the black educators on their campuses after the administrators on some of the campuses had refused to help. Various chapters of predominantly black fraternities and sororities and other national and local black organizations also gave us some assistance.

Our major source, however, was the black grapevine. We secured names from our personal friends, from old school acquaintances, and from colleagues we met at conferences, in workshops, and in cocktail lounges. We talked to blacks on airplanes, in airports, in barbershops, on tennis courts, at dances, at college orientations, on consulting trips, on speaking engagements, and at every other place where we could find one black who might know the identity of another working in a college or university. Every black carrying an attache case was a target from whom we might seek a name. Public school teachers, our family doctors, dentists, attorneys, and insurance men were all fair game as persons who might supply us with the names of subjects. We also used conference programs which listed the names of the participants, sometimes with accompanying photographs. We looked for the photographs of blacks in daily newspapers, professional journals, school newspapers, college catalogs, yearbooks, and programs of athletic events. We asked speaker bureaus to send us the names of blacks from among whom we might choose a speaker (some day). When our sample was completed we still occasionally found a scrap of paper or a business card with a name on it.

Ultimately, we identified more than six thousand blacks in almost eighteen hundred two-year and four-year colleges and universities. While this number represents slightly more than two blacks per institution, it is still the largest listing ever assembled of blacks in predominantly white higher education institutions. It is an irony that these unsophisticated techniques resulted in as many names as were culled from the preliminary survey questionnaires which we sent to the presidents of 2289 predominantly white colleges and universities listed in the 1972 *Directory of Junior Colleges* and *Comparative Guide to American Colleges,* fifth edition.

Considering the difficulty of assembling this list, it is not surprising that the black faculty member or administrator feels alienated. His own college officials maintain that even when blacks are on campus, their numbers, assignments, and, in many cases, their identities are unknown, or they are used to make up the goals needed to satisfy affirmative action guidelines.

In the last twenty years, more than a dozen researchers have investigated the problems of black educators in predominantly white colleges and universities.* Most of the research has unfortunately fallen into oblivion. The findings from these studies constitute an exposure of the extent to which blacks have been systematically excluded from the faculties and administrative ranks of higher education; such information embarrasses the academic community and forces it to rationalize its behavior. Public distribution of such research "runs contrary to the vested interest of the professoriate. And for obfuscation, foot dragging, and sabotage, when its vested interests are at stake, the professoriate has incomparable gifts" (Hexter, 1969, pp. 60–77). The studies have not had wide distribution in major educational journals; they are primarily in black publications. David Rafky's article, "The Black Professor and Academic Freedom" (1971a, pp. 170–182) is a good example. "Other avenues of publication open to whites are not as available to blacks. The buddy system, for instance, favors whites. When articles for journals or books are commissioned, close friends or associates are often chosen to write them. Since blacks rarely mingle in the social circles of their white peers they are rarely given these chances" (Staples, 1972, pp. 46–47). Manuscripts chosen for publication may be chosen or rejected as much for friendship and political reasons as for their scholarly contribution and relevance to education. Paradoxically, many studies related to what some call

* Atwood, Smith, and Vaughan (1949, pp. 559–567); Bellis (1968, pp. 23–25); Bryant (1969); Brown (1965); Egerton (1968); Greene (1946); Mommsen (1970); Moss (1958, pp. 451–462); Moss and Mercer (1961); Rafky (1971b); Rose (1961, pp. 432–435); Rose (1966, pp. 18–26); Taylor (1947, pp. 369–372); Thompson (1956).

black pathology are not considered "too controversial" to publish (Jensen, 1969; Banfield, 1969).

Those studies that have posited a black pathology complicated our search to establish a roster of black educators. The most studied people in the United States no longer want to be researched. Even black educators who work and reside in black and white communities, while voicing recognition of the need and importance of research, suspect the motives and attitudes of the people who do it, the uses made of it, the profits made from it, and the fact that the participants receive nothing as a reward for their participation, not even a copy of the findings.

An associate professor responded thus: "It seems that questionnaires never cease. Since those of us who complete these forms, those without whom there would be no results, never receive anything out of them (other than the somewhat questionable privilege of being a statistic) and the conductors of the surveys receive money and/or other benefits, it would seem reasonable that at least we could receive the results."

More than two hundred people who wrote to us informed us they would not participate but wanted to know how we got their names and how we knew that they were blacks. We were somewhat aware of the feelings among blacks relative to research, but we had no idea of the level of tensions and the depth of their concerns. We now understand. So intense is the suspicion and so pervasive is the reluctance to participate in more research to picture blacks as the "wretched people in society," as one black writer has put it, that scores of people demanded proof of our identity as blacks before they would agree to complete our questionnaire. We encountered this situation so often that in the cover letter accompanying our research instrument, we assured the respondents that the investigators were black. Even that assurance was in some cases not enough. One of the investigators has the surname Wagstaff, an uncommon one for blacks, evoking suspicion that one of the investigators was of an ethnic group other than black. A Stony Brook respondent asked in refusing to complete his questionnaire, "Is this for the FBI or the CIA?"

A black face alone is no longer the sole criterion to establish creditability in a black community or among black educators.

The people now seem to be aware that some black investigators have exploited them as much as white ones. Some asked if we were the errand boys from the university or if we were doing the research on our own. We have learned that we were investigated by the black grapevine to determine if each of us was, indeed, his own man. We submit that question to them as a referendum.

So general is the feeling of alienation, discrimination, unfairness, anger, and frustration among black educators, that those who did not share unpleasant experiences and felt they were being treated fairly in their jobs also felt the need to apologize for their lack of suspicion and feelings of satisfaction. We think the behavior of both groups has serious implications.

Fear of some kind of reprisal does not appear to be the reason why many black educators are refusing to take part in research. Rather, it is disgust; the research on blacks and their communities has been concentrated almost solely on the so-called black pathology and does not, in any way, portray blacks as living or participating in a healthy environment. Resistance to research is one of the ways in which black educators and the residents of black ghettos are putting the academic community on notice that they will no longer aid and abet the production of research which helps to turn the minds of blacks, especially youths, against themselves and their communities.

Our correspondents say this best in their own words: "I'm sorry but I will lend neither my name nor my support to another study of black people" (Ph.D., New York University).

"Haven't we been researched enough? I didn't know there was anything left to study. The persistent curiosity of these educators invites suspicion of blacks. I simply will not fill out questionnaires" (administrator, University of Massachusetts).

"You know, first it was the slum blacks—the disadvantaged —that was the subject of everybody's study; then Moynihan [1965] and those other so-called experts started on our families; the sociologists have completely prostituted our life style. They have the world thinking that all of our communities are filled with pimps, hustlers, entertainers, and athletes—they don't even point out that we have many complete families, factory workers, and teachers. No, I'm sorry, but I will not permit another professor to take an ego trip at my expense and at the expense of my black brothers" (counselor, Michigan State University).

"About the only thing that has been researched as much as we have is the white rat. I think the rat is running a poor second. No more research for me" (division chairman, Forest Park Community College).

We must admit that some respondents softened their attitudes when they were assured that the investigators were also black.

"When whites do research on blacks, it is not the conclusions at which they arrive but the premise from which they start that I resent. I have been in this business long enough to know that your conclusions usually support your hypotheses. A black brings a different point of view" (assistant professor, Yale University).

"When I read Chapter Ten in that trash Jencks and Riesman wrote [1969], I became convinced of the harm white professors do with their biased speculation and their nondocumented statements. These two men wrote a scathing report on blacks and their colleges using gossip as their source of data. Some of what they wrote might have been the truth but that is not the point. They showed a complete disregard—if not contempt—for scholarly responsibility. It appears that when whites write about black pathology, how they determined it is unimportant. Because of the prestige of these men too many of their statements have face validity. National policies and decisions which affect the lives of millions are often made on the basis of the findings, conclusions, and publications of such men. I would like to see more blacks doing research on blacks. You mean someone we can trust finally decided that we have an opinion and took the time to ask us about it?" (instructor, Broward Community College).

"Black brothers are doing the study? That's different! Our white friends are always studying us; some of them become instant spokesmen for, and experts on, black people. If we must have spokesmen and experts I prefer that they at least come from my frame of reference. Count me in" (assistant professor, University of Michigan).

"More blacks need to do their own research on blacks, or at least, team up with whites so that they can keep the research free of white bias and stereotyping. Whenever this happens, the findings are more positive and sometimes even startling" (professor, Ohio State University).*

A number of black scholars are taking the position of this last respondent. They are maintaining that research on their group should be done by them in order to prevent exploitation and misconception. Andrew Billingsley, a university administrator and sociologist, has been particularly outspoken: "The current ruling elite in social science is largely comprised of white males over forty, [who] should be overthrown" (quoted in Fraser, 1972). This, he maintains, would allow black scholars to "clarify" social science realities. He indicates that the black community has been characterized by a plethora of misconceptions. "Many misconceptions grow out of the values and techniques of the best social scientists in the country."

In another of his publications (1970b, p. 127) Billingsley wrote: "American social scientists are much more American than social and much more social than scientific. They reflect all the prejudice, ignorance, and arrogance which seems to be endemic to Americans of European descent. Furthermore, because of their skills at communication and their acceptance as authorities on race relations, social scientists do even greater damage to the understanding of black[s] . . . than do ordinary citizens."

S. E. and Zella Luria are even more explicit (1970, p. 79): "The social scientists attempt, in principle, to follow the same patterns [as the natural scientists], searching for laws that rule human events and deriving predicting schemes, on the basis of which a social technology may evolve. But here the distinctions are more easily blurred. The perception of social events and their interpretation are deeply influenced by the fact that the social scientist is a part of the society that he studies. Furthermore, experimentation

---

* There is data to support this idea on interracial teams. The interracial team of Susan Harris Ward and John Braun in their study, "Self Esteem and Racial Preference in Black Children." *Journal of Orthopsychiatry*, 1972, found that contrary to all of the previous studies done by whites alone, black children prefer people of their own color to whites. Others have found that when blacks deal with blacks the respondents achieve better. H. G. Canady, D. O. Price, Ruth Searles, and T. F. Pettigrew have found this to be so. See also Peter Wilson, "IQ: The Racial Gap," *Psychology Today* (September 1972), p. 48.

in the affairs of society can seldom be done under the relatively neutral conditions available to the natural scientist since all experimentation involves active involvement in the process of social change. The question of responsibility cannot be separated from the testing of hypothesis: Studying society in a scientific, experimental way means interfering with the course of events. There can hardly be value-free social inquiry and experimentation."

There is little question that this has happened as researchers have studied the black family. Robert B. Hill's research efforts (1972) refute Daniel P. Moynihan's characterization of the black family. There is considerable evidence that the best studies of blacks are by black scholars (Billingsley, 1970b). Few will deny that the works of E. Franklin Frazier, St. C. Drake, Camille Jeffers, Lewis Watts, and Daniel C. Thompson have been outstanding. Nor can it be denied that some whites, such as Robert Coles, Jessie Bernard, and Gunnar Myrdal, have shown insight when dealing with the black community.* Joyce Ladner, another sociologist, reminds the academic community that black sociologists tend to increasingly criticize the way in which white sociologists have handled problems of blacks, indicating that the handling has been in a stereotypical, mythological way (Fraser, 1972; Ladner, 1971). Sociologists, we were told, are constantly looking for a new angle to describe the pathology of a much exploited group. They never move beyond or give a second glance to their timeworn definitions and their statistics of black pathology, which almost always misrepresent the *majority* of blacks in this country. There is little question that the various controversial reports (Moynihan, 1965; Jensen, 1969; and Coleman, 1966; to name a few) have done and continue to do great harm to blacks, other minorities, the powerless, and the alienated who have no way to defend themselves from such scholarly attack.

Joan Baratz concludes (1972): "This state of affairs has resulted in the cry oft-heard in recent months, 'no more research on the poor . . . let the blacks research themselves'."

Although Baratz disagrees with black sociologists who insist that they should do the research in the black community, she does recognize the underlying logic concerning exploitation and lists it

---

* Others include Frazier (1932a, 1932b, 1948, and 1962); Drake (1962); Jeffers (1967); Watts (1964); and W. Thompson (1960).

as follows (1972): "(a) research does not immediately substantially help the large majority of the poor, black community improve their living conditions; (b) doing research is insulting to the community in that it singles out the members of that community and their problems as special; (c) the research findings are insulting in that they portray the differences between the community and the white mainstream, thus justifying the original 'singling out' of the community for research; (d) white social science professionals get paid more to study black people than the black people earn working in the white mainstream; (e) a white bureaucracy makes policy decisions on the basis of such research; therefore, (f) the black community is exploited."

It is because of these feelings that so many people believe blacks should involve themselves in the research on black Americans to give research a black perspective. Preston Wilcox (1970), Jessie J. Johnson (1969), and Darwin T. Turner (1968) support the concept of blacks doing their own research. This concern of black scholars and the charges of black students should not be minimized. Across the country white sociologists who study and specialize in ethnic and race relations have found their motivations and competence publicly challenged by blacks "who claim that only a black can understand the black experience. The antagonism toward these white sociologists has also spread through the black ghettos, making it difficult for them to continue their research" (*Time*, 1972a). Wilson Record of Portland State University in Oregon interviewed one hundred forty of the estimated seven hundred fifty white sociologists specializing in race and ethnic relations on campuses and found that nearly a fourth have abandoned the field of race relations (*Time*, 1972a).

We sympathize with the problems of scholars in their pursuit of knowledge; we, too, encountered great difficulty in identifying persons and gathering data from black Americans. We must, nonetheless, concede that distrust of white researchers by blacks is not ill founded. Some of the most eminent scholars have also been some of the most outstanding racists. Historians such as A. Dunning and J. W. Burgess of Columbia, Albert Bushnell Hart of Harvard, sociologist Howard W. Odum, and social scientist G. Stanley Hall, who founded the psychology laboratory at Johns Hopkins University, are examples (Winston, 1971). "Sociologists, like historians, are learning that much of their past analyses were facile, over-simplified, and at times biased when they dealt with black Americans" (Goldstein, 1971, p. 2). Rhoda Goldstein is a white sociologist who "understands the necessity of allowing black people who have 'lived the life' to write their own interpretations of these social phenomena." Black educators are no longer willing to submit to what they call *deviant perspectives* of blacks, which some white scholars hypothesize in their research. Obviously, most black educators disagree with W. Grier and P. Cobbs (1968), who state "The black intellectual must accept his exclusion from this battle."

Although the blacks we surveyed saw merit in doing research on their own racial group, they also indicated the very real value of collaborating with their white colleagues (20 percent have been asked to coauthor a publication with a white colleague). They were quick to recognize that studies about blacks which reflected their own black bias were as vulnerable to criticism as studies by whites which reflected a white bias. They suggested that when black and white scholars work as teams, each has something to learn from the other. Each has an opportunity to see and appreciate the competence of the other. Each can provide the checks and balances for his counterpart.

Black scholars cite other reasons why interracial research teams can be desirable when blacks are the subjects of research. They point out, for example, that blacks can interpret situations and behaviors of Afro-Americans which whites, regardless of their astuteness, do not appear to understand. They can help white investigators choose and include language in their reports that will not offend blacks. They can help white scholars to understand the value systems, goals, and objectives to which blacks aspire. And it is blacks who, by personal experience and some technical training, are best equipped to understand, articulate, interpret, and prescribe in the area of the black experience and the black community for those who are, or sense that they are, oppressed. A dual perspective —black and white—adds significantly to the academic enterprise. The presence of interracial teams helps to minimize criticism from blacks and whites and balances against what nonwhites call the ingrained habits of researchers.

While many blacks recognize the need for more collaboration, their comments still reflect the depth of the distrust they have of some research and researchers. We have already noted their criticism of sociologists (and psychologists). Although they are aware that these professionals do not possess special wisdom which will allow them to solve the problems of black faculty members, administrators, or blacks generally, they are equally as aware that some sociological and psychological research supports much of the stereotypical behavior attributed to blacks by the majority group. Sociologists are charged with identifying the sole role models of blacks as being social deviants, athletes, and entertainers (Wilcox, 1970), and, by omission, deny that there are factory workers, technicians, accountants, doctors, and attorneys who are models among blacks. Psychologists are rejected for accepting the premise that black students are psychological cripples who possess an ingrained sense of incompetence.

Afro-Americans are not only in conflict with these researchers and their disciplines, but they often function in conflict with other whites and nonwhites. The black administrator or faculty member is frequently marginal in two cultures, one black, one white. He cannot be separated from either. Marginality creates a feeling of nonacceptance, or alienation. The black educator senses this marginality in the colleges from the behavior of blacks and whites and is forced to deal with the dilemmas of the problem.

The black educator must always deal with the blacks. With black students, the relationship can be extremely frustrating. If he behaves in a fashion that is too middle class, black students may reject him; if he disagrees with them, they may threaten reprisals against him; if he chooses to live in a predominantly white neighborhood, he is accused of not identifying with the black community; if his possessions reflect upward mobility, they charge that his success is the result of their demands and at their expense; if he requires them to earn whatever grades and other rewards they get while "liberal" white colleagues give unearned rewards, he is told that he is more demanding than the white oppressors; if he tells black students that he does not give any points for being colored black, he is reminded that racial bias is what segregation and discrimination is all about; if he dares to pursue his own interests, promote his own scholarship, and attempt to make a contribution to his own discipline, he is told that what he is doing is not relevant; if he insists that he is an educator and is not interested in politics, he is told that he is denying reality; if he rejects some of the philosophy of revolutionary writers, he is accused of a slave mentality; and if he appears reasonable in his dealings with whites, he is called "handkerchief head," "Oreo," and "Uncle Tom." This kind of dilemma has caused some blacks to quit, others to destroy themselves (Flint, 1972).

Students represent only one dimension of the black-to-black dilemma. Some middle-aged blacks who attended predominantly white colleges still remember the attitudes of African students toward them. African-born blacks, like other foreign-born whites and nonwhites, chose their friends, sometimes their homes, and their colleagues from among the majority group. Some Africans who attended predominantly black colleges did not identify with the black community. Foreign blacks seemed to take their cue from domestic whites and behaved accordingly. When someone, inadvertently or logically, identified an African as a Negro, the African immediately repudiated the identity and disassociated himself from the group with whom he was identified. The blacks from Africa on the campus during the forties, fifties, and up through the mid-sixties, had deep contempt for their American black brothers. At that time, to be anything was better than being Negro. The college community, too, showed deference to the more exotic blacks from Africa. They took them home as houseguests, to restaurants, to church, and to other places where Africans, especially in native costume, had contact with whites. These amenities and opportunities given African-born blacks only reinforced their negative attitudes toward American blacks who were denied these experiences. It must be recognized that some Africans who were on predominantly white campuses represented royalty. As such, they may have behaved according to the dictates of their station and class. Although such behavior may be understood, it was inappropriate, ill advised, and counterproductive in the black community. Other Africans claimed royalty and, in fact, had none; the claim was of considerable social benefit. One dean, a black woman, informed us that she never met an African while she was a college student who did not claim to represent royalty. While African blacks did not all move permanently into the American mainstream, a few of them did move into education in both predominantly white and black colleges.

And too, Africans were not always treated with greater respect than American blacks, especially when they left the antiseptic environment of the college campus. One has but to read the autobiography of Kwame Nkrumah, the late president of Ghana, to be convinced of this. He explains a Baltimore experience (1959, p. 35): "I was parched from thirst and I entered the refreshment room at the [bus] terminal and asked the white American waiter if I could have a drink of water. He frowned and looked down his nose at me as if I was something unclean. 'The place for you, my man, is the spittoon outside,' he declared as he dismissed me from his sight. I was so shocked that I could not move. I just stood there and stared at him for I could not bring myself to believe that anyone could refuse a man a drink of water because his skin happened to be a different colour. I had already experienced racial segregation in the buses and in restaurants and other public places, but this seemed to me to be stretching it rather far. However, I said nothing but merely bowed my head and walked out in as dignified a manner as I knew how."

Even when American blacks knew about such slights to African blacks they were unsympathetic because their African brothers attempted to act superior to them. In spite of the time lapse and the events of the late sixties and early seventies, older blacks still carry around more resentment than one might suspect.

The following comments were taken from the questionnaire of an Ohio State University respondent: "What bothers me is that they [African blacks] are in programs all over the place— even Black Studies. When did they ever know, or want to know, anything about us? While they were going first class, we were in the back of the bus. We struggled and suffered, and some died under Jim Crow laws and practices. We contributed to the NAACP because that was all we could do until the kids started to raise hell in the late fifties. I never saw an African demonstrate for our cause. Right here, right now, on this campus, when the kids confront the system and make demands of it, our black brothers with the British accents are the first to disappear. But they are there to pimp on the gains we have made. I know with all the talk we hear about unity that my views aren't popular. But I have a long memory and I have as much right to state my case as anyone else. I hear these kids call some fine men 'oreos,' men who made it possible for *them* to make demands. And I see these Africans cash in on everything we have done without paying any dues!"

Young blacks (under thirty) do not appear to hold the same kinds of resentments toward their African brothers. Many were surprised to discover that their parents and some of their middle-aged black teachers felt this way. Black female faculty members (over thirty-five) recalled how African students who did associate with blacks did so primarily with women. Because some African graduate students did not have sufficient funds, they cultivated friendships and received assistance from black women, especially professional women. Few married these American black women. They exploited black women, but most married white women. As soon as the African students got their degrees, most departed for Europe and Africa, leaving their black female benefactors behind. Since most young blacks have not experienced Jim Crow laws, since Africa has become one of the symbols of the black movement, and since young blacks see conflicts between American-born blacks and African-born blacks as a "family affair" that can be worked out, they do not expend their energy in damning the past, but in exhalting the future. This attitude is difficult for older blacks. Rush and Clark explain it (1972, p. 13): "Many older blacks have felt the razor edge of discrimination; they are often those with the most scars and concomitant bitterness, though suppressed."

Whites in the college challenge the black educator in some of the same ways as the black students do. If the black educator refuses to intercede when black students challenge the faculty or administration, he incurs the disfavor of his administrators; if he supports students in certain of their demands, he is reminded that he represents the institution and should be loyal to it; when he insists that the secretarial pool and other personnel treat him the same as they treat his white colleagues he is told he is oversensitive; if he asks that commitments to him be made in writing, he is accused of distrust. When he insists that he is not an expert on blacks, some administrators do not know what to do with him; if he refuses to play the role of "supernigger," he is treated as an incompetent. If he produces in his field, he is compared to other black scholars, not simply to other scholars. If he wears an Afro hair style, dashikis, and other trappings associated with black militancy, he is charged with setting a bad example; if he is aggressive rather than docile, he is said to be uncooperative.

His white colleagues still want him to continue the credit-to-your-race behavior of the twenties, thirties, and forties, while the blacks of the fifties, sixties, and seventies insist that he should "do his own thing." These attitudes distress black scholars, but they are also intrigued by some of the racial attitudes and behavior of some of their colleagues which alienate them. In spite of the recent breakthroughs for blacks in higher education, the tincture of racism remains. Our data indicate that 57.1 percent of the educators we surveyed feel that overt bigotry from white colleagues is a serious problem in their institution. They indicate that college officials actually look the other way and permit racist practices to take place on their campuses. Some black administrators have told us, for example, that they have pointed out the condescension and acquiescence in their colleagues who permit Jim Crow dormitory operations on their campuses to satisfy the desires of the black separatists among their students. Here one witnesses a strange irony: white racism being used to aid and abet black racism.

Black racism is as destructive and counterproductive to the goals of blacks as is white racism. Many blacks maintain that there is neither logic nor morality in arguing the legality of segregation perpetrated by whites when it is justified if done under the aegis of black student demands. Black educators have suggested to their colleagues that concessions to racist demands by blacks promotes segregation and the worst kind of racism because it is under the subterfuge of liberal response to student concerns and pressures. The same administrators who grant these concessions do not permit other students to break the law.

The blacks we talked to seriously questioned the administrators who claimed to support the law but were willing to disregard it and perpetuate one of the most devastating and dehumanizing practices America has produced—segregation. The blacks claimed to have been ignored when they advised their administrators not to permit their institutions or black students to play into the hands of segregationists. Scores of blacks believe that people who really care about you will not knowingly support you in activities that may be harmful. Equally as many told us that is not unusual for faculty or a junior administrative officer to have his advice ignored. Most say they expect it.

Amid such dilemmas, only the strong survive. Most black educators find that they are not black enough for blacks and too black for whites. Expected to act as the intermediary between the white academics and the black students and black community, the black educator bears an unfair burden. To be praised by one group is to be condemned by the other; to be rewarded in one role is to be punished in another; and to be involved and committed in one frame of reference is to be abused in another. Stated more simply, he finds himself always doing the wrong thing—or the right thing wrong. The only way he can cope with all of this is to be his own man, and to be one's own man is to be alone.

Another of the problems that the nonwhite educator says contributes to his feelings of alienation is the feeling that he never really knows where he stands in relationship to his white colleagues and how they feel about him and his areas of interest. As an example of this, a black history professor wrote us that after a meeting on Black Studies held by the social science department he inadvertently intercepted a memorandum from one to another of his white colleagues. He read the communique: "I didn't want to mention my feelings during the department meeting because our friend was there. Frankly, I can see very little academic or social value in Black Studies. How could you build a viable curriculum for it? After all, blacks have not made a significant contribution to the world or to America. And all of their [the Black Student Union] threats and violence simply proves that they are not ready. You must admit black students do not show outstanding abilities."

The black professor was the "our friend" in the note, of course. He made several copies of the memorandum for his files; then he sent the original note on to its intended destination with attached comments of his own to both the sender and the recipient.

He gave us a copy of his comments, from which the following excerpts are taken:

> I hope your intent is positive; I wish it were more open and honest. In a university, any subject is worth examining, isn't it? But as I shall be spared the preachments of others, I wish I could say, so shall I spare you mine. But I cannot. While black students have made what seems to me open, honest, and legitimate demands for a body of study and knowledge, it appears that my colleagues have responded to them with resistance, hostility, and dishonesty. The forefathers of these young people were uprooted from their homes and systematically robbed of their culture, their names, their families, their heritage, their religion, and forced to live under the worst kind of slavery the world has ever known; you think of their heirs as villains because they want to know what happened and why. It is even more ironic that academicians would deny the heirs of the victims, who still bear some of the scars, an opportunity to learn about themselves, their history, and their exploitation. I am sure that scholars recognize that such study would be of value for all students. My fellow historians, perhaps you already know who cut the trees and built the roads and railroads, who hewed the wood and drew the water, but I guess this would be of "little academic and social value" (to quote you) to the sons of the masters. I guess I could go into blacks discovered this and blacks invented that, but since I am not sure what you consider significant I will not do so. It is strange that you would mention violence in relation to blacks who have suffered so much of it from the God-fearing people of America. Still, no black in America has ever assassinated a president, started a war, dropped an atomic bomb, placed one race in slavery, another in concentration camps, and practically committed genocide against a third one. No black has ever murdered a senator, killed the recipient of a Nobel *Peace* Prize, or polluted a river. A record like that ought to be worth something. You are certainly in good company when you indicate that blacks are incompetent. As a historian, you know that it is well documented that Washington, Lincoln, and the author of the Constitution agreed with you.

The professor told us that he was ashamed of his own behavior, but he resented the hypocrisy of his colleagues. In our personal communiques we encountered many such stories, most of them documented as was this one.

Afro-Americans indicate that hypocrisy takes other forms. The concept of *qualified* is a form most pervasive. "We cannot find qualified blacks." No statement made by white educators so infuriates blacks as this comment, especially the word *qualified.** Blacks feel that the word has been vulgarized and simplified; it is full of political ambiguity; and as it has passed from person to person it has been the basis for academic prejudice. It has allowed educators to reject the entry of blacks, other nonwhites, and women into higher education. It has permitted administrators to rationalize and justify inequitable behavior. And it embodies many contradictions. Where the college officials on one campus maintain that they cannot find qualified blacks, the officials on another campus in the same state or city can find all of the black staff they are seeking. "That word *qualified* is the monkey on my back—on the backs of most blacks in higher education," states a University of California administrator.

The problem with the concept of *qualified* is that no one seems to know what it means, except the person who uses it and those who are the victims of its use (Birenbaum, 1971; Moore, 1970, 1971). Minority group members have effectively been denied access to higher education because of various definitions of *qualified.* From all sections of the country black educators indicate that they never hear the word *qualified* applied to candidates for positions in their colleges unless the candidates are black. In short, the term *qualified* has become the rhetoric of rejection for blacks, an implicit assumption that a black will not be competent. And all over they see college people embed the word in the most cabalistic parliamentary machinations to deny blacks entry into the world of higher education. These are but a few of the reasons why the word *qualified* carries with it the same emotional meaning as *busing* or the phrase *law and order,* since "it must be remembered that law

---

* Of our sample, 893 or 28 percent indicated that this word was the euphemism whites used most which they believe had a hidden or special meaning for them. Women indicate this slightly more than men in both two-year and four-year colleges.

and order is an experience the black American has never had"
(Slater, 1970, p. 26).

Blacks who do succeed through the hiring process encounter
yet another problem: social and professional isolation. Black educators say that they share few social or professional activities with
their white colleagues. At least 53 percent of our respondents in
two-year colleges revealed that they live in segregated housing, in
restricted neighborhoods, attend segregated churches, their children
are enrolled in segregated schools, and they belong to segregated
clubs. Even the 43.5 percent of blacks who live in the same community as their white colleagues have different social outlets. In
four-year schools 60 percent of the blacks live in the same community as their white colleagues. Still 72.3 percent of the blacks
in community colleges and 67.1 percent in four-year colleges seldom
if ever engage in social activities (dinner, theater, dances, parties)
with their white colleagues. They may have lunch with their white
colleagues, but they involve themselves in few other social activities.
Blacks in large urban colleges report that they do have more social
contacts with their white colleagues, especially in far western,
eastern, and large midwestern communities, than do their black
colleagues in suburban, rural, and southern colleges.

Professionally, a similar dissonance occurs. White faculty
and administrators in engineering, law, and dentistry departments,
for example, have a reputation among blacks for being conservative,
intolerant of dissent, indifferent to social needs, elitist in their
approach, and, therefore, highly discriminatory in both their students and their colleagues. Out of the 2174 black respondents in
predominantly white four-year colleges, 1 percent or less were in
these particular departments: thirty in engineering, twenty-five in
law, and five in dentistry.

In community colleges, white educators in the vocational
programs do not spend much time socially or professionally with the
few black educators that are admitted. Many white faculty members
and administrators identify with blue-collar workers, union members, and union officials. Because of the discrimination in vocational
and apprentice programs, the educators working in them manifest
some of the attitudes if not the behavior of trade unionists. Much
of their behavior is aided and supported by state and federal author-

ities organized in joint apprenticeship committees. And then too, blacks are invited to take part in social activities at some places, but because they feel uncomfortable and because of other personal reasons they choose to segregate themselves.

Black administrators do not perceive themselves in quite the same way as black faculty members do. They are even more isolated. They find that their roles are ill defined; their positions lack authority; they suspect the rationale for their recruitment; they make few, if any, real decisions; and they are disillusioned. Many perceive their major responsibility as one of keeping the black students in line and pacifying the black community. One white female administrator informed us that when her bosses seek a black administrator, "they look for one who is middle-aged, middle-class, and sexless." She indicated that her supervisors felt that these criteria would guarantee that the applicant would not take risks (or provide a threat) either professionally or socially. Many of them have guessed wrong. Nonetheless, black administrators are well aware of the lack of power in their positions. They are fully aware in some cases, and suspicious in others—that some of their white colleagues praise them in public and engage in carping criticism in private.

Black administrators confirm that their white colleagues often expect them to provide corroborative information on all kinds of subtle and evaluative questions about other blacks in varying positions and departments. Numerous black administrators commented to us that they were involved in some type of black or ethnic study program and were told by their deans or division chairmen that their program did not have the support of the black faculty members and administrators on campus and, therefore, might be in danger of losing funds. In checking with other black faculty members and administrators the respondents found, as we did, that the white administrators and others had, indeed, asked black faculty members how they felt about the program. Further checking revealed that this strategy had been used on many campuses. Blacks resent their colleagues and administrators who attempt to use them in the process of discrediting and discontinuing Black Studies programs. One black said to us, "I don't think English 101 is worth a damn; but I don't believe they will use my appraisal to get rid of it. And I don't believe they ask the French members on the staff what they think of teaching French history and literature."

The majority of black administrators fall into that category of "assistant to"—never in charge, but an assistant to the person who is. Less than a dozen predominantly white two-year and four-year institutions are headed by blacks. There are a few full deans who are black with a slightly larger assortment of associate and assistant deans. By far the greatest number of black administrators are coordinators and directors of special programs and projects with unusual and prestigious-sounding job titles which mean very little in terms of authority and decision-making power.

Faculty members, on the other hand, have clearer roles. Few, however, are on the most important faculty committees, are members of the faculty senate, or are tenured. A sizable percentage of our sample of black faculty members are assistant professors or below and are serving in other nontenured and nontenure-accruing positions (see Chapter Six for more details). Those in two-year colleges gain tenure from longevity and need not go through the promotion and ranking system characteristic of the four-year college. In spite of the lack of job security for many blacks, a surprising number are militant.

Activists among faculty and administrators consider themselves the most alienated of all black educators. They feel feared, resented, rejected, avoided, and isolated; never ignored; but considered a kind of pathology; a problem, not a solution; fanatical, not realistic. Nonetheless, those concerned with equal opportunity for blacks in higher education agree that an excess of imagination and of moral passion is preferable to the absence of either in their colleagues. Only 4.1 percent of our sample consider themselves activists; 75 percent of these people are in four-year colleges. The overwhelming majority consider themselves left of center (active but not extreme) and moderate.* This percentage of blacks surveyed (77.9 percent) is greater in two-year colleges than in four-year colleges.

Activist blacks on the campus are different from the traditional middle-aged, middle-class blacks who are willing to submit to the average college administrator's symbol of "Negro Progress." While the forty-five-year-old middle-class black who is better edu-

* ACE (August 1973) found 44 percent see themselves as conservatives.

cated and economically more solvent is willing to withhold some of his criticism and demands and to remain silent in exchange for higher academic rank and other such rewards, militants refuse to do this and show a cool ruthlessness in rejecting compromise. They are not willing to renounce their heritage as a social error and strive with the rest of the Joneses. While militants recognize that some moderate blacks will painstakingly, and probably without some of the verbal extravagance, succeed against improbable odds, militants feel themselves representing the authentic new voices.

We found the activists to be assertive, militant, defiant, and self-affirming. They are quick to note, as Kenneth Clark has, the white "liberal" educators' "struggle to reconcile their affirmation of racial justice with their visceral racism" (Clark, 1965). They will not permit the dichotomy between word and action to go unchallenged. They refuse to remain silent and allow educators to contradict in behavior everything they put in print. Black activists rarely appear to be locked in the ambivalence characteristic of moderate blacks and whites. Whenever they perceive a vast deception they publicize it.

Administrators do respond to the concerns and demands of black activists, in spite of their militancy, with more dispatch and action than they respond to the expressed concerns of more moderate blacks. Some black activists perceive that they are privately feared when they confront the academic establishment; because of this fear they feel many of their demands are met.

Much of the resentment toward this group concerns their confrontation behavior. Their rhetoric is direct and challenging. Their tactics usually circumvent the typical procedure for interacting with the college administration. Often in manner, sometimes in dress, and almost always in speech, a perpetual hostility permeates the behavior of activist black educators.

Still it is significant to note the positive reaction and response to these educators from white and black students. Most of the black educators we surveyed indicated that they felt more acceptance from white and black students than from white colleagues.

We have explored some of the reasons why alienation, cynicism, disillusionment, and contradiction are reflected in the moods and behavior of many blacks in higher education. The black educator in the white college must come up the hard, self-tutored way. He soon recognizes, perhaps painfully, that his color creates an elaborate division of labor that has always been cruel, is currently impractical, and, unfortunately, is still operative. His senior white colleagues rarely reach out to help him nurture and fulfill his talents. They seldom offer him any serious criticism for his work. His scholarly achievements or outstanding accomplishments as a teacher in his discipline get only passing attention.

Some black educators seem reluctant to write (J. Johnson, 1970, p. 33). Frazier observed this more than a decade ago; he attributed it to the shortsightedness of black administrators (Frazier, 1962b, pp. 32–33). Our findings are more encouraging. While past publication efforts on the part of blacks in higher education have not been significant, 78.5 percent of our two-year college respondents and 70.1 percent of our four-year college and university respondents reported that they are involved with activities which *will* lead to publication. Black educators indicate that while an insignificant minority of their white colleagues provide them with assistance and with thoughtful, fair, and respectful appraisal, the vast majority do not. The black educator's white colleagues, as far as we can tell at this juncture, have not been able to distinguish him silhouetted against their own value system. And they have yet to distill the importance of his place with them. The black educator sees the contradiction between the prejudice and eccentric behavior of white authors and their written theories.

Blacks note that their white colleagues have an aversion to facts which contradict or challenge the credibility of some of their deeply held beliefs. In spite of their training and empirical propensities, their behavior reveals that it is easier for them to preserve earlier learned stereotypes and attitudes than to face the current facts. Many are remarkable for their stubborn perseverence in permitting habit, automatic reaction, and hardened, set ways to take precedence over reason. They are not the super liberals they are reported to be. They have rejected pluralism and parity with blacks, other minorities, and women in their ranks. Even under the leadership of the acclaimed Robert Maynard Hutchins, there was strong opposition to the appointment of blacks to the faculty of the Uni-

versity of Chicago (Bond, 1966, p. 554). The opposition came from
the faculty members, not the students. This behavior by white
faculty members is contrary to logic and the philosophy of a
university.

The community of scholars is a subculture. It demands
conformity, establishes hierarchy, expects homage, and evaluates
itself. Those who want to get in must submit to a relatively choice-
less life style, at least until awarded tenure and a high rank. In
this community blacks have found that for the tenured, only one
right exists: the right to decide about others (who is competent,
what is scholarly, who should be ranked and promoted). The nontenured faculty members have a frequently unrecognized but simply
conceded right to survival, only because their existence is necessary
to the existence of those who they assist—the tenured. The nontenured do not resist change; the exploited are not deafened by the
rhetoric of oppression; the poorly paid faculty members do not get
used to poverty. If they invade, violate, or attempt to change the
system that exploits them, they are usually shut out with impersonal
ruthlessness. Black educators feel this happens to them just because
they are there, regardless of their attempts to modify the system.
Their very presence is the threat.

Some white scholars still isolate and insulate themselves from
black educators although such behavior is no longer tenable. In
the past, people in higher education have not been profoundly
agitated by inequity because they have had so little regard for the
victims of inequality. They have not stood on the floors of college
senates and fought for the right to have minorities among their
colleagues. How could they when they do not appear to believe
minority and female educators deserve what they reserve for themselves?

The black intellectual cannot forget that an integrated
academic world is not a current reality (Cruse, 1967): "The
tentative acceptance the Negro intellectual finds in the predominantly white world allows him the illusion that integration is real—
a functional reality for himself and a possibility for *all* Negroes.
Even if a Negro intellectual does not wholly believe this, he must
give lip service to the aims of racial integration, if only to rationalize his own status."

The black educator exists almost independently in white academe enduring a variety of insults and generally being judged incapable. He is still asked about being black, about the black life style, and about the black experience and what makes it unique; he is asked to explain and justify being black.

W. E. B. DuBois long ago noted these questions with disarming insight: "Between me and the other world (white) there is ever an unasked question, unasked by some through feelings of delicacy, by others through the difficulty of rightly framing it. All nevertheless flutter around it. They approach me in a half-hesitant sort of way, eye me curiously or compassionately, and then, instead of saying directly, 'How does it feel to be a problem?' they say, 'I know an excellent colored man in my town'. . . . I smile, am interested, or reduce the boiling to a simmer, as the occasion may require. To the real question, 'How does it feel to be a problem [black]?' I answer seldom a word" (1967, p. 13).

The need to defend one's color is a despicable enterprise. The nonwhite educator sees those around him at first reject and later refuse to accept the inevitability of unwelcomed social changes. Accordingly, he observes how tradition has become a kind of rational scar tissue impervious to the events of the times. Increasingly, he finds that he can be what he is on his own terms; he does not have to accept the versions of himself that others dictate. Unlike the most militant among his peers, he does not find it necessary to talk black, to try to strut or to walk and move black. He already knows how to think, act, and be black. He has something that most who work with him and who write about him have failed to notice. He has a distinctive sense of self and place that no amount of sociological and other academic double-talk can change.

His main problem of alienation is the incongruity between what his white colleagues imagine of a black academic and what he feels as a "distinctive sense of self." When he submits to this conflict, he finds himself inextricably caught between heaven and hell and knowing nothing of either. The conflict is a constant reminder that the social and professional distance between himself and his institution and white colleagues has only narrowed superficially.

The term *black experience* is a cliche of our time. The

expression is bandied about in polite and not-so-polite conversation by the initiated and uninitiated as each looks knowingly at the other. The initiated are usually black and the uninitiated are usually white. Most whites have a limited understanding of the black experience and raise incredulous questions about it, such as, "What's monolithic about the black experience? Don't blacks have the same range of problems, feelings, and emotional responses as other groups? Why can't we think of people as people and attempt to understand and relate to them likewise?" Blacks respond indignantly to questions of this nature and feel that they represent further evidence of the insensitivity of whites.

Black experience has special meaning for blacks. The black person in America has the full range of experiences as other Americans. He is human and experiences all the drives, motivations, and needs that other humans experience. He is a citizen and holds all of the concerns for pollution, environmental protection, quality of government, and taxes that other citizens hold. He is spouse, parent, child, aunt, uncle, and all the other categories of relationships within the nuclear and extended family, just as any other person. He is religious and nonreligious, virtuous and nonvirtuous, heroic and scoundrelly, militant and moderate, and intellectual and antiintellectual. In these ways the black experience is no different from the human experience.

But the black experience is different and encompasses more. Its difference is primarily one-dimensional but, by comparison, subordinates all the other experiences blacks have. It is unique because all blacks, regardless of educational level, social station, political persuasion, religious affiliation, and economic status, are made one and the same by it. The assimilating component of the black experience is *bigotry*. Bigotry that expresses itself in denial of opportunity, exclusion from the mainstream of social, economic, and political activities, insults to the human spirit, and transparent hatred. Malcolm X succinctly summarized the black experience when on one of his speaking engagements he asked a black scholar who was harrassing him if he knew what whites called a Negro with a Ph.D. The man responded that he did not know. Malcolm X replied, "Nigger" (Staples, 1972, p. 48). Such is the black experience. It is the arrogance and feelings of superiority of whites aligned against and denying the hopes and aspirations of blacks.

Does the white academician differ in his relationships with blacks? Is the black experience different in the white academy? We asked black professionals to describe the conditions that prevail in their institutions and they gave us some candid answers. Good human relations are usually built upon feelings of confidence and trust. Persons who have genuine feelings of confidence and trust have few anxieties and can engage freely and creatively in social, professional, and other activities. Our respondents in both two- and four-year institutions reported they have difficulty trusting their white colleagues; women were less trusting than men. Only 16 percent of our respondents felt that they could trust most of their white colleagues; 31 percent felt that they could trust some of them, 40 percent felt that they could trust a few of them; 13 percent felt that they could trust none of them. We are not fully informed as to why these feelings of distrust have developed in the black professional, but we can infer plausible reasons from other information we have received.

Many of the debilitating practices of society have spilled over into the academy; blacks, even in this rarefied environment, are victimized. More than 62 percent of our respondents in four-year institutions and 56 percent in two-year institutions experience bigotry from their white colleagues on a scale from moderately serious to very serious. They seem not to have this problem with white students, who have little reluctance to accept and interact with black professionals. It seems that those who have come to be taught must do the teaching.

The feeling of isolation is strong. Though blacks have limited away-from-the-job contact with their white colleagues, they do not perceive it as a problem; the majority are more frustrated by the impotent efforts of their institution to increase the small number of black professionals and students on their campuses.

Though blacks did not expect to find nirvana in the white academy, they tell us they have been amazed at much of the treatment they have received from the white intelligentsia of America. There is name calling—not the crude, vulgar, derisive kind employed by the unlettered, but the gentle-sounding kind cloaked in euphemisms such as *your people, qualified,* and *militant;* there is segregation standing stark-naked and ugly and polarizing both student and faculty groups; there is lack of redress for minority grievances—the resources found to support many frivolities are seldom available to optimize opportunities for blacks and other minorities; there is paternalism, that ogre of white mentality which blots out rational thinking about nonwhites and assigns them child-like qualities for which someone white must accept responsibility; there are efforts to limit black contact with white persons of the other sex. All of these things occur with discomforting regularity. Beyond this, our respondents say most of their white colleagues do not support efforts to change negative views about blacks, particularly when the efforts are initiated by blacks. Their white colleagues take a dim view of the black awareness movement.

Black awareness for most blacks has deep meaning. For many it is a form of rebirth. It is an opportunity to come to grips with oneself and develop a positive view of one's blackness in contrast with the negative view society has generally imposed. We have alluded to the many studies made on all aspects of black life and the way these studies have generated volumes which portray blacks as caricatures of society. Very few studies have presented blacks as contributing members to society. Blacks generally have felt, therefore, that there was something inherently wrong in being black. Several studies describe high rates of self-hatred among black children and youth, and many adults are not immune. The self-effacing jokes, lack of confidence, efforts to change hair, facial features, and color are all commonly known. But blacks decided that black is beautiful, and by logical deduction, so are they.

Most people know of the black awareness movement, and most react to it. Many understand the importance of identity and know that a person and a people must define themselves before they can have pride in who they are. Blacks have been struggling with their identity crisis and have manifested their search in diverse ways. For many, Africa became Mecca, and they changed their names and dress to correspond with those of Africa. Others decided that the natural look was better than results from efforts to emulate white standards of beauty. New norms were developed for black beauty and dress. Black was in; white was out. Nowhere did these new norms grow and develop more than on college campuses. Whites were faced with a new kind of black student and forced to interact with him.

Our respondents in both two-year and four-year institutions indicated that the reaction of white academicians has been more negative than positive. Only 27.1 percent of the respondents in two-year institutions and 27.8 percent in four-year institutions perceived a positive reaction to the black awareness movement by their white colleagues.

We return to the question posed earlier: Is the black experience different in the white academy? Our respondents tell us, there is no significant difference. Malcolm X said it well.

Chapter Two

••••••••••••••••••••
••••••••••••••••••••
••••••••••••••••••••

BLACKS IN THE
ACADEMIC
MARKETPLACE

••••••••••••••••••••
••••••••••••••••••••
••••••••••••••••••••

*B*lacks were practically non-existent in the academic marketplace of predominantly white colleges and universities until the 1970s. So insignificant was their presence and so tiny their numbers, that only three sentences are devoted to them in Theodore Caplow and Reece McGee's provocative volume, *The Academic Marketplace* (1965, p. 194): "Discrimination on the basis of race appears to be nearly absolute. No major university in the United States has more than a token representation of Negroes on its faculty, and these tend to be rather specialized persons who are fitted in one way or another for such a role. We know of no Negro occupying a chairmanship or major administrative position in our sample of universities."

The exclusion of blacks in higher education was thus summarily dismissed. The authors had recorded in passing this academic paradox of discrimination in the community of scholars but did not propose any change in the all-white character of higher education institutions. They simply noted and acquiesced to the prevailing convention. Because of the times, perhaps, they did not feel compelled to focus on the need and use of black scholars.

Times have changed. It took a turbulent decade to change them. The enactment of civil rights laws, student dissent, the demand for and emergence of Black Studies, government funding, and the resulting mandate for affirmative action plans have exposed academic resistance to the recruitment, selection, and hiring of minorities. To avoid a collision course with these forces, some administrators in colleges and universities began to look to the black marketplace and to vie with one another to attract blacks. This action should not have been necessary. Regardless of any of the recent social changes, "freedom from discrimination, like academic freedom, is essential [in the academic community] to the free search for truth and its free exposition" (Konheim, 1972, p. 161). The American Association of University Professors (*AAUP*) confirmed this concept, which dates back to five and a half decades ago in the organization and was reaffirmed implicitly in the 1940 Statement of Principles on Academic Freedom and Tenure.

The demand of white institutions for black scholars is more myth than reality. The number of available blacks is smaller than it should be, but the demand for them is far less. Many administrators say that black educators are hard to find. Although highly trained black college teachers are in short supply, they are in greater demand in predominantly black colleges than in predominantly white colleges (McGrath, 1965). The Office of Special Projects of the Ford Foundation conducted a survey of black men and women who hold a doctorate and found that less than 1 percent of the earned doctorates in America are held by blacks (Bryant, 1970, p. 3). "Holders of the doctorate (in particular) are sought as faculty members both by predominantly black colleges seeking to raise their academic standards and by white colleges seeking a new level of minority representation in the faculty" (Bryant, 1970, p. 5).

While black faculty members and administrators are in short supply, their numbers have increased. This is more and more apparent in predominantly white schools. Blacks are not faced, however, with a "continued demonstration that the doors to these institutions . . . are open to them" (Moss and Mercer, 1961).

The process, or, more specifically, the politics of recruitment, selection, and hiring of faculty members and administrators have been well documented (Caplow and McGee, 1965). Black Americans distrust, and realistically, the traditional closed system and bureaucratic mechanism through which professors are located, approved, and hired (Williams, 1969). It is reported that black Ph.D.'s are being grabbed up at a premium rate (Goodman, 1972, p. 112). To the system's credit we have found few blacks who were appointed to positions above that which their credentials warranted. To its discredit we found highly credentialed blacks in positions which were little more than clerical. Still, some say: "The biggest buy on the academic market these days appears to be the black scholar with a Ph.D. White universities are falling over themselves to snatch him up, frequently for a window dressing betokening their liberalism as well as for his talents" ("Black Brain Drain," 1972, p. 39).

Some blacks have been recruited away from predominantly black colleges, a strategy labeled the "black brain drain" (Poinsett, 1970; Conyers, 1968; Jencks and Riesman, 1969). Black students have become increasingly anxious and concerned over the scramble of white institutions to recruit blacks to satisfy student and alumni agitation for black professors, while some white institutions have vigorously sought these same individuals as a unique form of status symbol to conspiciously represent a lack of racial prejudice (Mommsen, 1972b).

Activities by white institutions to recruit blacks obscure a catalog of paradoxes. "Until relatively recent years, a virtually impermeable racial barrier excluded Negroes from white universities and their superior facilities for teaching and research" (Winston, 1971).

Many of the black scholars who are now the targets for recruitment were considered on the "intellectual periphery" when they were in all-black colleges (Shils, 1967) and were the object of academic discrimination and racism when they attempted to move into white colleges. In spite of the reported zealousness of white institutions in recruiting, there is still gross underrepresentation of black Americans in institutions of higher education.

There is, of course, some overreaction hiring of blacks. A

sizable number of blacks with whom we had contact believed that their appointments were, in great measure, the result of some crisis situation, in which angry blacks were demanding black faculty, more black students, Black Studies, and black administrators (Moore, 1971). This was true in both two-year and four-year institutions. Young faculty members and administrators freely admit this and do not consider any other alternative, credentials notwithstanding. Older educators feel that their credentials and experiences were the factors which gained them entry. Young black educators point out that many of the older black educators were qualified for years and were not approached by representatives from predominantly white institutions in any way until the campus crisis of the sixties. The selection of staff, particularly in relation to blacks, is still in a tentative period. It got started around 1968, slowed in 1971, and by 1972 was a mere trickle. Even if an institution is trying, traditional methods for selection of college staff appear to be obsolete and do not produce acceptable results when seeking either blacks or anyone else other than Caucasian males.

Search committees, other ad hoc arrangements, vitae and resumes, placement agencies, and journal advertisements produce a low yield in locating black candidates. The majority (80 percent) of our respondents heard about job vacancies from other blacks and nontraditional search procedures. Only 12 percent were brought to the attention of the institution through its traditional sources. Black lay organizations provide the names of more potential applicants than any of the above sources.

In our original survey which went out to presidents of two-year and four-year colleges, we asked: Are there one or more Negroes (blacks, Afro-Americans) on the faculty of (name of the college)? Are there one or more Negroes (blacks, Afro-Americans) on the administrative staff of (name of the college)? We requested a simple yes or no response. Many of those presidents who answered no also entered unsolicited reasons and comments. We asked several black educators about a few of these statements, and they have labeled them for us. Here are a selected number of the verbatim labels and statements: (1) *the efforts without results plea:* "We have tried to recruit blacks but we have been unsuccessful"; (2) *the parochialism dodge:* "This community is not ready for blacks";

(3) *the numbers game:* "This community is only a small percent black so we don't feel a mandate to hire Negroes at this time"; (4) *the budget pressure:* "We cannot afford to hire blacks at our place; the large institutions can pay them two or three thousand dollars more than we can afford to offer"; (5) *the too-qualified-to-work rationalization:* "The blacks we have been able to locate have been overqualified for the job"; (6) *the supply and demand rationale:* "There are simply not enough (blacks) to go around"; (7) *the elusive decision:* "The faculty makes the decision" (four-year college); or "The administration makes the decision" (two-year college); (8) *the self-exoneration protest:* "If it were left up to me, I'd hire blacks tomorrow, but it is out of my hands"; (9) *the digital restraint plea:* "I personally would like to hire blacks but the system ties my hands." Blacks tell us these are statements which they have come to expect.

There is an element of truth in most of the above statements but to one of them blacks react violently, namely, that a person is overqualified for the job: "Man, my wife was pregnant, we only had enough money left to pay a month's rent and I was standing there, in the middle of my wardrobe, fresh out of graduate school. This little man sat there, a king above all the gods, and told me I was overqualified for the job. As much as I resented him I felt sorry for a guy who combs his hair over his bald spot because he can't face reality. If white administrators never learn anything else, I hope to God they learn better than to tell a man who needs a job that he is too qualified to work."

It is not a compliment but hypocrisy of the highest order to tell a man who wants a job and who wants to work that he is overtrained. Some administrators use this tactic to leave a rejected applicant feeling good. If the intent is to spare his feelings, avoid the truth, or hide bigotry, this strategy accomplished the exact opposite effect: it insults the intelligence of the candidate. The respondent who was last quoted asked an interesting question: "Can you imagine a hospital administrator telling a heart specialist that he is overtrained to work in the cardiac ward? Or, can you envision a patient telling a surgeon, 'you're too well trained to remove my appendix'?" If the candidate cannot do the job, then he should not be hired. We think that to refuse him employment because he has more skill than the job calls for should not be a decision for the employer but for the candidate, unless the candidate requests salary remuneration and other benefits in excess of what the job offers. A candidate deserves to know the true reason why he is refused a job. Some blacks work hard to become qualified as the academic community prescribes only to be told that they are too qualified for the job. Still they know that credentials are the game.

Credentials in the black marketplace and in the black community have never meant the same as they do in the white educational institution, although "upward mobility among Negroes seems to have depended more on professional credentials and less on entrepreneurial or managerial talent than is the case among whites" (Jencks and Riesman, 1969). Still some black educators feel that there is little relevance in credentials even in white institutions. Ralph A. Dungan suggests (1970, p. 148): "If credentials placed the professional stamp of approval on qualities that were important to the higher education process, we would be delighted with them. The problem with credentials is not that they exist, but that they are irrelevant in too many cases."

Many blacks appear to subscribe to what Nathan Hare has repeatedly emphasized: "A scholar is a man who contributes original ideas, new insights and information to the existing fund of knowledge—whether or not he has a string of academic degrees or executes his activities in a manner appropriate to the traditions and conventions of the existing world of scholarship" (1970, p. 58).

Those in the black marketplace are well aware that higher education will recruit those who have the best formal education, who most nearly approximate the existing ideals, who perpetuate traditions, and who will assist in maintaining the status quo. They recognize, as Arthur Pearl has (1970, p. 39), that because we are a credentialed society and portion out wealth, prestige, and status disproportionately, those who successfully complete a formal education become the primary vehicles for the maintenance of racism.

Some historical antecedents have influenced the indifferent attitudes of blacks toward the purported prestige of credentials. Up to the beginning of the last decade, blacks who did pursue the doctoral degree were forced to teach and administer in poorly equipped and inadequately financed institutions. The administrators and the persons in the communities where they worked often treated them with disrespect, if not with contempt. Black scholars found themselves in departments headed by persons with far less experience and frequently with half their academic preparation. They found themselves overburdened with excessive class loads; sabbaticals, research support, and opportunities were nonexistent. By white standards they were considered academic caricatures. Because of this, many talented young men did not go on to try for higher degrees that led only to professional dead ends. Only 593, or 18.4 percent of our respondents, held the Ph.D.; and 64 of them were in community colleges. Almost half of our respondents, 1031 or 47.4 percent, who currently work in four-year colleges hold the master's degree. This has serious implications for promotional opportunities, for the work they will be allowed to do, such as dissertation direction, for salary, for tenure, and so on. In two-year colleges, 66.3 percent had the master's degree (the highest degree required), including the sixty-four Ph.D.s.

In the past, blacks who sought the Ph.D. and were employed in the public schools were ridiculed. They truly became overqualified: they were the professors of tenth grade algebra, the linguists who taught freshman Spanish, the botanists who explained the difference between plants and animals, and the backfield coaches for the freshman football team, as well as hall sentries, ticket takers, and study-hall monitors. In the St. Louis Public School System in Missouri, for example, even as late as 1966 a new Ph.D. received a two-hundred-dollar increase in his salary. Until the end of the 1960s, very outstanding young Ph.D.'s found themselves teaching in high school, some even in elementary school with its self-contained classroom and its gum-chewing clientele. For all practical purposes, little distinction was made between Ph.D.'s and other school teaching personnel in terms of salary and prestige; the black Ph.D. received no appreciably greater salary increase or job responsibility than a person who held a master's degree.

Other blacks who earned the Ph.D. were forced into taking positions with the federal government. The salaries were higher, but most of them never rose above the lower grade levels.

Many blacks in two-year and four-year colleges have indicated to us numerous inconsistencies regarding credentials. Some of them view credentials as irrelevant because they often have little to do with the actual job. Others have written that their colleges have made academic certification more important than the function such certification is supposed to serve. They complain that their departments are more interested in credentials than experiences; they resent the ineffective people qualified on paper who spend their time attempting to distinguish themselves for their peers while neglecting their students. Blacks also note that some well-qualified persons lose their nontenured positions because they are more interested in teaching than they are in research and publication. A number of them reminded us that the accreditation of colleges may be withheld because there are an insufficient number of Ph.D.'s on the staff. Such are the paradoxes that disturb our respondents as they appraise credentials. We would be remiss, however, if we did not point out that some blacks both outside and inside of the academic community respond differently to what Dungan calls "credential madness."

The black community does not have many heroes in higher education, who have made it, who can hold their own academically, socially, and professionally with any group. Fewer than three thousand blacks in the United States hold the Ph.D. degree. As a consequence, when blacks do find someone to act as their spokesman, they want him to be academically pure both to quiet the people who would question his qualifications and because higher education is psychotic about credentials. The black administrator or faculty member must be strong, stronger than his white counterpart, because he has tougher battles to fight.

Those in the black marketplace are keenly attuned to the realities of their situation. They will not allow themselves to forget that before the midsixties the label "Negro professional" was more cliche than reality. The term simply meant that the person had earned a degree from one of the American institutions of higher learning. And as Leslie Campbell has emphasized (1970, p. 25), "For all of his scholarly efforts this man received a position of importance in his inferior community and usually an income slightly higher than his downtrodden brothers." There is ambivalence in the black marketplace about credentials, but those with and those without credentials both know that there is so little distance between them when they are viewed by the larger society and, in many ways, by the university. Still they are aware that "black faculty and administrators [in black colleges] have given more of themselves, their talent, and energy [to black students] than have white men and women of half their worth, who have received twice the financial and social rewards from our society" (Billingsley, 1970a, p. 136).

Blacks speak of the arrogance of credentials with disbelief. They remind us that they have found that simply getting a degree is not enough; where you get it is also very important. We must agree that one of the first questions blacks (and whites) are asked by those in the academic community is, "Where did you do your work?" (Translated: "did you get your Ph.D. from a prestigious university?") We believe that degrees from ivy-league schools still carry with them a halo effect for whites although the blacks we talked to did not consider where the degree is earned to be as important as the fact that you have it. Until fairly recently, whether the degree was from an ivy-league or a bush-league institution, for blacks it amounted to the same. They all ended up in predominantly black colleges. There are a surprising number of ivy-league degrees hanging on the walls of the ghetto. Those in the black marketplace are appalled at how the colleges and universities accept paper instead of performance as a measure of a man's worth. One former dean puts it this way: "The preoccupation with credentials in our institutions reminds me of the preoccupation with grass in the suburb where I live. The people there measure a man's worth and character by the length of his grass." Credentials, of course, are only a part of the considerations black educators in the academic marketplace must keep in mind. A whole range of professional activities such as publishing and professional meetings are also supposed to be a mark of competency, growth, and professionalism.

Candidates from the black marketplace are said to participate minimally in publishing and professional organizations. Publication is a part of the credentialing process. Blacks in higher education publish less than whites (Rafky, 1972). Reasons for this include a lack of enthusiasm among publishing houses and especially college publishers for the black point of view and a lack of financial support for blacks who want to do research (T. Johnson, 1971). Closely related to the scholarly production of books, articles, and other academic work is the availability of scholarly resources. John Hope Franklin, the noted historian, has spoken and written of the isolation and humiliation of black scholars at the hands of archivists and librarians. Up to the mid 1960s, in some cities and states, particularly in the South, black scholars could neither use university nor public libraries.

The involvement of black educators in professional meetings is not dissimilar. D. Thompson (1956) indicates that black professors are unlikely to attend professional meetings or hold office in professional organizations. J. A. Moss and N. A. Mercer, interpreting Thompson's data, speculate (1961) that these nonparticipating black educators are insecure, are likely to be less aggressive scholars and, as a result will not risk failure by attempting to secure positions in predominantly white colleges, although blacks from integrated schools of the North are likely to be more aggressive. These investigators are probably incorrect. Thompson does not take into consideration "the historical barriers erected against blacks in the professional associations" (T. Johnson, 1971). Blacks were not wanted. Martin Kilson gives one explanation (1969, p. 304): "Because of the racism in American life, Negro professionals practiced largely within an all-Negro context . . . had their own . . . associations which serviced their members in dealing with white society . . . they hoped ultimately to integrate, both as professionals and members of the middle class, into white institutions."

Apparently, neither Moss and Mercer nor Thompson were aware that the secretary of the AAUP had once asked black members to come in the back door of a southern hotel in order to attend the convention sessions or that some black educators could not attend professional meetings because their colleges were not accredited. In some states accreditation automatically carried with it membership in the accrediting association. Such a membership entitled the college to representation at conferences, and the majority of the white members objected to attendance by blacks (Winston, 1971, p. 678). They did not know that many black colleges could neither afford to send their faculty members to conventions nor pay them a sufficient salary to finance their own convention trips. It has been charged that administrators and faculty members attend conferences to recruit staff, to look for new positions, and to get on committees to bring status to themselves and their colleges. Often, they do not spend as much time exchanging information about important educational problems and the exploration of innovative solutions as they do in cocktail parties. And finally, much of the trivia which takes place at many professional meetings may not be of interest to blacks. Our sample revealed that 76.9 percent of the blacks in two-year colleges and 76.3 percent of those in four-year colleges belong to professional organizations.

Publications, attendance at professional meetings, and research are a part of the credentialing process. Blacks have come to recognize that the academic community will not suspend these criteria as prerequisites for employment of minorities except under very unusual circumstances. What strikes us is how ludicrous some of the prerequisites can be. In one large university, there is a proposal that a faculty member (black or white) cannot be awarded tenure until he has published a *hardback* book. We must confess that we do not understand what the rigidity of the book cover has to do with the quality of its content. Regardless of the rationale for such a policy, any black who hopes to be recruited into a predominantly white institution had better learn the ground rules. Most institutions look for special things in their recruits.

Many colleges and universities set up elaborate mechanisms for the recruitment and hiring of faculty and then promptly ignore most of those structures (Barzun, 1968, pp. 34–62; Caplow and McGee, 1965, pp. 93–117). The procedures vary greatly from one institution to another, from one department to another, as well as from one applicant to another. There is no set pattern. Preferential hiring (for blacks and whites) is the rule rather than the exception; that is, the position and vacancy is not open, announced, or applications invited. Rather, the prevailing procedure is to seek applicants known to existing faculty and departments, friends of persons in the department, the "closed" grapevine, and so on. The vast majority of potential black applicants may never know of the vacancy. Another procedure is to appear to openly invite applicants, while the persons to be interviewed, evaluated, and selected already have unofficial approval and a gentleman's agreement. We found blacks who had been recruited and hired where the recruitment and selection committee of the institution had not evaluated the credentials of the applicant. In some cases, the committee did not have a copy of the applicant's vita. The selection and choice of the candidate was more from subjective evaluation than objective criteria. On the other hand, we found an unusual amount of time and effort of many persons was utilized only to finally choose the individual arbitrarily based on criteria other than the individual's academic qualifications. The right sponsors—prestigious men in a field, men from outstanding departments in other colleges, board members, powerful administrators, men who edit journals and serve on publication boards, advisory committee members (in community colleges), sources in the government who have access to and authority to award funds—can often provide much influence in recruitment, selection, and hiring. One thing is unmistakably clear: selections are more subjective than objective.

To recruit black faculty members into white colleges, headliners in the field, professional associations, respected friends, graduate professors, and other traditional sources are almost totally ineffective. None of these sources have had much intimate and continuous contact with black educators. Until fairly recently, Afro-Americans were excluded from most of the professional associations; respected friends did not always include blacks among their "respected" friends. Many black educators, especially those over age thirty, tell us that, as graduate students, they were never informed when recruiters were inquiring about applicants for faculty positions.

Administrators and others are adamant in their contention that they cannot locate qualified blacks to hire. This is not surprising. The problem of searching out black Americans to work in predominantly white colleges can be a unique problem, one which requires a solution and methods just as unique. Most of all, the solution to the problem requires genuine effort and commitment. We are impressed, for example, with the efforts of football coaches and their assistants, whose commitment and tenacity in recruiting black athletes is not matched by academicians in the recruitment of nonwhite and female faculty. We are told by men who work in schools *so unknown,* and in places *so remote,* that football scouts literally come in with a guide. They might be exaggerating, but we do know that scouts have identified players and have gone to find them in places where the scouts had to sleep on pallets, use the outdoor privy, and wash themselves on the back porches of shanties where the facilities were so primitive that they had to pump the water and use a washpan. The president of Dartmouth, John George Kemeny, created a computer system to help football coaches keep track of scouting data (*Time,* 1972b, p. 57). One would not expect a full professor to make such efforts and endure such inconveniences, but it is nonetheless clear that the identification and location of black professionals requires special effort.

Our data show that the blacks who are currently working in white colleges have been contacted in a variety of ways. We found that 921 of our respondents (42 percent) in senior institutions and 480 in community colleges (45.5 percent) learned about their positions from personal friends. Another 1193 found out about their jobs through informal sources and acquaintances. (See paragraphs which follow.) Eight hundred and nineteen of them (37.7 percent) were in four-year colleges and 347 (35.5 percent) were in community colleges. A quick computation of the above figures and percentages will reveal that 2594 of our respondents (80.3 percent) did not find out about their positions through the college and university sources (e.g. advisors, university placement, graduate schools). Only 12.0 percent used such sources. Nineteen persons (0.6 percent) used a commercial agency, 36 (1.1 percent) used journal advertisement, 100 (3.1 percent) used mass announcement, and 91 persons (2.8 percent) did not respond. As might be expected, some of them were contacted at the black colleges and offered more money, better working conditions, and a range of fringe benefits. Less than 20 percent in either two-year or four-year colleges left black institutions for these reasons. After relocation, these blacks were a source of referral for the identities of others. Black educators who have an opportunity to travel, make speeches, work as consultants, write books, lead civil rights organizations, and achieve high visibility through other means are frequently offered positions.

Some blacks take the positions, but even if they do not take the jobs, they know other blacks who may be interested in a faculty position or vacancy. The black social organization is also an important source for the identification of black educators. While white professionals tend to limit much of their association with those in their professional fields, blacks associate a great deal across professional fields and disciplines. More specifically, black doctors, lawyers, and other such professionals are likely to socialize as much with black teachers as with members of their own professional group. The social class lines in the black community are much more fluid. Because of the housing patterns of blacks and their sparse numbers in the professional ranks, they are well known to each other. They have few options for recreation and entertainment. They are not country club members, most do not belong to such groups as the Rotary, Kiwanis, and so on. Hence, they turn inward—to their fraternities, sororities, social clubs, old school pals who still meet and enjoy the camaraderie of their youth. One can still find many places where doctors, lawyers, and college professors as well as college dropouts, waiters, bus drivers, and government workers spend some of their free time together in warm companionship. In such places, one's position, income level, and other such symbols of class are known but seldom mentioned or introduced.

The people who constitute this mixture of professionals and social classes also attend many of the same social functions and maintain similar leisure-time schedules. Another reason for this mixture is the historical education pattern of the sexes in the black community. The number of college-trained black women is considerably higher than the number of college-trained black men (Shearer, 1967, p. 4). Boys were taken out of school to work and help finance the education of the females, since the education of the black male did not appreciably increase his employment opportunities. As a consequence, a disproportionately high number of black females over age thirty are educated. These women often married black males who were not their educational equals— waiters, cab drivers, and janitors, as well as professionals. Their spouses accompanied them to social functions, causing a class plurality of the black community.

In the white community, waiters, cab drivers, and janitors are not likely to be at the social events of doctors, lawyers, and other professionals. Social mixtures such as this are not found throughout every black community either, but they are more often found among blacks than among whites. As a result, a recruiter can ask a black professional in almost any field where he can identify another black who has credentials and who may be interested in joining a predominantly white college. Active members of Greek organizations are also good sources, because so few fraternities and sororities are predominantly black, because membership in them required college attendance, and because the majority of college-trained blacks are in a limited number of professions, such as education, sociology, and related behavioral disciplines.

The informal sources for locating black faculty are virtually inexhaustible. Affirmative action officials are a rich source; they know both persons seeking positions and institutions searching for minorities to hire. Whites who worked in predominantly Negro colleges or who were classmates of blacks are acquainted with many blacks in higher education. Foundations such as Ford and Danforth have assisted many blacks in higher education and keep a record of the recipients of their philanthropy.

Blacks themselves have learned about the jobs they hold from many unique places: a chance meeting at a cocktail party and similar social affairs have been fruitful for some. Our respondents made the following statements about the positions they now hold: "I ran into a man on an airplane who gave me his card and asked me to call him."

"My former supervisor took another job and asked me to accompany him."

"At my graduate institution we were told to get in the 'BB [bulletin board] habit.' So I kept on the alert for brochures and other announcements and applied for a job when I saw one come through that I had both the interest and the qualifications to match."

From a single "buzz" session at a Washington conference, the participants around the table related the way they made the initial contact with their institution: "In my area [Illinois], they were opening community colleges every week or so; so when I read in the newspaper that a new one was scheduled to open I simply made an application."

"I knew the secretary at the college who informed me of an impending resignation. I suspect that I was the first in line."

"My predecessor had to find his own replacement. He was invited to take another position at a different college but was required to find his replacement before the college would release him from his contract. The strange thing is that I met him at a supermarket."

"I went to the Hilton Hotel to see a friend attending the AAHE conference and while waiting for him, this personnel man came up and asked me to interview for a job right here in town [Chicago]."

"A textbook representative told me about the job I hold."

It is without question that some blacks hear about the jobs they take by accident.

Not all college officials offer excuses for not locating blacks. Those who really want to get the job done find ways. One administrator said that he read the reports on dissertations in progress in certain journals and then gathered information about the specific graduate researchers. When he discovered that a particular graduate student was a minority member, he would contact him immediately. He invited the person in for an interview, sometimes as much as a year prior to his graduation, and in the interim he filled the position with a part-time person. One director of personnel secures the lists and identifications of all of the students scheduled to graduate in specific fields and determines if there are blacks in the class. Still another administrator checks with the personnel man of a large city system to determine experienced teachers who may be working on advanced degrees. One department head informs us that when he attends a conference he seeks out the room where the inevitable black caucus is scheduled and asks a black entering the meeting to take in his business card and a copy of the job announcements from his institution. Another college sends a black recruiter to national and regional meetings with instructions to visit black caucuses and other gatherings of minorities where he might identify blacks who may be interested in his college. A large midwestern college pays its recruiter an extra three-hundred-dollar bonus (the recruiter calls it a bounty) for every competent individual that he locates who can successfully make it through the faculty screening process and be hired. Black publications will reveal the names and location of many minority persons; a Texas administrator uses this technique. Still another administrator uses directories of black organizations and sends announcements of vacancies in his college to each of the organizations listed. One is only confined by his lack of imagination in the process of locating competent blacks to serve as faculty members in predominantly white colleges.

The majority of our respondents, however, heard about the positions from other blacks: faculty members at the college, former teachers, football coaches, sorority members, and members of black organizations which have contact with colleges and universities. Blacks who are already working in predominantly white colleges are without a doubt the best sources.

The public schools of our major cities are a fertile reservoir of black talent for community colleges. More than 30 percent of all recent two-year college teachers come from these schools (McConnel, 1970, p. 223). The overwhelming majority of black teachers and administrators in community colleges are former public school personnel. When contacted and offered positions in predominantly white colleges, many young blacks are ready to leave the autocratic environment, the greater teaching load and other responsibilities of the public school. Titles, promotions, sabbaticals, some travel, minor research opportunity, clerical assistance, reimbursements, and other fringe benefits are sufficient inducements to attract former high school people—especially blacks—into the ranks of the two-year and four-year institutions. They know little of the internal stresses in the hierarchy of postsecondary institutions. Blacks are often unsuspecting of the discrimination and rejection they encounter in institutions of higher learning though they are never completely surprised. One thing is readily apparent, regardless of how the black faculty member or administrator is treated: most, if not all, of them move *up* the institutional prestige ladder, unlike what has happened in the past (L. Wilson, 1942). Major-league educational institutions have traditionally sent most of their higher education and research graduates *down* the institutional prestige ladder (Caplow and McGee, 1965). Blacks coming from public schools or from predominantly black colleges are considered by their white colleagues to be moving up.

Because of the reported short supply of blacks, those who already have positions in predominantly white institutions receive many offers. Mommsen (1970) found that 91 percent of the black Ph.D.'s sampled in 1970 received one or more "offers or inquiries of availability." In spite of the many offers to some blacks, Mommsen discovered that some blacks feel that even "well-qualified" blacks will be excluded and discriminated against by whites, particularly in the top hierachies. Well-qualified blacks who are considered extremely militant are not likely to be recruited if the seeking institution is aware of their activism. Many institutions would rather not run the risk of encounters and thus will not hire a black who is his own man and who is politically active.

While the supply of blacks may be insufficient to meet all of the needs of some white institutions which claim to be seeking them, in certain disciplines, such as education and the humanities, there are no shortages. In other disciplines such as mathematics and physics, the numbers are much smaller (Wispe, Awkard, and others, 1969; Conyers, 1968).

Some administrators say that they do not look for blacks because they cannot afford to pay for them. Considerable debate revolves around this point. Robert Staples writes (1972, p. 42): "Daniel P. Moynihan once remarked that the most sought-after person in the labor market was a black Ph.D. I once heard a white sociologist remark that the going rate for a black Ph.D. in sociology was twenty thousand dollars a year. This at the time was a revelation to me, as I was earning about half that amount."

Yet our findings indicate that blacks actually earn less than has often been reported. In four-year colleges 729 men (47.9 percent) and 469 women (74.5 percent) earn less than $14,000. In these same institutions, 247 men (16.2 percent) and 27 women (4.4 percent) earn more than $20,000. The remainder of the men and women earn between $14,000 and $19,000. In the two-year colleges, 312 men (41.9 percent) and 309 women (70.4 percent) earn less than $14,000; 80 men (13.3 percent) and 19 women (4.3 percent) earn $20,000 or more, with the remainder earning between $14,000 and $19,000. Over all, 56 percent of the blacks in senior colleges, and 60.1 percent of those in junior colleges earn less than $14,000.

Even a cursive review and comparison of faculty compensation as reported and rated by the AAUP indicates that blacks are not compensated disproportionately higher than faculty members as a whole (see the *Chronicle of Higher Education,* April 30, 1973, pp. 1–7). In fact, the AAUP scale is based on the academic year, while most of the blacks in our sample (58.1 percent) work the calendar year. Therefore, while the salaries of blacks generally are comparable to others who work as professionals in two-year and four-year colleges, over half of the blacks in our sample work a calendar year to earn what colleges report they pay their professionals in an academic year.

In a surprisingly large number of colleges in our sample, the administrators reported that they did not have regularly appointed blacks on the college staff. Many of the same colleges, however, did have blacks who were visiting lecturers and other such part-time teachers. The part-time teacher is a unique phenomenon in both two-year and four-year colleges.

Typically, part-time professors and other such teaching personnel neither have the personal investment in the institution nor enjoy the benefits of the regularly appointed. Most of them are moonlighters. They do not have committee assignments, keep office hours, advise students, do research at the institution, attend faculty meetings, or (except in two-year colleges) involve themselves in collective negotiations. On the other hand, they neither get tenure, insurance, retirement benefits, advantage of the research facilities of the institution, opportunity to involve themselves in the decision-making of the institution, nor the camaraderie of stimulating colleagues.

Another classification of part-timers work full-time. They perform all of the duties of the regularly appointed faculty but on special contracts; they are not really full-time, not really part-time staff. A large number of blacks find themselves trapped in this twilight zone. Some have worked in these impermanent positions for a long time. Many black part-timers are extremely bitter, even those who work only as moonlighters. In an interview, one expressed his feelings in this way: "How do I feel about being a part-time staff member? That's easy. We're crapped on. We work at night, we get no orientation, no counseling service, no office, and no equipment service such as audiovisual aids. I get a piece of chalk, and I am expected to teach. I have only seen the chairman of the department once. If I have a question it goes unanswered or I provide my own [answer]."

For the "pure moonlighter," one who is interested only in the money, a part-time position in a predominantly white institution is a gravy train. Those blacks who are currently high school teachers but who are also working toward advanced degrees see more value in part-time work and view such work as a valuable experience to add to a resume.

Both two-year and four-year institutions exploit the part-time section of the black marketplace in two ways, however. First, part-timers are paid less money for the same student contact time than regularly appointed teachers working an overload or other extra time. Second, the black part-time faculty are exploited when they are counted as employees in order to meet affirmative action guidelines. Blacks, of course, are not the only part-time personnel who are used for the self-interest of the colleges. The use of teaching assistants is a corollary. The institution makes no commitment and seeks no special loyalty beyond a day of work for a day of pay and the pay is at a lower rate than that paid a regularly appointed staff member to do the same job.

Special projects are filled with persons from the black marketplace. Counselors without training or credentials are common in programs for the disadvantaged and Black Studies. Beyond common sense, intuition, some knowledge of the disadvantaged culturally different community, and the ability to speak the language, interpret the innuendos, and anticipate the behavior of this group, these blacks do not have any special student personnel skill. Many say that the skills they do have are not possessed or ever learned by white counselors working with black students. Still, it is difficult to understand why the academic community "believes" that untrained blacks make good counselors for the so-called disadvantaged and low-achieving student. This student needs the most skillful and well-trained person available.

Nonetheless, some untrained blacks make good counselors; some communicate better than trained counselors. As peer counselors, untrained persons have proved to be effective (Jackson, 1972, p. 280) and have been instrumental in improving grades and classroom skills (Vriend, 1969). In community colleges, they have succeeded in helping students adjust to their academic environment (Pyle and Snyder, 1971), and they have assisted students in developing social skills and the ability to fight loneliness (McCarthy and Michaud, 1971). Students from minority groups (blacks and others) have emphasized the inability of trained college personnel to understand and accept their unique needs and life styles. Present counseling efforts are designed to cope most effectively with the problem-solving need of a motivated middle-class clientele and have little value to an increasingly heterogeneous student population, especially the minorities (Warnath, 1971).

Too many special-project counselors are not regularly appointed staff members who accrue tenure, other security, and benefits. These counselors could be better described as paraprofessionals. We are told that some of them have come to the university out of poverty, social action programs, and other such government and foundation experiments which have hired the unlettered and the untrained from the black marketplace. Many federal and other monetary grants to colleges and universities carry stipulations that a certain portion of the staff be from a minority group or groups. Our respondents in this category revealed that they are used as consultants, lecturers, speakers, workshoppers, and facilitators in encounter groups as they are asked to "train" and sensitize faculty members to be more effective in working with minority group students.

These paraprofessionals represent a kind of "tell it like it is" unit. In recent years we have seen these participants at national meetings, performing for the collective academic communities of a nation. Their behavior is studied and their words are taped. Their comments are later included as quotations in scholarly volumes to add authenticity, realism, drama, pathos, and urgency to what, in some cases, turns out to be an extremely dull book. A Los Angeles City College peer counselor explained this to us: "I say what the professor can't say because his life is dictated by his peers. He is too damn self-conscious to be real. The language he uses confines him, and his education restricts him instead of expanding him. If I want to say shit, I say it. If he wants to say shit, he quotes me."

The professor not only uses this person's material but also gives the credit to an alias. Faculty members also use the tapes as teaching aids in their classes and pass them among departments and colleagues on other campuses. We know an educator who took one such tape home to entertain his party guests. Sometimes the paraprofessional from the black marketplace gets some recognition for his statements and is invited as a consultant or a speaker at another institution. They go and entertain. "At a hundred, sometimes two hundred dollars a day—why not?" stated one respondent, a counselor in a tutorial program of a midwestern college. "The students seem to learn something even if their professors don't." The paraprofessionals know they are being used, however. They talk about it, are hurt by it, resent it, and a significant number seem bitter.

The blacks in special programs often come and go. Those who take the jobs soon recognize that they have no power, little or no influence, no security, and no professional recognition. They are hired to do what they do: keep the program going and the natives quiet.

Very often these persons in the black marketplace can make an excellent contribution to an institution if that college appreciates and utilizes well the natural talents of the individual. They are often able to do what trained persons cannot do with students, especially students from poor and black communities. Institutions have not learned to team up the professional white and black counselors with the paraprofessionals in order to make the best use of the human resources. One of our respondents says: "I know I am not a trained counselor, but if the professional counselor here would tell me what he knows about counseling and I told him what I know about these people we are both trying to work with, maybe we could help them. The gentleman with the degrees can't forget that he has them and seems to get a little uptight and does not want to share his secrets with me. He is heading for a fall. He can never learn about these black dudes from a book. That book is not the real world; it is a report on the real world—and the guy that wrote the book is just like he is. Working with blacks requires some special skills of sensitivity."

Charles Warnath confirms this from personal experience (1971): "If a counselor is fortunate enough, as I have been, to spend some time with a black counselor who is willing to demonstrate the differences in verbal and body language between whites and blacks, it will quickly become apparent that many of the characteristic gestures and word usages of the blacks are quite incomprehensible to the whites, while common reactions of white professionals are viewed as putdowns or status reinforcers by the blacks. The black student and the white professional may converse using English words and yet be talking completely different languages. The whites will be receiving only very carefully screened messages but will be unintentionally sending out negative communications which reinforce the distance between himself and the black student. At present I feel white professional counselors may act as advisors to minority students in regard to the system or the institutional structure, but very few are capable of acting as effective counselors."

Almost to the man, our respondents who serve as counselors, who serve in nonprofessional, nontenured positions in special programs, agreed with Warnath. Trained black counselors were also in agreement.

Many of the persons who work in the soft-monied programs come from the black marketplace, especially those working with the underachieving and minority group student. At the same time, we must stress that minority groups other than blacks are also working in similar compensatory programs, including some programs for whites, especially in California and Colorado colleges and in colleges in the Appalachian regions.

The majority of compensatory and other remedial programs in colleges were staffed with blacks. We do not have data which will shed light on why this is so. Some respondents suggest that some of the black faculty members who have been recruited from secondary schools in urban areas and from predominantly black colleges have more experience working with students in these programs. Others suggest that the traditional white educator, whether he is in a two-year or a four-year school, is not equipped or committed to the kinds of involvement necessary to provide instruction for slow performers. Still others indicate that their nonblack colleagues resist teaching students who can be identified as remedial and suggest that such students should not be in the college at all. An assignment to teach remedial courses or to be required to teach remedial students in their regular classes lowers their status in the eyes of their colleagues. Our subjects said that some of their white (and black) senior colleagues refuse to teach high-risk students. Their refusal did not always apply to black students alone, but to any student whose ability did not appear to warrant college admission. These attitudes were as prevalent in community colleges as in four-year institutions. One respondent suggested that postsecondary people know nothing of the "new" student in higher education.

Since some blacks do, in fact, have some experience in working with such students and the college community offers more money, more free time, and more academic freedom, they often accept such assignments as an entree into other programs and departments of the institution. Considerable evidence from our respondents, however, supports the idea that blacks with experience in working with remedial students often come from colleges which are considered compensatory.

It would be erroneous to believe that only the part-timer, the special-program worker, and the Black Studies personnel are recruited from the black marketplace. Many outstanding scholars and administrators have been lured to the predominantly white university. W. E. B. DuBois, George Washington Carver, Carter G. Woodson, Charles Thompson, Charles Drew, and many, many others had to live out their days, develop their talents, and make their contributions under the most adverse of academic conditions in underfinanced and poorly equipped institutions, but other blacks, such as Kenneth B. Clark, Allison Davis, John Hope Franklin, and many others have become outstanding figures in predominantly white institutions (Winston, 1971). From coast to coast we found outstanding blacks in two-year and four-year colleges.

The presence of prestigious blacks on a campus brings as much positive attention to the institution as it does to the individual. In administration, we found presidents, vice-presidents, provosts, assorted deans, department chairmen, personnel directors, and so forth, in some of the largest and most prestigious institutions in the country. We found that black faculty members and adminstrators were on the boards of national professional organizations, presidential committees, and heads of national programs. We found them represented on publication boards and other influential educational sources. In short, blacks can be found in all types of positions. But they are very, very few in number. Many of them are better known nationally than they are on their own home campus.

Over half of the black faculty members and administrators are clustered in urban colleges and large state schools. Wyoming, Montana, Rhode Island, and the Dakotas are among some of the states which do not appear to attract blacks. We did not receive a single response from blacks who hold jobs in two-year colleges located in those states. There are blacks living and working in some institutions in those states, but the number is extremely small. All of the two-year college presidents in Montana and South Dakota, 3 of the 5 in North Dakota, 6 of the 7 in Wyoming and 2 of the 3 in Rhode Island who responded to our survey indicated that they did not have a black professional on their staff. We were not able to determine to what extent institutions in these states tried to recruit from the black marketplace. Some college officials with very few black students do not recruit black personnel. The rationale is that if there are no black students, there is no reason to hire black staff members. Administrators still do not recommend staff solely with respect to their fitness for the task to be performed and without reference to race or creed.

On the other hand some of our subjects indicated that they did not bother to interview for positions in such communities. The few who did were unhappy with what they saw. Others who worked in such communities quickly became disenchanted with them. One sums up his experiences: "Housing, entertainment, and community involvement are nonexistent. Our children must attend hostile schools, and merchants watch you like you are a thief when you go in the local trading post. Finding a dentist, doctor, or barber, or even a baby-sitter requires an act of Congress. I have to drive seventy-three miles to get a haircut. You walk down the street and people look at you as though you're the village freak. If you do not fly the American flag from the front yard or attend the local sweet potato socials you are considered subversive. I obviously can't qualify for the Elks, nor my wife the D.A.R.; not that we would have any ambition to join those racist cults even if they changed their policies. These poor, scared, eccentric people brag about being suspicious of strangers like it's the eleventh commandment. Why would I want to remain in a community like that or recommend it to another brother?" Schools in these types of communities, hoping to recruit blacks, do nothing to prepare the community or the applicant for the mutual encounter.

A surprising number of blacks who were formerly in predominantly black educational institutions plan to return. They made some interesting comments and observations about their former colleges. It was noted that for all of the autocratic behavior charged against administrators in black colleges and universities, the staff members always knew where they stood (Billingsley, 1970a). Repeatedly, these respondents emphasized that black administrators were more decisive. White administrators seem to seek a referendum and a vote of confidence before they will "make" a decision; in black schools administrators may seek input but they do not apologize for making a decision if they are responsible for the outcome. Definite actions are taken. If a committee does not do its work, the assignment is taken away and given to another committee. If the second committee also fails to do its work, the administrator decides what to do about it. Many blacks like this decisiveness. The mood of the sixties suggests that blacks not only want input into the decision-making but also want some control over the things which affect their lives. Nonetheless, they believe that when people seek a decision, those charged with the responsibility should make them. When asked about the democratic and shared approach to decision-making in white colleges, the response implied that a democratic process did not always guarantee democratic behavior or results.

People in the black marketplace are required to develop unique kinds of savvy as they deal with the academic community. They have discovered that the academic community is no place to be a slow learner. "Get it in writing" has become a guiding principle although college administrators are reluctant to put their promises in writing, especially those in four-year institutions. Blacks need to interpret and define every title, term, requirement, statute, and university rule, lest they find themselves the victims of a loophole. Two-year college people are more direct in what they do. We found *many* cases where the institution would assist a white faculty member or administrator with moving expenses and would not even make the offer to blacks. Because blacks were not aware of the options available to them, most never inquired about them. If policy would not permit paying moving expenses, the college would put the person on salary a few months earlier. If policy permitted the paying of moving expenses, it was left to the discretion of the administrator. In some cases, this assistance-in-moving cost was determined by the rank of the person to be hired. In either case, few black personnel were given the option.

Blacks have also learned not to get trapped in the institutional politics during the interview. To be asked what one thinks about Black Studies in an interview for a position in mathematics, for example, is inappropriate. Mathematics is neither black nor white.

We found that whites were assisted, both formally and informally, in locating housing much more often than blacks; the wives of white faculty members and administrators would call on the wife of the new white member of the staff and offer their assistance, show her the city, take her to lunch, ask her to shop with the group, exchange home visits, luncheons, and so forth. With blacks this was more the exception than the rule; the overwhelming majority of our respondents said that this did not happen to them. Visits were exchanged about once a year when, "It's my time to have a party." There was virtually no contact among the children of black and white faculty members and administrators except in isolated cases. Repeatedly our black respondents told us that the brochures sent, the Chamber of Commerce hard sell, the advance public relations work of the realtors, the recruiters for the Elks, Kiwanis, Rotary, League of Women Voters, and the rest of the social service clubs and business vanguard of the community were not intended for them. A surprising number of our sample said that they did not feel welcome in church. One rarely hears or has to deal with the old "I'm the only one on the block" syndrome once attributed to upwardly mobile blacks. Being the lone black in a neighborhood, church, or college is not a distinction but a frustration.

As the black marketplace gets feedback from the blacks who have already taken assignments in predominantly white institutions, those in the market become a little distressed. One of the things they hear is that the black educator does not have time to be professional. He is asked to recruit black faculty and students, counsel and advise black students, serve on committees which deal with the problems of black students, act as a liaison person with the black community, and so on. In 83 percent of our sample in both two-year and four-year institutions, black staff members are asked to help resolve problems involving black students. Not every black is either prepared or desirous of working with black students or any student for that matter. Some, like their white colleagues, would prefer to do research in their academic disciplines and leave the advising and tutorial functions to others who have both the temperament and the skill to handle black student problems and who can act as public relations agents in the black community. These blacks, however, are severely criticized by students and other persons in the black community.

A random look at the black marketplace indicates that black educators are like nonblacks. Some of them are sober, narrow, tepid, ordinary men, distinguished only in their mediocrity. A closer look will also reveal some eccentric, bitter men—men who prepared themselves in law, education, physics, architecture, and other disciplines but who find themselves working in government, on the police force, in the Post Office, and as minor civil service employees. Their misapplied and undiscovered talents are lost to the society and to their own group. A few of them, understandably, do develop a nagging sense of inadequacy. Finally they reach a mental set where they are undisturbed by ambition. Theirs are the minds that are wasted in society. They are the men who have been relegated to the tireless exploration of the little minutiae which punctuate life. They do their jobs and get through the day. Many of them long ago submitted to the structured indignities prescribed for them. Outfoxed and overwhelmed, they lost the wisdom of choice and would be bewildered with what goes on in the innards of an educational institution. Their lives have been either one of the unintended ironies or deliberately planned hoaxes of society. Captured in the bitter bondage of race, some have given up.

Many community colleges, unlike four-year institutions, have recruited some of these blacks, provided them with some intense in-service training and have provided them with new careers. These institutions find that former college-trained men who, for a number of reasons, were "forced" to become policemen (for example), can teach police science better than a university-trained theorist; that a practicing nurse teaches nursing better than a classroom nurse; and so on. Blacks who chose the military services because they could not secure jobs commensurate with their training in civilian life have also been recruited into two-year colleges after they terminate their military careers. Many of these blacks who have been plucked from rank obscurity possess a fascinating repository of experiences and skills which are extremely useful to the students of a comprehensive community college. We found black men and women in the community college with degrees in architecture, for example, who could neither secure employment with architectural firms nor in four-year colleges. These persons were teaching drafting. The paradox is that these blacks were called in as consultants in both architectural firms and four-year institutions. In one case the design of a major structure carries the name of a white architect while the work was done by a black one. This, of course, is not new, even though it may not seem ethical. Professors have long been accused of taking the research and writing of their students and publishing it as their own. Black musicians, who moonlight as teachers, explain why they sometimes turn their backs on the audiences when they perform. One community college official who is also an outstanding musician indicated that professors of contemporary music send their students to watch how a performer will finger his instrument to achieve a certain musical effect in order to imitate it. In some cases, the students were being sent to learn from those who were "not qualified" to teach at the college.

All of this shows there is talent, torment, and tension in the black marketplace. Skepticism still abounds. Black educators do not believe that much has changed in the mainstream of society generally or in predominantly white colleges and universities in particular. They know that black educators exist on the underbelly of higher education and seem destined to always remain the professional survivors. They consider the purported changes new myths while they continue to encounter the old realities. They hear of the new moods but they cannot dispel the old memories. They see educators use tradition as a refuge rather than an instrument of illumination. They read a miscellany of contributors to professional journals who never mention the tragedy of the black scholar; they see buried in oblivion the work of the very, very few who do mention the problem. They vocalize how the agents of higher education are too sure of their own superiority to be greatly troubled by the lot of the average black educator. Talking with the persons in the black marketplace convinces one that there are some blacks in the predominantly white colleges who would like to get out, some outside who would like to get in, and there are many who are not sure.

There is pessimism in the black marketplace. The progress of the 1960s has been stymied in the early years of the 1970s; the women's movement has gained momentum in pursuit of the same goals as blacks in higher education; government spending for colleges has been seriously curtailed; equality of opportunity seems no longer a popular cause to support; and foundations are finding new innovations to fund. The academicians who were silent and gave neither their personal nor their professional support to the efforts to get black educators into their ranks are now screaming "reverse discrimination" when others make the efforts. Taxpayers —through their legislatures—are not providing funds for higher education the way they did during the last two decades. An oversupply of teachers and professors is reported in two-year and four-year institutions respectively. Students are no longer making nonnegotiable demands.

It is understandable, therefore, why the black educator is concerned. Blacks tell us that the academic community is retrenching. The signs of reversals are already apparent. Programs which never had real college status are being dropped. "The time has come to phase out these bastard programs," one administrator emphasizes. Untenured blacks are also being phased out. Department heads are receiving "confidential" memoranda which describe how they can legally fire personnel and avoid being taken to court. Already there is much discussion about a restriction on the number of persons awarded tenure (Jacobson, 1973, pp. 1–5; VanDyne, 1973, p. 7).

The Commission on Academic Tenure recently wrote in their report: "If institutions continue to award tenure to 60 to 80 percent, or more, of eligible faculty, and if faculty size does not grow proportionately, many will find themselves, within a few years, with tenure staffs so large that promotion for younger faculty will be increasingly difficult. The effort to bring increased numbers of women and *minority-group members* into the higher teaching ranks may be frustrated" (Keast and Macy, 1973, p. 7, italics ours).

There is also the problem of preferential retention of tenured faculty as a result of funding problems and lack of program growth. The statement issued by The Association of American Colleges recognizes and emphasizes that "Strict adherence to preferential retention of tenured faculty members or strict recognition of seniority, for example, may result in disparate rates of reduction for women or members of ethnic or racial minorities and thus jeopardize recent progress toward fairer representation of these groups in the academic community. Staff-reduction decisions may also raise problems in relation to laws and regulations governing discrimination" (Association of American Colleges statement, November 8, 1971, p. 4).

Since blacks were the last to come and most of them have not been in the academic promotion process long enough to be awarded tenure, they will be the first to encounter some of the proposed restrictions. Black educators see such a move as another of a long list of cruel and intended practices where they, who were the last to be discovered, are destined to be the first to be abandoned. Mattie T., a Chicago community college teacher, warned a group of new jobholders several years ago, "Simply because you have a new job with the men in America's gothic houses, don't invest your soul just yet. You should know better. Those boys will break your heart—a day at a time." The black men and women who work in special projects, who got their positions because of open admissions to accommodate the so-called disadvantaged students, who were appointed because the institution was getting federal funds, who were appointed in response to student demands for ethnic studies, who are new in higher education in predominantly white institutions, and, who therefore, are in the lower academic ranks, and those administrators with undefined roles and no authority—all the last to be hired—know that they will be the first to be fired. Nationwide, the signs are unmistakable. One respondent emphasizes, "The black purge has started, and it does not take long for the academic establishment to get back to business as usual."

A number of blacks, sensing the handwriting on the wall, are beginning to move back to predominantly black colleges, although some are returning out of a sense of commitment (Blau, 1973, p. 55). One thing is certain: black educators have been most thorough in their exploration of white institutions and exceedingly merciless in their findings. Those blacks who teach, or want to teach, do not appear to be as cynical as those who administer, or want to, and who know at best they will likely become assistants to other line and staff administrators.

Chapter Three

●●●●●●●●●●●●●●●●●●●●●
●●●●●●●●●●●●●●●●●●●●●●
●●●●●●●●●●●●●●●●●●●●●●

AFFIRMATIVE
ACTION

●●●●●●●●●●●●●●●●●●●●●●
●●●●●●●●●●●●●●●●●●●●●●
●●●●●●●●●●●●●●●●●●●●●●

*R*esistance to the employment
of blacks by white higher education institutions has forced some
blacks to appeal to the federal government for assistance in bringing discrimination suits against these institutions. Affirmative action
is the means through which these lawsuits are initiated. Affirmative
action has been used by a few blacks both as a threat and a
mechanism to combat faculty and institutional resistance, but it
has had little impact on selection and hiring. White women have
been more successful than blacks of both sexes in using affirmative
action to secure equal employment opportunities and the accompanying benefits. Most of the blacks with whom we had contact did not consider affirmative action a threat or a vehicle that
would be used successfully on their behalf.

Perhaps no single procedure to eliminate inequality in hiring
in higher education has surfaced the attitudes, fears, anxieties, and
bigoted behavior of academicians as has the affirmative action
concept. Affirmative action is considered by many white males in
the academic community to be the *enfant terrible* of all governmental involvement in higher education and is to be resisted at all

cost. Black educators of both sexes, however, tell us that, regardless of their qualifications, this plan is the only vehicle they have left to gain entry into the faculty and administrative ranks of predominantly white institutions. The vehicle is not an effective one; we are told that the federal government must enforce it, to make it work.

Except under extreme crisis the academic community has not taken steps to ameliorate the inequities in higher education. Discrimination against women has been far more publicized than discrimination against blacks in higher education. No conferences have been scheduled or held to promote equal treatment for blacks parallel to the fifty-fifth annual meeting of the American Council on Education (1972); no charges have been made by blacks to match the charges of women against three hundred sixty colleges and universities ("Faculty Backlash," 1972); no detailed government report has been made to specifically describe the discrimination against black educators, as those that were published in the interest of women (U.S. Department of Labor, 1969, p. 161). The *Junior College Journal* (Olson, 1972), the *Report on Higher Education* (Newman, 1971, pp. 51–56), *Newsweek, Science* (University Women's Rights, 1972, p. 151), *Change* (Moog, 1972, pp. 1–2), The *Journal of Higher Education* (Chalmers, 1972), The *Chronicle of Higher Education* (Fields, 1972a, 1972b, 1972c; Sievert, 1972; Semas, 1972), and hundreds of other professional and popular publications have responded to the plight of females and have publicized the barriers to them in higher education. No such documentation of and copy against injustices from such a wide variety of sources have been offered on behalf of black educators. We see mammoth studies which devote only lines (if any copy at all) to the plight of black scholars and their struggle for entry into higher education. Black educators have come to an obvious conclusion: the academic community is still morally calloused and responds only to threat and crisis.

The historical roots of affirmative action can be found in the Civil Rights Act of 1964 (under Title VII). Growing out of this act was an executive order (No. 11246) issued in 1965 by President Lyndon B. Johnson, and later, No. 11375. Both of these executive orders were designed to guarantee that institutions provide equal opportunity in employment for minorities and women. *Affirmative action* is the popular name for the plan to implement the executive orders. The plan has not been as potent in insuring black recruitment as they had hoped. Affirmative action can be both a corrective measure and a dilemma. It is a corrective measure because it is an effort of the federal government to establish guidelines to insure that the institutions which receive federal funds will include minorities and women among their applicants for faculty and administrative positions. It is a dilemma because any plan to modify the traditional sovereignty which exists in the departmental structure of colleges and universities creates a major problem. The biggest problem is to determine how blacks can be hired and integrated into colleges and departments without discriminating against whites, primarily white males. Whereas the problem is a real one and an issue which is incompatible with traditional faculty prerogatives, it is not an insurmountable one. We believe that academicians are a privileged class and they exist in a clearly established caste system. They could give up some of their privileges in order to establish and insure the rights of those who are not currently members of their class and caste.

The original executive orders generated neither much concern nor activity in the academic community. As the director of the Office for Civil Rights put it, "the higher education establishment remained unruffled" (Pottinger, 1972, p. 24). Order No. 4 from the Department of Labor finally shook the academic community from its posture of indifference. This order outlined affirmative action requirements and supplemented them with guidelines. Revisions of the order were issued in 1971 and 1972 to handle some of the problems encountered in the application of the guidelines. Educators insisted that the guidelines were unclear. Essentially, Order No. 4 declares that the government finds women and minorities underutilized in specific occupations. The order also threatened to withhold the federal funds of institutions which did not develop affirmative action plans to recruit and hire minorities and women. It was believed, perhaps naively, that the threat of a cutoff of federal funds would stimulate some and force other administrators to comply with the regulations.

Academicians did not respond to affirmative action enforcement procedures wtih magnanimity or equanimity. Instead of looking for ways to make affirmative action plans work and providing leadership which would help to bring about equity in the employment of minorities, some of them looked for reasons why such a plan would not work. They conjured up real and imaginary problems which they said would not permit an educational institution to accommodate such a plan.

They immediately took to the podium and the printed page and charged or implied that those in the black marketplace who wanted entry into the academic community were unqualified and incompetent. Most of them did not resort to academic jargon—or what Mike Royko (1972) calls *educatorese*—the language "spoken and written by educators, to prevent those . . . who aren't educators from knowing what they are up to." Their denouncements have been direct, free of ambiguity, and unvarnished. They also denounced the federal government for instituting such a plan. Affirmative action guidelines were vehemently condemned by educators, notably by such men as philosopher Sidney Hook of New York University, political scientist Paul Seabury of the University of California at Berkeley, and John Bunzel, president of San Jose State College. These men suggest that the guidelines will lead "inexorably to the hiring of unqualified persons for irrelevant reasons" (Goodman, 1972, p. 114). Once HEW began to apply pressure to educational institutions, popular and professional publications printed statements from educators to the effect that an educational institution was not a business and could not be run like a business.

Robert Perrins puts it this way (1972): "The federal government has been slow in realizing that employment descriptions and practices in an institution of higher education are not as easily quantifiable as, say, those in an automobile plant."

J. Stanley Pottinger, the Director of the Office of Civil Rights of HEW, noted (Goodman, 1972, p. 118): "Universities have 'been slow to develop systematic ways of keeping track of who is in their employment ranks . . . decisions as to who will go and who will stay are not always susceptible to measurement.' Institutions of higher education have been singularly reluctant to admit any sort of external influence on the policies and practices which govern their operations and their faculties in particular."

Others insist that accounting is impossible in colleges and

universities and that affirmative action demands a kind of account-ability which colleges and universities cannot meet at present. Some maintain that it is impossible to even collect certain data in large colleges and universities. Others insist that head count and ethnic identity (required by affirmative action officials) was against the law in the 1950s and 1960s and the current demand for it is a step backward.

Some educators go to to core of the matter and ask about their departmental prerogatives to determine which candidates are qualified to teach in their disciplines. Academicians did not turn inward and appraise what could be done; rather, they accepted tradition as a commandment and they worked strenuously to keep it. Words like *quota* were introduced; phrases like *conflict of interest* were suggested to describe competition between minorities and women. Repeatedly we read, "We cannot find qualified blacks." Questions about the lowering of standards and academic excellence were asked, and many irrelevant assumptions, hypo-thetical situations, and predictions were introduced.

Although administrators are often charged with the respon-sibility for racial discrimination in higher education institutions, in reality they are frequently the scapegoats, defenders rather than perpetrators of the unlawful and illegal practices. The Committee on Discrimination from the AAUP recognizes that "In too many cases it is the faculty itself, or a significant portion of it, which has opposed change in such areas as appointment policies. Improperly utilizing the principle of preserving quality, faculty members re-sponsible for recommending appointments have denied entrance to the academy to women and to persons of minority race and back-ground. Faculties have likewise doubtless been influenced by exist-ing patterns which lead to discrimination based on improper considerations in such matters as salary, retention, promotion, and service on decision-making bodies" (Konheim, 1972, p. 162).

We must make it explicit that we subscribe to the concept of excellence; persons should be chosen on the basis of their quali-fications and other criteria for the finding and hiring of competent faculty members, exclusive of the consideration of skin color or sex. We want to be equally explicit in advocating the affirmative action concept. The two ideas are not in conflict, but it appears that a significant number of educators subscribe to the first and reject the second.

We have not found any evidence in articles or elsewhere that blacks and women who want access into the teaching and administrative ranks of higher education are unqualified. Neoacademic demagogues are playing to the base fears of people, i.e., job security, loss of university traditions, discrimination of white men in order to hire blacks and women, and retaliatory actions for failure to provide redress for past discrimination. Using trigger words and phrases such as *quotas* and *the lowering of standards* which have the same emotional content as *busing, open housing, abortion,* and *amnesty,* educators have abandoned scholarly approaches and are behaving like columnists (Chamberlain, 1972) and labor unionists, if not bigots. Stretching interpretation, quoting out of context, substituting one word for another (e.g., *quota* for *goals*), speculating on outcomes, emphasizing that exceptions must be made in professional criteria, speaking for others, and defining the desires and intent of others without consulting them are prevailing examples and familiar techniques of the demagogue. These men are using a string of adjectives which are superficial and factless, emotional and thoughtless, vitriolic and tasteless—in sum, disagreement by tantrum. Their techniques and behavior are useless in reaching an equitable solution, if any solution at all. That all of this is coming from the pens of educators makes it all the more reprehensible.

A number of distinguished authors who we can cite have been guilty of such activity. In Bunzel's article, "The Politics of Quotas" (1972, p. 34), he writes: "One of the most critical issues is the extent to which the commitment to increase the percentage of minorities in college faculties can coexist with the maintenance of professional standards in hiring and retention."

Why is this a critical issue? Is there any reason to believe that standards will not be maintained? The hypothetical and controversial suggestion implied by Bunzel's statement seems to lack empirical data.

All of the available evidence that we have been able to collect indicates that those institutions which have been challenged for discrimination have, indeed, applied a double standard. An example is the case of the University of Michigan, which awarded women salaries disproportionately lower than those awarded men while at the same time admitting that they were as competent as their male counterparts who held the same rank.

Bunzel further writes: "Giving faculty appointments immediately to large numbers of relatively unqualified persons will do a serious disservice to all graduate students presently pursuing their degrees, and, indeed to all students." And he suggests that there are "other questions which have to do with the consequences of establishing dual sets of criteria for faculty appointment and retention."

Who is asking that such steps be taken? Why does one's race (or sex) require an additional set of criteria?

Bunzel's inconsistency is observable in comparing two of his articles. In a 1968 article (pp. 35–36), he responds to an educator who suggests that Black Studies should have black professors, by asking two questions: "Is the color of one's skin more important than the substance of the course? Is color the test of competence?" We say no to both questions. And our respondents indicate that, "the best qualified, irrespective of race," should teach courses in a black curriculum. It is only when blacks and whites are equally qualified that they believed that the black should be given preference; 87 percent reject the idea that only blacks should teach Black Studies.

Bunzel's questions and statements in the 1972 article suggest that skin color and sex *do* indicate inherent incompetence and a threat of lost standards. According to Bunzel, those who represent the black marketplace and women will be "relatively unqualified persons [who] will do a serious disservice . . . to all graduate students." Our data show that 38 women sit on dissertation committees, 24 of whom are allowed to chair these committees. Similarly, 211 men sit on dissertation committees, and 171 of them are permitted to chair them. While Bunzel does not define what he means by "large numbers," 249 persons are not likely to seriously challenge or harm graduate education in America. Also, it does not seem logical to give "faculty appointments immediately" to any "relatively unqualified persons," regardless of their race and sex.

Only 148 of our respondents in four-year institutions have the full-time responsibility of teaching graduate students. While it is possible that these men and women may "do a serious disservice to . . . all graduate students presently pursuing their degrees," to quote Bunzel, the facts which would substantiate such a broad and sweeping assertion have not, to our knowledge, been offered. There is another question: "Who will decide who is relatively unqualified?"

Philosopher Charles Frankel goes even further when he says ("Faculty Backlash," 1972, 127): "If you hire unqualified women [and by inference we think he also means minorities], bright white males don't get jobs." Maybe Frankel is right. However, many of those, like the authors, who challenge the rationale for such a statement believe that Frankel would be on sounder ground if he offered evidence to substantiate the reason for his concern. What is disturbing is his chauvinism. Hiring unqualified persons of either sex and of any race would result in a number of bright white males, bright white females, and bright minorities of both sexes not getting as many of the available positions. Frankel, however, seems only concerned about "bright white males."

In a 1968 article Dr. Bunzel writes, "It has only been recently that colleges and universities have succeeded in removing *politics* as a test for hiring and firing." This is a naive statement, and the author would be hard pressed to prove that politics have been successfully removed from colleges and universities as a test for hiring and firing. His own writings belie and contradict it. Perhaps he should read some of the recent literature which indicates that administrators are beginning to be keenly conscious of faculty applicants' dress, hair, politics, and so forth before hiring them (Budig, 1972, p. 648). The Harvard firing of nontenured economists who were considered radical is another such situation (*Newsweek*, June 5, 1973, p. 67). If by politics, Bunzel could possibly mean that the old quota system designed to limit the number of Jews in the academic community is no longer operative, he may be correct. If he means, however, that colleges and universities no longer discriminate against minorities and women, he is not familiar with the practices of the educational institutions of this country.

Articles which omit facts, distort information, use scare tactics, resort to innuendo, predict doom, and pose questions to confuse rather than to illuminate are inherently political. "What makes you think professors are any different from other white people?" questioned one of our respondents. "They are as much like Archie Bunker as any other group you can identify; of course they are political." It does appear that affirmative action is a political procedure notwithstanding its moral and legal implications.

We have read the affirmative action guidelines, including the controversial Order No. 4, from the Department of Labor. Some excerpts follow: "An affirmative action program is a set of specific and result-oriented procedures to which a contractor commits himself to apply every good-faith effort. The objective of these procedures plus such efforts is equal employment opportunity. Procedures without effort to make them work are meaningless; and effort, undirected by specific and meaningful procedures, is inadequate. An acceptable affirmative action program must include an analysis of areas within which the contractor is deficient in the utilization of minority groups and women, and further, goals and timetables to which the contractor's good-faith efforts must be directed to correct the deficienies and thus to increase materially the utilization of minorities and women, at all levels and in all segments of his work force where deficiencies exist."

While the language is hardly breathless prose, one thing is clear: it does not indicate in any place that an institution is expected to lower its standards, hire unqualified persons, or to set quotas.

Pottinger offers a rationale for the quota distraction (1972, p. 24): "Every crusade must have its simplistic side—a galvanizing symbol, a boogeyman, a rallying cry. The word *quotas* serves these rhetorical purposes in the present case. Since quotas are not required or permitted by the executive order (11246), they are for the most part a phony issue, but very much an issue nevertheless."

Pottinger admonishes college administrators that they ought to do their hiring "without a compromise of quality" (Goodman, 1972, p. 118). And the Committee on Discrimination of the AAUP reports, "A properly conceived affirmative action effort, it must be emphasized, neither requires nor implies the placement of unqualified persons in any position, nor does it require the dilution of valid standards for appointment or promotion to any position" (Konheim, 1972, p. 163).

Paul Seabury, on the other hand, cloaks his resistance in some of the same logic as John Bunzel, but adds a social dimension.

Seabury writes (1972a): "They [universities] are now required to redress national social injustices within their walls at their own expense. Compliance with demands from the federal government to do this would compel a stark remodeling of their criteria of recruitment, their ethos of professionalism, and their standards of excellence" (Seabury, 1972, pp. 38–44).

This statement should not go unchallenged. National social injustices are not the issue; racism and discrimination within the walls of the university are, although the two ideas may be two sides of the same issue. The black faculty members with whom we talked are not asking predominantly white universities to redress social problems of the entire nation, but they are demanding that white faculties and administrators redress their own practices of injustice within the walls of the institution.

Seabury's assertion that universities are required to do redress "at their own expense" is hardly accurate. The author himself noted, "as early as 1967, the federal government was annually disbursing contract funds to universities at the rate of three and a half billion dollars a year" (Seabury, 1972, p. 39). And the Carnegie Commission has recommended that this amount be tripled.

If compliance with federal guidelines, that is, publicizing vacant or new faculty positions in colleges and universities and making them accessible to *all* of those who are qualified and who apply requires "a stark remodeling of their criteria of recruitment," then the recruitment criteria were perverse in the first place. And if the purported hundreds of thousands of excellent minds which populate American colleges and universities cannot devise recruitment procedures which eliminate race and sex as a handicap, then one must seriously question the quality of those minds. As to the "ethos of professionalism," one of the meanings of the word *ethos* is "the universal or objective elements of a situation or condition as distinguished from the emotional or subjective elements." Scholars are supposed to seek the truth, accommodate reality, and deal with objective evidence; it is difficult for those who are less scholarly to understand how academicians ignore intellectual rigor and permit irrational behavior and statements to take precedent over reason. We believe that Seabury is irresponsible when he says, "Large numbers of highly qualified scholars will pay with their careers simply because they are male and white" (*Newsweek*, Dec. 4, 1972, p. 127). He was bitterly attacked for this statement (*Newsweek*, Dec. 11, 1972, pp. 4–5). Such a statement is as unfounded as his attitude appears to be deep-seated. White males in America will never suffer while blacks and females of any color enjoy preferential treatment.

Seabury and others organized a movement to end the policy of what he calls "reverse discrimination" in higher education. The instrument of this movement is called Committee on Non-Discrimination and Integrity (*Newsweek*, Dec. 4, 1972, p. 5). Women and blacks appear to believe that this committee is nothing more than a front or straw organization, a distraction to blunt the charges of discrimination, racism, and sexism against the individual members and to cover up the charges of bigotry. They are asking, "Where was the committee of five hundred scholars and their moral outrage . . . when blacks and women were systematically excluded from employment on college faculties?"

While Seabury talks a great deal about the standards of excellence (1972b), he does not define it nor do we hear it defined by other critics. Each discipline, each institution, even each person has his own concept of excellence. In fact, we hear more about the prestige of an institution where a candidate comes from than about its standards. About the only standards we are able to consistently identify in four-year colleges and universities as they seek an applicant is that the individual must hold the Ph.D. in his discipline, must have good letters of recommendation, and have a pleasing personality (Caplow and McGee, 1965, pp. 108–115). In community colleges, he should have the master's degree or its equivalent. It appears that good letters of recommendation are expected by all institutions. From that point on everything is negotiable. Often the candidate's publications are not read (Caplow and McGee, 1965, p. 111; Van den Berghe, 1970, p. 88). If the department wants the man, however, he meets the standards. E. L. Chalmers indicates that the criteria or standards employed to evaluate faculty "are difficult to verbalize and virtually impossible to qualify" (1972, p. 523). And William Boyd's report, *Access and Power for Blacks in Higher Education,* from the Educational Policy Center, notes that there is an absence of reasonable and stable reference points or standards. The document states, "Standards set for blacks tend to be rigid, arbitrary, and discriminatory, or to be so flexible, unpredictable, and patronizing that they become meaningless" (1972, p. 10).

When some white educators do eventually concede that qualified minorities can be found, they also indicate that giving consideration to them as a method of remediation for past injustices amounts to a social welfare program: "To say that the minority people to be hired will be 'qualified' is to evade the issue. If they are indeed qualified or qualifiable, and affirmative action is taken, they will move at a certain pace into these positions anyway. But the inescapable assumption of the ascriptive approach, of the literal quota, is that minority people are *not* qualified or qualifiable, that they *cannot* compete even if given a competitive margin. The proposers of such a quota system are calling, then, for a social welfare program, pure and simple, which indeed should not be performance-connected. . . . Is the belief to be developed that performance should be abandoned on every level as a criterion, not only of accomplishment, but of a sense of accomplishment? This would involve not only a basic shift in our values as a society, but a cruel and destructive hoax on expectations" (Raab, 1972, p. 43).

Both Seabury and Bunzel quoted an excerpt from Justice Harlan's statement when the jurist dissented from the "separate but equal" doctrine in the case of *Plessy* v. *Ferguson* in 1896. The Supreme Court endorsed the concept. In dissenting, Harlan wrote in part: "Our constitution is color-blind." While the constitution may be "color-blind," the historical outrages against minorities provide overwhelming evidence which suggests that too many of the citizens who should administer this concept of color blindness are, in fact, blinded by color. Higher education is not exempt. Seabury also quoted Felix Frankfurter, who was purported to be impressed with how the selection system in colleges worked. An excerpt from Frankfurter's statement follows: "What mattered was excellence in your profession to which your father and your face was equally irrelevant."

Perhaps Frankfurter is regarding his own autobiography and experience as precedent; it is certainly not history. Since the jurist was neither a black nor a female who had been denied an equal opportunity to join a college or university staff, it is possible that he never encountered the extent to which one's face and sex *is* relevant in the "community of masters." He was Jewish, and that fact alone has been considered by many Americans to be an affliction and just reason for discrimination. As such, the justice must have known the extent to which one's father *is* relevant. He was on the bench during the famous *numerus clausus* which was used to restrict the number of Jews admitted to the faculty ranks and the professional schools. This was a quota system, and it has since been eliminated in most colleges. Seabury notes in his *Commentary* article, "HEW and the Universities" (February 1972), "with the triumph of equal employment opportunity over quotas, the last bastions of discrimination collapsed" (Seabury, 1972a, p. 44).

The Women's Equity Action League (WEAL) apparently did not know that "the last bastions of discrimination [had] collapsed" since this organization filed charges against three hundred sixty colleges for alleged discrimination ("Inside HEW," 1971, p. 270; "Faculty Backlash," 1972, p. 127). Certainly the *Report of the President's Commission on Campus Unrest* indicates the feeling that discrimination is still around. Racial injustice on the campus was one of the major focuses of the report. "They [students] denounce the university's relationship to discriminatory racial practices" (*Report of the President's Commission on Campus Unrest,* 1971, p. 4). Kenneth B. Clark, who has served on the board of trustees of two colleges, is a well-respected professor of psychology, a consultant to the U.S. Government, a member of the New York Board of Regents, and has testified before congressional committees, also disagrees with Seabury. Clark indicates (1970, p. 7): "The fact that race is a significant, if not *the* significant, factor in American education certainly seems no longer to be debatable."

While Seabury tells us in one article that the bastions of discrimination have collapsed, a few months later, in a second article in *Commentary* (December 1972), he leads us to believe that discrimination is inherent in American society. He does not deny that discrimination exists and that it should not exist. Rather, he suggests that those discriminated against should not be provided with *legal* means to apply the same tactics against the discriminators. We are compelled to remind him that discrimination and segregation in housing, schooling, employment, and in many other facets of American life have *legal* precedent. Seabury seems to be saying that two wrongs do not make a right; we suggest that neither will one wrong make a right. It also appears to us that he is saying to the victims, "Do not trespass; but forgive those who trespass against you." He does ask (1972b, p. 44), however, what we think is a good question: "Is discrimination as objectionable when pressed on behalf of previously disadvantaged minority groups as when pressed on behalf of advantaged ones?" The response from most (not all) of our respondents is a resounding yes. Seabury offers no options or alternatives beyond the procedures currently used, and these have been employed to discriminate against minority groups in the first place.

Daniel Bell, who also rejects affirmative action, insists (1972, p. 41): "As a principle, equality of opportunity denies the precedence of birth, of nepotism, of patronage, or any other criterion which allocates place, other than fair competition open equally to talent and ambition." We submit that this principle is as laudable as the Ten Commandments, but the implementation in both cases leaves much to be desired.

It is clear that Bunzel, Seabury, Bell, and others mainly speculate about the evils of affirmative action and project a fear that borders on paranoia of the unqualified black and female onslaught. They and few of the other opponents of affirmative action deal with the facts which have given rise to such an action and even fewer seem to offer suggestions, solutions, or even helpful comment. While these academicians are purported to deal with objective data, they have not produced evidence which would support their claim that compliance with affirmative action guidelines will require institutions to hire unqualified persons, lower the standards, and lose excellence. This is a point so obvious that its implications seem completely overlooked.

Since the opponents do not offer facts, here are a few facts: (1) colleges and universities have discriminated against minorities and women (Caplow and McGee, 1965, p. 194; Astin and Bayer, 1972); (2) colleges have been involved in *preferential hiring practices* which excluded minorities and women (Caplow and McGee, 1965, pp. 94–96); (3) colleges have paid disproportionately higher salaries to men than to women (Olson, 1972); (4)

colleges and universities do employ a closed system to identify potential faculty and administrators (Caplow and McGee, 1965, p. 115); (5) higher education institutions do award tenure to persons who have not published (Barzun, 1970, p. 43); (6) colleges and universities have limited the enrollment of minorities and women in Ph.D. programs (*Trends in Educational Attainment of Women,* 1969, p. 16; Newman, 1970, p. 73; 1971, p. 52); (7) institutions have passed over the person who is most qualified because he was a threat to the nonproducers in the department (Caplow and McGee, 1965; Van den Berghe, 1970); (8) colleges have hired younger and less qualified persons because they were cheaper to get (Caplow and McGee, 1965; Van den Berghe, 1970); (9) community colleges do allow discriminatory programs to exist on the campuses of public-supported institutions; (10) minorities and women do wait longer than white males for tenure and promotion (*Careers of Ph.D.'s,* 1968).

When confronted with these facts, academicians retort that they are not responsible for what happened in the past, and even the courts support them in some cases. Their protests are understandable. While some may exonerate them from injustices perpetrated against minorities and others in the past, however, we and others (those in the black marketplace) hold them responsible for maintaining the discriminatory practices, for perpetuating the injustices of the past, and for justifying these practices under the guise of tradition. Still others are appalled that they take no action and offer no leadership to help ameliorate the inequity in the academic community. Clark Kerr has warned us to expect this (1964): "When change comes it is rarely of the instigation of this group of partners [academicians] as a collective body. The group is more likely to accept or reject or comment, than to devise and propose."

It is ironic that Bunzel, Seabury, and other eminent scholars who emphasize publication and research as the criteria for excellence and the mark of qualification never mention teaching as a criterion. Lack of concern for teaching has been of special note for some scholars (Barzun, 1970, p. 69). Students resent the fact that teaching is no longer the central concern of postsecondary institutions (Kerr, 1964, p. 104; Van den Berghe, 1970, p. 37). Faculties in both two-year and four-year colleges appear unconcerned about teaching in two ways. The first is instruction. Too many of them are not punctual, are slipshod in marking papers, ill prepared in lectures, and careless about assignments. They do not follow the procedures of good instruction—establishing sound objectives and giving sufficient time and attention to preparation, presentation, application, and evaluation. The second lack of concern in teaching is manifested in withholding or withdrawing service to students. A number of faculty members refuse to keep office hours, will not serve as advisors to students, refuse to teach or will only teach students they select; many take sabbaticals and other leaves while serving on the committees of students who are in the process of completing their degrees.

Yet teaching is probably one of the strongest skills of black educators. Many of them have had considerable experience in giving instruction. They have taught heavy classloads to large numbers of students who, by white standards, would not be considered prepared for college and would not, in many instances, be admitted to college in the first place. As we have said, black educators have worked under the most adverse conditions, in poorly equipped and inadequately financed schools. These colleges have been considered compensatory and the majority of the students, by any measurement criteria in popular use, rank lower than their white counterparts. Yet, it is a tribute to their loyalty, commitment, and skill that more than 90 percent of all of the black Ph.D.'s in America today earned their undergraduate degrees from predominantly black schools. Many of the black educators who currently teach in predominantly white institutions and are considered qualified by their white colleagues not only came from faculty positions in predominantly black colleges, but also were themselves the products of such schools. Whether or not blacks who come to the college are good teachers does not appear to be the paramount concern among scholars. There seems to be more concern about how many will be allowed to come.

The critics of affirmative action maintain that blacks, among other minorities (and women) who may seek employment in higher education, and who may be hired as a result of such action, will be unqualified. We have not been informed as to how those critics have made their assessment of future applicants, nor have we seen any empirical data that assesses the competence of blacks currently working as professionals in predominantly white institutions. Are the opponents of affirmative action simply speculating that black educators who may get their jobs as a result of the provisions under the Civil Rights Act of 1964 and its subsequent Executive orders (11246, 11375) will be unqualified? Or are they basing their decisions on the performances of the black educators who are now working in the academic community? If the explanation is the former, it must be rejected and condemned for lack of evidence. If it is the latter, then we would ask several questions with regard to black educators currently serving in predominantly white institutions: Are they poor teachers, deficient researchers, and incompetent administrators? Are they men and women without talent whose students complain about the quality of their instruction, their refusal to advise, or their failure to keep conference hours? Have their supervisors complained of their inefficiency? In short, are they qualified or not? If they are not qualified, they should not be there. But they should know, specifically, who decided their status, on what basis, and the procedures used; and they should certainly know they are being evaluated. On the other hand, if they *are* qualified, what makes them such? They should know this also. We believe that these questions deserve answers.

It is widely held by affirmative action opponents (and others) in the academic community that one is measured or evaluated by his colleagues. This idea belongs more to rhetoric than to reality, more to public relations than to policy and practice. We have been unable to find a black scholar who reports that he has had his teaching observed by a teaching colleague, a department chairman, or, in the case of two-year colleges, a division chairman. The real or pretended academic courtesies and traditions are pervasive (for example, the belief that a colleague knows and can teach his discipline) and do not permit one's colleagues to observe the instruction of another without invitation. In senior colleges, professors know that their classrooms, laboratories, and other teaching stations are "off-limits" to all but assigned students, persons who get permission from the professor, and individuals who are invited. Some would suggest that this is granting teachers immunity from responsible appraisal. In two-year colleges, the same situations prevail, but many of them have an added guarantee—through collective bargaining, they know that very little if any observation and evaluation of their teaching activities will be carried on by administrators and other supervisory personnel. We are not arguing that one's colleagues should spend time evaluating him; although perhaps they should. What we are suggesting is that they do not. It does not appear, to us at least, that academicians really want to evaluate themselves; and the response of scholars to proposals that they be evaluated by others is rather well known. In sum, accountability in higher education seems little more than an academic argument. And since the academic community appears to have neither the means nor the disposition to evaluate its members, how does it determine who, among those outside and inside, may be qualified? It administers no examination to an applicant beyond an interview; it has no guideline as to the quantity and quality of publications one must produce in order to be qualified; it does not indicate what field services are the important ones for professionals to perform; it does not suggest what professional organizations are the best ones for colleagues to hold membership in; its definition of merit is vague and has not found consensus even within its ranks and among its members.

In summary, if the critics of affirmative action, who are a part of higher education, have not evaluated those blacks (and others) inside the academic community whom they obstensibly know, how can they evaluate those black professionals petitioning for entry into higher education whom they do not know? Perhaps the scholars are so concerned about the number of blacks who may seek entry into higher education that they have refused to be confronted with such obvious considerations. They do seem almost paranoid when they speak as if a "quota system" is being forced upon the higher education enterprise.

Some eminent scholars seem most disturbed by the word *goal* as it is used in the affirmative action language. They maintain that it is a code word for *quota*. Blacks agree that code words hide much that is perverse in education.

White male faculty and administrators often insist that the *goals* required by affirmative action guidelines are *quotas*. They resurrect all of the unjust practices related to quotas which some of those in higher education have used to limit for some people (certain ethnic groups) and deny to others (certain racial groups) individual rights, employment opportunities, and personal and economic rewards which they themselves enjoy. According to 80 percent of our male and female respondents in community colleges and 70 percent of those in four-year colleges, incompetent blacks have not been hired "to meet some numerical or stipulated goal or quota." Yet, some academicians charge that quotas are being established and that the federal government is less than honest when it refuses to call a quota a *quota*.

The black men and women who were our respondents feel that the professors and administrators are also dishonest. They tell us that they understand the distaste academicians have for the word *quota;* they have the same distaste for the way college people use the word. They point out that while academicians do not want a quota system to apply to the number of blacks, other minorities, and females recruited and hired in the colleges and universities, the professoriate is using the word to accomplish the same ends for which the word *busing* has been used. We have also observed the uncomfortable parallel between the behavior of public school officials and teachers and university adminstrators and professors: just as *busing* has become the rallying word for many people to cover up their real attitudes and justify their behavior in regard to bringing black children into their schools, so has *quota* served the same purpose for faculty members in two-year and four-year colleges in regard to bringing black faculty and administrators into previously all-white colleges. Just as politicians have used the busing issue to further their own ends and to resist and defy the "all deliberate speed" mandate of the Supreme Court, so educators have used the quota issue to stall affirmative action plans. Just as those who resist integration of public schools predict that bringing black children into previously all-white schools will require the schools to lower their standards and will result in inferior schools, so educators insist that the hiring of black professors will require colleges to lower their requirements and lose their standards of excellence. And just as public school officials use the "all deliberate speed" language and loopholes of the 1954 *Brown* v. *The Board of Education* decision of the Supreme Court to evade the spirit of the decision and to implement or oppose it according to their own proposals, time-tables, and desires, so college administrators, supported by the professoriate, use the "every good faith" language and loopholes of Order No. 4 of the Department of Labor to evade implementation of Executive Order 11246. Comparisons are seldom perfect; the two issues may be difficult, but the parallel is unmistakable.

Another thing black educators find disturbing is the tendency of those who are critical of affirmative action to ridicule some of the efforts of the government because of the distortion of the quota idea. Roche reports that Seabury "has developed two hybrid labels which put the [*quota* v. *goal*] question in perspective: the *quoal*, a slow-moving quota-goal; and the *gota*, which is a supple, fast-moving quota-goal" (1973, p. 48). Roche also notes that another professor, whom he did not identify, proposed a sociological caucus (with regard to quotas) composed of "two blacks (one man, one woman); one Chicano (or Chicana on alternate elections); one person to be, in alphabetical rotation, American Indian, Asian, and Eskimo; and sixteen white Anglos. Of the latter, eight will be men and eight women; fourteen will have to be heterosexual and two homosexual (one of these to be a lesbian); one Jewish, ten Protestant, four Roman Catholic; and one in alphabetical rotation, Buddhist, Mormon, and Muslim; fifteen will have to be sighted and one blind; eight must be juvenile, four mature, and four senile; and two must be intelligent, ten mediocre and four stupid." We do not believe that blacks we know would consider either of the above statements humorous.

Few will deny that some of the HEW guidelines have been considered confusing at times; some of the actions taken have seemed capricious to the adversaries of affirmative action; and all of the procedures have not yet stood the test of time and operation in the attempt to ameliorate discrimination in the academic community. But it seems unreasonable to expect HEW officials to anticipate and answer each question, to plug each loophole, and to satisfy every unreadiness.

Regarding public schools, even a comedian is aware that the results of the 1954 decision are unsatisfactory. We need no reminder that the public schools are more segregated now than before. And in regard to the institutions of higher education, unless the federal government enforces the affirmative action guidelines, the outcome of the Civil Rights Law of 1964 and Executive Order 11246 are predictable. Those in the black marketplace fully expect the academic community to behave like partisan politicians, that is, to let their own personal advantages supercede principle as the arbiter of racial discrimination.

We do not wish to suggest that the affirmative action problem is not difficult. It is even more difficult when one considers the job market in higher education in the early 1970s. Adding to the difficulties is the problem of women versus minorities. We believe Seabury is right when he notes (1972a) that HEW officials "now scent sexism more easily than racism in the crusade to purify university hiring practices. Minority-group spokesmen grumble when this powerful feminine competitor appears, to horn in. In the dynamics of competition between race and sex for scarce places on university faculties, a new hidden crisis in higher education is brewing."

Blacks are certainly aware of this problem; some of them interpret the great attention to women as one strategy to minimize their efforts and to promote females in preference to them. "After all," as one black faculty member astutely states, "white women may be considered the lesser of two evils when compared with blacks of both sexes."

Institutions should maintain equity for all persons irrespective of race or sex. It will require extremely hard work by all persons concerned to seek a solution that is fair to all. We believe the academic community has the expertise to do the task. But at this juncture the community of scholars is doing more to create barriers to an equitable solution than to suggest ways that a solution might be reached.

It is apparent that white women are in a better position to accomplish their goals than are minorities. They have done voluminous research on discrimination in higher education against their sex. There are more of them who already have many of the credentials that academic departments seek. Their movement has overshadowed the black movement for the present. And those in the black marketplace suggest, unless we are completely naive, that they are well aware that the chances are better for a white female than they are for any minority person—male or female.

At present, however, affirmative action plans to insure equity and to prevent discrimination in higher education are no more successful in colleges and universities than they are in the construction trades. Perhaps the situation is worse. The academicians should know the intellectual and moral implications of their behavior. Colleges and universities seemed more responsive to hiring blacks as a result of student activism than because of the moral persuasion and veiled threats of HEW. Our data show that 51 percent of the two-year college respondents and 57 percent of the four-year college respondents felt this way; more men than women (57 percent of the men, 43 percent of the women in two-year colleges; 66 percent of the men, 57 percent of the women in four-year colleges) chose this response. For the most part, affirmative action guidelines have neither been followed nor enforced. The 1972 guidelines, attempts to clarify earlier directives, minimized some of their effectiveness and created loopholes (Fields, 1972a; *Newsweek,* Dec. 4, 1972, p. 5).

Society never creates loopholes for the victims. Thousands of college departments still do not have a single black or female faculty member or any other minorities. Opponents of affirmative action ask, if preferential hiring should take place for blacks, why not for the Irish? Italians? or Germans? We, in turn, asked our respondents the same question. A Miami-Dade Community College respondent answers the question: "The next time somebody asks that question, you ask him . . . the nationality of the guy at the next desk, in the adjoining department, the man in the admissions office, and the thousands of presidents, deans, and boards of trustees members who are not black." Those in the black marketplace look at discrimination against females and Jews quite differently; the outcome as well as the nature of the discrimination appears to be different.

Women who manage to get hired in colleges and universities and who attempt to move up the rank hierarchy clearly have a harder time than men. Women who achieve the rank of full professor in biological sciences, for example, wait two to five years longer for promotion than men, as much as ten years or longer in the social sciences. Correspondingly, married women wait five to ten years longer than single women (*Careers of Ph.D.'s,* 1968). Women average lower salaries than men in each of the academic ranks (*Salaries,* 1966, pp. 3–4). And contrary to what male academicians would have you believe—that discrimination against women in higher education is declining—"the plight of the woman in higher education in the job market has not improved, but worsened" (Newman, 1971, p. 55).

White females, unlike blacks of both sexes, have been in the academy for a long time, but not many of them. At least they were hired. While they were employed, they were used, refused promotion, given a disproportionately lower salary for the same work as their male counterparts, and many of them were denied tenure.

The women are now fighting back. They have initiated investigations by HEW compliance officers and have demanded investigations by the Equal Educational Opportunity Commission under Title VII. Affirmative action programs have been demanded. They have claimed and have been awarded back pay in proven cases of sex discrimination in salary. They are having their day in court, and many institutions of higher education are responding to their demands. Voluminous research on their plight has been done, and much is still under way. The findings demonstrate conclusively the extent to which they have been discriminated against. Fortunately, they have had some within their ranks who are already in the academic community and who not only have the research skill but also the time and resources, especially the resources of the institutions where they work. Others among them are married to academicians who can identify the vulnerable points they might attack in the academic armor.

Jews have also largely won the battle against the quota system which was designed to limit their numbers in the community of scholars, although there are still institutions without Jewish representation. The system was abandoned because it was demonstrated that the very fibre of higher education lacked integrity by maintaining it and because the system could produce neither a valid rationale nor academic criteria to justify the exclusion of an ethnic group that is so well known for its scholarship. Now many

Jewish academicians, supported by powerful organizations such as B'nai B'rith, oppose affirmative action ("Minority Hiring," 1972, p. 4; Poinsett, 1973, p. 35). Some of them perceive many of their hard-fought gains under threat. At the dedication of the Johnson Library, President Lyndon B. Johnson said it well when he said, "Those who have struggled long to gain advantages for themselves do not readily yield the gains of their own struggles so that others may have advantages." Although affirmative action poses no threat to the gains of Jews, some of them oppose it, primarily male Jews. The cluster of fears, anxieties, insecurities, and hostilities seem unfounded.

Blacks have a very different story and a different problem. Blacks were not denied on the basis of a quota system; they were denied altogether. Both their faces and their fathers were black. And contrary to Frankfurter's insistence that these two criteria are not relevant, the evidence of their relevance is overwhelming.

Some of those resisting the hiring of blacks into higher education are describing and labeling their own graduates as "unqualified." Many of the blacks are called unqualified by the same institutions at which they obtained their graduate degrees, by the same professors who advised them, and by the same departments that directed their dissertations. Mommsen's investigation (1972a) indicates that 95 percent of the blacks who hold the doctorate have obtained them from white institutions.

It appears that the crime of black educators is that in the past the overwhelming majority of them were forced to go and teach in predominantly black colleges where they had neither the means, time (due to excessive work loads that included as much as fifteen to twenty contact hours of teaching), nor the institutional support to do research and publications. While 11 percent of the doctorates among whites are held by women, black women hold 21 percent of the doctorates among blacks. A significant number of these women are apparently considered in the ranks of the unqualified, according to the critics we discussed. They must deal with double jeopardy since they are both black and female.

Blacks have had neither the research, influence, political power, media, litigation, nor the interest of the academic community in their plight for representation on faculties and in administration on college campuses. Only the militant black students pressed the issue. Their militancy and mood of the 1960s are now dissipated along with their hopes.

"To a large number of people, and mainly the young, the decade [1960s] seems now to be littered with the ruins of great expectations: many of its more decent commitments dismantled; its moral language largely discarded; its political sensitivity held in contempt; its outlook upon the world withdrawn; its racial promises revoked or betrayed; its moral sense driven up against the wall" (Anderson, 1971, p. 27).

In contrast to women and Jews, blacks have almost an insurmountable problem—the race barrier. The overwhelming majority of Jews in America are white. Whites who can prove that they are being denied their rights for equal treatment and who can call attention to the fact that they are being discriminated against will get someone to listen and someone to act. All of the Caucasian ethnic antecedent groups have been able to move into the mainstream of American life while preserving much of their cultural heritage. Those who did not have the group pride or the desire to preserve their ethnic identity could change their names from Cohen, Malinanski, and Fantini to Smith, Jones, and Wilson and exist within the anonymity of their whiteness. No such refuge is available to those with black skin or with names of Wong, Garcia, and Running Bear.

In spite of the discrimination against white females, the numbers of their sex in higher education have always been greater than the number of blacks of both sexes. A few years ago there were more white females in one large state college system (four-year) than all of the blacks (men and women) in predominantly white colleges and universities in the entire nation (*Faculty and Staff Statistics,* State University of New York, May 1971, p. 3). And while Jews represent about 3 percent of the total population, they constitute a far greater proportion than that on the faculties of American colleges and universities. In fact, they have become quite influential in helping to perpetuate the very system which denied them entry for a considerable period of time. In some institutions they appear to be the major discriminators. So influential are members of this group in the educational hierarchy in one city that blacks and whites call the building where they are located the "Jewish Pentagon." Florence Moog has summarized this position on Jews, blacks and women with uncompromising candor (1972):

> That Jews are now abundantly represented on faculties of American colleges and universities is owing to the enhanced emphasis on science in the Second World War and to the subsequent expansion of higher education itself. No thanks at all are due to the exercise of academic freedom by the complacent caste that was the tenured professoriate into the fifth decade of the twentieth century.
>
> But even in the eighth decade, black scholars are still largely segregated in small poor institutions serving their own race. Half a century ago academic and nonacademic whites alike thought—to the extent that the matter crossed their minds at all —that Negroes were satisfied with second-rate opportunities or worse. In the 1930s, however, Eleanor Roosevelt used her great influence to make people see the merciless pervasiveness of discrimination against blacks. Although some whites became thus sensitized to the existence of this canker in the body of democracy, there is little evidence that the tenured professoriate anywhere used the protection of academic freedom even to question, much less alter, the customs or regulations that barred blacks from academic opportunities. In this case too, off-campus events, involving especially the increasing militancy of blacks themselves, are the real force behind the changes that are finally going forward.
>
> It is the position of women, however, that epitomizes the unwillingness of the beneficiaries of tenure to notice what goes on under their own noses. Welcomed as graduate students and rejected as colleagues, women scholars constitute a problem that has become evident to the white male professoriate only through the recent vigorous application of the Civil Rights Act of 1964.

So now, as before, blacks must go back to the courts and wait. "We cannot depend upon the conscience of the academic community to be equitable. It doesn't have one," states a respondent from the University of California at Berkeley. His observation seems consistent with responses to our own data.

We asked respondents to rank in order three of the following phrases (used by the various political groups and others) as a means of addressing discrimination in higher education: (1) by any means necessary, (2) nonviolent confrontation as a means, (3) time as a means, (4) education as a means, (5) leave it to the laws and courts, (6) the conscience of the academic community, and (7) other (please specify). Item 6 was not only not ranked, but it also received more negative comment as being an option without any creditability. Items 3 and 5 ranked in the lower half while Items 2, 4, and 1 respectively, were the ranks and order chosen.

Perhaps if the academic community could convince blacks, other minorities, and women that higher education did indeed have a conscience, that it would apply "every good-faith effort" (to use affirmative action language), government plans would not be necessary.

Our respondents have convinced us that they cannot depend upon voluntary efforts of the academic community. As long as the hiring of black scholars was left solely to the white males, nothing was done. Even now, for the most part, the status quo remains just that—status quo.

Chapter Four

••••••••••••••••••••••••
••••••••••••••••••••••••
••••••••••••••••••••••••

THE
"ASSISTANT TO"

••••••••••••••••••••••••
••••••••••••••••••••••••
••••••••••••••••••••••••

*I*t is said that persons who take positions as administrators become bastards the day they accept the job. This appraisal seems to find consensus with school people at all levels of education and people of all races and at all types of institutions. Such a characterization may not be accurate, but it is prevalent. Black administrators as a specific group are no exception. Unfortunately blacks have not had their own forums or strong advocates in national organizations, publications, and other resources available to them to give rebuttal.

Until fairly recently, most black educational administrators have functioned primarily as principals in segregated public schools and as administrators in all-black colleges and universities. Only recently have they been hired in predominantly white educational institutions, but their roles, status, authority, and performance have not been an area of empirical investigation or scholarly speculation. The only major research on minority administrators we have been able to locate is Stephen B. Lawton's "Minority Administrators in Berkeley: A Progress Report" (1972). And this report was for public schools. We know of at least one other major investigation now underway. The major problem in refuting much of the criticism of the nefarious opponents of minorities in higher education is the almost exclusive reliance on logical arguments and limited observational data rather than comprehensive research evidence. The few researchers who have given attention to blacks in higher education have concentrated their efforts on the number of doctorates held by blacks, their academic origins, their distribution in the disciplines and the total population, their incomes, and other such demographic profiles. And these investigations have dealt primarily with black faculty. We identified and cited several sources of this research earlier. Much of the data on blacks in higher education is still generally in the hands of blacks in predominantly nonwhite colleges. Rufus E. Clement,* Horace Mann Bond, Thomas D. Jarrett, and Mack Jones, all of Atlanta University, have kept rosters of black doctorates for years. Recently some others have developed and maintained rosters of Black Americans who hold doctorates in their disciplines, notably James E. Conyers (sociology) and Mack Jones (political science). Melvin Sykes of the University of Texas is compiling a directory of blacks in higher education. And, of course, we hold an extensive list of blacks in higher education in both two-year and four-year colleges and universities.

By far, the researchers who have given attention to non-white professionals in higher education were in all-black colleges and were black themselves. Their findings, with a very few exceptions, have been published in *Phylon, Journal of Negro Education,* and other all-black publications. Whites who could not get their materials on blacks published in white professional journals have also used these sources. Publication in these journals by both blacks and whites has been by both design and necessity. White academicians have typically ignored these publications except as a last resort after they have been turned down by more prestigious and widely known publications. Yet, while the *Journal of Higher Edu-*

---

* Rufus Clement was a former president of Atlanta University. As a member of Kappa Alpha Psi fraternity, he once spoke to the St. Louis Alumni Chapter of Kappa Alpha Psi and explained the importance of keeping information on blacks who had achieved academically so that when the time came for Black Americans to have an opportunity to move in the mainstream of academic life, they could be identified and located. Few, at the time, shared his foresight and optimism.

cation, Phi Delta Kappan, and the *Junior College Journal* have greater visibility and wider distribution, few would suggest that the intellectual and scholarly content of these publications are of the same quality as the black publications cited.

While white scholars have not given their time, talents, and attention to black administrators in predominantly white colleges and universities, they have been quick to describe and offer opinions about the black administrator in all-black institutions. Again, to quote one of our respondents: "They come all the way down here to the black institutions—the black academic ghettos, as it were— to observe black administrators and their purported deviant behavior. We never see a line of print or a page of research on black administrators in their own [white] institutions." Not much significant empirical data but a lot of criticism of black administrators is penned by whites. Black administrators in nonwhite institutions have been singled out and severely criticized for their purported authoritarian behavior. Christopher Jencks and David Riesman (1969, p. 459) indicate that many black colleges "are run as if they are the personal property of their presidents." The management of some black colleges, such as Southern University in Louisiana has appeared to be under the administrative control of a single family for decades. It is also true that one can find nepotism in some black colleges. Such favoritism can also be found in many white colleges, and many times of a more nefarious nature, because it is frequently not only familial but also ethnic, regional, sectarian, and racial. Nonetheless, many blacks indicate that they believe that Jencks and Riesman show great contempt for black administrators and for black institutions generally. And these two authors are not alone in their negative appraisal of black administrators. *The Negro and Higher Education in the South,* a report of the Commission on Higher Educational Opportunity in the South, suggested that black administrators, pressured by fiscal problems, white governing boards, and the black community, were forced to assume strict control of every aspect of the college. The report goes on to say that these administrators were unable to find qualified second and third echelon administrators. As a consequence, the report continued, "patriarchal administration was inevitable" (1967, p. 19). Another author proclaims that black administrators have displayed a certain mount of pigheadedness, authoritarianism, backwardness, timidity, and antiintellectualism (Billingsley, 1970a). And many blacks themselves have called black administrators Uncle Toms.

"Uncle Tom as an epithet, is assigned by radical and revolutionary blacks to any blacks less militant than they. It is a way of dismissing and discrediting the views of those who are still committed to an interracial and integrated society and do not in all cases support violent or other militant tactics" (Trow, 1970, pp. 17–18).

Staples has suggested (1972, p. 44): "Most of these college presidents represent a cross between Stephin Fetchit and a Latin American dictator."

Vivian Henderson, too, notes (1971) "[Negro] college administration is often characterized as being a one-man show— that man being the president of the college. He is often accused of being a strong-armed, sometimes benevolent, dictator who is inflexible when it comes to the delegation of authority and sharing decision-making."

Clark Kerr, who is more diplomatic, writes (1970, p. 114): "Negro colleges are seeing the once masterful presence of the president—indispensable ambassador to the white power structure— reduced in stature as both faculty and students are less impressed than they once were."

And Tilden and Wilbert LeMelle say that black colleges are characterized by "presidentialism" (1969, p. 3). The traditional black administrators, like many of their institutions, have become the victims of the times and the social and political determinants of change. Those who refused to accommodate change have found that the faculties, students, and lower echelon administrators who formerly submitted to their authoritarianism were compelled to rise up against them and the concomitant oppression. That is but one side of the story, characterized only by black administrators in predominantly black colleges. It should not be forgotten that black administrators were serving a power structure which demanded that many behave the way they did. And it was due to the efforts of some of these men that many black students had an opportunity for any type of posthigh-school education in the South, border states, and even some sections of the North. In many ways the powerful black president functioned in the same way as the black mother who beat her children to make them respectful to whites, to forcibly remind them to say yes sir and no sir, to go to the back of the bus without protest, and to respect the laws of segregation regardless of how dehumanizing these laws were. Although her behavior was harsh, the perceptions and fears which motivated her actions were real and her love was never questioned.

The black authoritarian presidents took their orders from the real authoritarians: the abolitionists and mission-minded men and women who financed and controlled black colleges (Drake, 1971) and the racist legislatures and other components of the existing power structure and the prevailing social order. The role of the black administrator was more than ambassador to the power structure; he was also the willing scapegoat for both blacks and whites for the posture he was willing to take and the image assigned to him. In many ways he was the victim who was assigned the role of villain.

Perhaps the most essential difference between black and white administrators is that black administrators seemed to get things done under the most difficult of circumstances. They were said to be abrupt, harsh, and not given to little charades of diplomacy and other social lubricants which obscured their real feelings, intent, and direction. They were tidy—open and shut. People knew where they stood. Respondents who were formerly in predominantly black colleges insist that psychologically this behavior can be by far kinder than much of the nebulous behavior they encounter from white administrators in predominantly white institutions. Some noted that one of their greatest frustrations in predominantly white institutions was not having their positions defined. They were frequently not told what was expected of them, were not informed as to how they would be evaluated, and in far too many cases, were not advised of the level of their performance until something was drastically wrong.

A frequent complaint of people who work within administrative bureaucracies is that their authority and responsibilities are vague ("Summer School," 1972, p. 18). Only infrequently could we find a black administrator who could give us a precise description of his duties. The same is true of his decision-making responsibilities. A few find that some of their superordinates allow clerks, secretaries, and other support personnel to give off-the-cuff evaluations of their performances; that their supervisors discuss them with the classified personnel; that the clothes they wear, the automobiles they drive, and the language they speak are all gossip items for secretaries and sometimes their own colleagues.

For all of their faults, and there were many, black administrators did not permit faculty members to do as they pleased on the one hand or tolerate departmental anarchy on the other. They did not submit to faculty self-governing to the extent that it would grind the institution to a halt. And they knew what was going on in their colleges. No black administrator would declare that he did not know if a certain class or race of person was on his campus or that certain conditions existed. It is rare that a staff member or student fails to see the college president during his entire tenure in a black college.

In another vein, the black administrator is not charged with correcting a mistake by passing it upward or making a committee accountable for his responsibility. We do not yet know how effective black administrators perform in predominantly white institutions because so few have had positions there. Most but not all of the negative appraisals of black administrators have amounted to superficial observations by blue-ribbon commissions, hearsay, and comments from dissatisfied faculty members and students.

While black administrators have an authoritarian profile, many of their accusers also concede these men had little choice in much of their behavior. Some do not accept the argument that black administrators are more dictatorial than whites. Our respondents in predominantly white colleges indicate that white administrators are more diplomatic though equally as authoritarian. They point to all the literature on governance that has flowed from the pens of educators. Every major professional publication as well as many scholarly books over the past half decade have addressed this problem, and some of the authors have insisted that administrators have been arbitrary, unresponsive, and capricious in their actions. This has been especially true of the proponents of collective bargaining. Some insist that administrators behaved as though they did not know that students had rights until their uprising of the late sixties when administrators were forced to negotiate with students. One of them summarized the feelings and experiences of many in regard to their past relationships with administrators— especially deans. "When you went to the dean's office during my time you were always in trouble. Now when these kids come in— the dean is in trouble." Even legislatures in all their conservatism recognize that administrators have not protected the rights of students. One black professor notes, "From the complaints we hear, unionism in higher education is not a result of a responsive, democratic administration; neither is the rebellion among teaching assistants, dissenting students, nor the observed hypocrisy a result of a democratic and sensitive administration." The Task Force on Faculty Representation of the Campus Governance Program indicates that administrators are too powerful on the great majority of campuses (Keeton, 1971). Regents indicate that deans and presidents stand between them and the campus. Deans complain that they are hemmed in by uncooperative and timid presidents (Keeton, 1971). While blacks on predominantly white campuses agree with Arthur Cohen (1969, p. 39) that "the administrator's control over the faculty is less than it was ten years ago," they still hold the power and authority. One of our colleagues remarked, "We wait on administrative decisions like welfare recipients to see what budget we will get."

In small colleges and in colleges in certain regions of the country administrators are as authoritarian as they ever were. Most of all, however, our subjects indicate how white administrators respond to them. While white deans and presidents are not as abrupt as their black counterparts, the end results are the same. They tell our subjects what they cannot do; rarely what they can do. They reverse decisions, resort to petty nit picking, and ignore the concerns of faculty members and students. While many white administrators are reputed to employ the democratic model, their critics (black and white) claim that they are no more effective in getting things done. One respondent, a former dean in an all-black college, pointed out: "How quickly we forget. All of this governance jazz and democratic hocus pocus is of recent vintage. Presidents and deans have reigned unchallenged. In many places they still do. On the other hand, these democratic models allow the institution

to go to pot. At my college, the whole governance of the college
has been held up for months because the senate cannot get a
quorum. The adminstration is willing to let the college go to hell in
order to appease a few faculty members. That would never happen
in a black school."

Neither black nor white administrators seem to be very well
trained for the specific job of management in higher education.
Collective bargaining is an area in which administrators seem
greatly incompetent (Bolman, 1968, p. 181; Moore, 1971; Lieberman, 1971).

Few black administrators are at the helm of predominantly
white two-year and four-year colleges. Seattle Central Community
College, Michigan State University, Montclair State College, and
Sacramento State College are notable exceptions. It must be noted
that there is great diversity in titles and positions and a lack of con-
sistency in the power and authority assigned to specific titles and
positions. We found that what was a line position in one institution
was a staff position in another. A better index of an administrative
position had to do with the kinds of decisions an administrator
could make. Summarily, the influence of his decisions defined his
job, his authority, his power, and the position. The types of determinations that the black administrator could make also put the college
personnel on notice as to what he could do. This determination of
power is made early by the various facets of the college. In far too
many cases, the black administrator could do little if anything. The
overwhelming majority of blacks who have moved into the administrative ranks of white colleges are assistants to the white line (and
staff) administrators. The black "assistant to" is the administrative
caricature in higher education. Even the worker in the kitchen, the
attendant on the parking lot, and the custodian sweeping the floor
know that most black administrators are without power and authority.

More than one-third (1171 persons or 36.3 percent) of our
respondent population are administrators. At first glance this gives
the impression of a concentration of power and authority in a group
that does not hold equal representation generally throughout the
institutions. Closer examination of the data, however, shows that

1095 (94 percent) of the positions can be characterized as some type of "assistant to" position and they were designated by sixteen different categories or titles. These were basically peripheral positions which were defined, continued, and supported at the pleasure of others. Only 76 of the black administrators held line positions. Specifically, 67 were deans, 26 of them functioned in two-year colleges, and 41 were deans in four-year colleges. Similarly, nine black administrators were presidents—five in community colleges and four in senior institutions.

The same black administrator who was considered a good president, dean, and principal in all-black institutions has become an "assistant to" in the administrative ranks of predominantly white colleges. His assignment has little to do with his qualifications and absolutely nothing to do with the title he holds. His duties have no apparent relationship to the job description (if he received one) when he took the job. The "assistant to" has become the convenient scapegoat in some colleges.

In one community college the black administrator on the staff in instruction told us that the college got word of a confrontation by black students planned for later in the evening. While the president of the college, the dean of students, and the dean of business, who controlled management, student behavior, and campus security respectively, went home earlier than their usual time, the black administrator was asked to remain and be on hand when the students came. In this case the black was asked to perform the collective jobs of the other administrators while they left the campus. This man was left in an untenable situation without power or authority to speak or take action for the institution. In another major university where students were in the process of revolt, a black junior administrator was given a promotion on the spot to go out and deal with the problem.

Trouble-shooting with black students appears to be the major function that the black adminstrator is expected to assume; 82 percent of those in two-year colleges and 83 percent of those in four-year colleges and universities indicate that they are called upon to intercede when black students are involved with some conflict situation. Bennie Wiley maintains (1971, p. 550): "They [black administrators] become convenient pawns which the college's real administration can point to when something goes wrong: 'We have Mr. Black handling that problem'."

In another two-year college in a multicollege district, we found an associate dean of continuing education, who was also in charge of a special remedial program, with primary responsibility for the recruitment of students, and, added to this, in charge of publicity. Each of the other colleges in this district had a man assigned to each of these functions. If any pattern is discernible of blacks in administration, it is the multiplicity of functions the "assistant to" is asked to manage. Compounding this situation is the fact that they have little authority to carry out many of their responsibilities. Our respondents in both two-year and four-year institutions agreed overwhelmingly that they were able to get the kind of information necessary to do their jobs, but they did not have the power and authority to make decisions related to many facets of their jobs.

The other high-priority areas for black administrators appear to be in black-oriented programs (Black Studies, Ethnic Studies, Urban Studies, etc.). The high visibility black administrator is needed in these areas for pacification. His complexion also makes him an ineluctable participant in admissions and in student services. Our investigation did not reveal a single black administrator working as a business manager or a dean of business, although we did find them working in financial aids.

Little can be determined from the titles of black administrators. Wiley insists (1971, p. 550): "If the university power structure wanted blacks to enter the mainstream of the university system, blacks would be hired in established positions. This has not been the case. Almost all blacks in university administrations fill newly created positions with little power and authority. Or they fill positions whose titles connote a superblack. Both types offer no potential for upward movement."

Many assistants to the presidents did not provide, as far as we could determine, any real assistance to the president. Some black staff administrators, in fact, were required to submit all communiques channeled outside of the college to a white administrator for approval before the communiques were sent.

Regardless of what other function they are required to do, no function takes precedent in quite the same way as Black Studies and black student behavior.

Pick up any higher education journal or national report; you are likely to find a discussion on Black Studies. Few educational areas have had as much publicity in popular and scholarly journals. "Black and nonblack scholars, columnists, and community leaders carry on a war of words over the relevancy of Black Studies. . . . The criticism and defense of Black Studies in schools cut across racial and generation gaps. Some of its major critics are black educators and leaders of black organizations; some of its stoutest defenders are influential nonblack schoolmen and scholars" (Cohen, 1971, p. 157).

Perhaps in no other area does the higher education establishment show its true conservative—if not racist—attitude in quite the same way as in this area. And, perhaps, in no other area does the black administrator find himself on the horns of a dilemma, the dilemma of trying to mediate a conflict in values and goals between the desires of black students and the academic community.

"The director of any Black Studies program performs his activities within the framework of an academic community, and he is most often himself an academician. . . . He has the concerns of tenure, publications, position advancement, and colleague esteem— all of which are related, in part, to the quality of his scholarly writing and teaching. But along with being an academician, the director is also a black man. The very fact of his racial identification carries with it membership in a racial group that has had a definitely subordinate relationship to the structure of white universities and white academia. . . . The stronger the black students perceive the director as aligned with the values and activities of the white faculty and administration, the less they perceive him as aligned with their goals and values. Thus I contend that he suffers a loss of legitimacy in the eyes of the black students because the students do not consider the values and activities of white academia as commensurate with their own" (Rist, 1970, pp. 620–621).

Community colleges have done more to include Black Studies in the curriculum than four-year institutions have done, and in two-year institutions the administrator is more successful

(Cohen, 1971). Yet, "if one were to judge by the number of courses in community college catalogs and schedules of classes, the verdict would be that black and white administrators have been exceedingly restrained, if not actually reluctant, to introduce Black Studies courses" (Rist, 1970). Still, in no other field of higher education is the black administrator more intimately involved. Many of them are reported to be hired in the institution in the first place because of Black Studies programs and the demands of black students. While white educators have ignored, damned, and criticized these studies, it has often been left to the students and the black administrators—especially black students—to propose, organize, and implement Black Studies in the face of some unusual odds. Consider these statements (Altman and Snyder, 1970):

"Probably the most shameful chapter in the recent history of higher education in America was the pitifully equivocal response to pleas by black students and others for studies that are relevant— Black Studies, Chicano Studies, and Ethnic Studies programs. To further complicate matters, many weak-kneed but calculating administrators acquiesced in a spirit of hypocrisy that to me was wrong. They made such statements to their students as: 'We will do as you say—find a Black Studies director; and then you may tell us what ought to be in the curriculum.' To me the cynicism implied here is disgraceful, and further it represents an abandonment of responsibility for professional and social leadership. . . . For all of these years American higher education has included selected ethnic and other specialized studies as part of the curricula with few giving it a second thought. Only when *black* and *Chicano* were placed in front of *studies* did the "intellectual lid" of indignation blow. Ever since, there have been those who have devoted a disproportionate amount of their energies to proving that Black and Chicano Studies cannot be considered valid areas of collegiate concern" (Charles G. Hurst, Jr., president of Malcolm X Community College).

"When black students on a campus propose to the administration an experimental program in Ethnic or Black Studies, they should first ask themselves if they can really develop the program they want. . . . What I see happening across the country is that as new experimental ideas are proposed, they are quickly translated into the same old campus power structure" (William Birenbaum, president of Staten Island Community College).

"The system has sought only to obscure the critical issues through mindless polemics, describing Black Studies as 'soul courses,' charging that Black Studies are political—as if white studies are not —and saying that Black Studies do not meet so-called objective standards" (Usuf Kaurouma, black graduate student of University of Colorado).

"Educators still continue to discuss publicly the issue of Ethnic Studies within the rhetorical framework of academia" (Richard Keyes, past chairman of Black Studies at Fresno State College).

"Black students who have been faced with the responsibility of demanding Black Studies, striking, picketing, and denouncing the racist administrations and faculties in order to get an audience are then being saddled with the responsibility of designing curricula, hiring faculties, and administering new programs, all the while having to attend their classes and pass their courses. No students in the recent history of higher education have assumed so faithfully such a heavy burden. The rest of us should be ashamed of ourselves" (Andrew Billingsley, Howard University; 1970a).

Sylvester Monroe writes (1973, p. 48) that the faculty vote to support Black Studies at Harvard "was an easy way of washing their hands of the whole matter, leaving to the students themselves the responsibility of educating black students."

"Supporters of Ethnic Studies are facing challenges from the public, from some college administrators, and from state legislators who feel the study of minority groups is a passing fad" (Sievert, 1973, p. 54).

Yet, while we hear about all of the resistance to Black Studies and about the mood to eliminate them, Jewish Studies are growing extremely fast. More than three hundred colleges have such courses, and this number continues to grow.

"Numerous colleges, including Ohio State and the University of Texas, have full-scale programs that permit students for the first time to go as far as the doctoral level in Jewish Studies" (Fiske, 1973, p. 8).

It is significant that while Jewish Studies have the same

questions of relevance, availability of qualified teachers, the need to evolve standards and so on, "the predominant mood seems to be in favor of them" (Fiske, 1973, p. 8).

The situation is the exact opposite for Black Studies. It is obvious that Jewish Studies are supported by Jews as Black Studies are supported by blacks. The irony is that the academic community accepts one and rejects the other. The dual standard is operative in the academic community even in Ethnic Studies.

Inherent in these comments is the dilemma of black administrators assigned to such programs. While there is considerable disagreement among black administrators about the goals, content, and organization of Black Studies, almost all respondents saw a need for it. It is also notable that many predict the demise of such programs as soon as institutions quiet down enough not to attract too much attention, and as soon as much of the outside funding is withdrawn. Already in the early years of the seventies, there are many indications that their perceptions are accurate.

Another of the underlying problems for the black administrator is that minority students have no faith in the people who administer institutions of higher education (Keyes, 1971, p. 120). They hear an administrator shouting that he is for them, but they have not seen him put himself on the line. They can only conclude that he is not trustworthy. A few of our more aggressive and hostile subjects suggested that white administrators (and some black ones) behave as though the establishment of Black and Ethnic Studies on campus, and giving the students a say in them, was tantamount to turning an asylum over to the inmates.

In spite of the trauma of rhetoric, black administrators note, as others have, that militant students are really conservative. Martin Trow says (1970), "Black militants often sound like radicals, making sweeping condemnations and demands when in fact their intention is to increase the numbers of black students and to gain somewhat larger resources for them in their institutions." Nathan Wright agrees (1972) that "black students are not seeking to have the educational establishment destroyed. They are insisting that it be inclusive of and that it work in the interests of all who would aspire to the fulfillment of their potential."

These goals of students do not make the black administrator's task any easier. One of the first demands that black students make of an administrator assigned to a Black Studies program is that he *be* black, not simply *colored* black. Second, they demand that he think black; third, that he is well imbued with what they call the "black experience." This means that the administrator should fit the image which they (the students) find acceptable. In different institutions, regions, and communities, the administrator's behavior may vary greatly, but the above three criteria appear to be constant. In most institutions the students want to choose the man, and he is expected to serve at their pleasure. On the other hand, they want a man who is his own man, who refuses to be the "house nigger" of the administration or of them.

It must be emphasized here that black administrators (and faculty) of both sexes, and in both types of institutions, insisted that they will take positions antagonistic to those which may be popular with black students. More specifically, 64.1 and 63.3 percent of the women in two-year and four-year colleges respectively took this position. Similarly, 71.6 and 75 percent of the men in these same institutions took the same position. And, 84.2 and 86.4 percent of those in two-year and four-year colleges respectively did not consider pressure from militant and activists students a problem—although they admit that black students can create a dilemma for them at times.

The administrator of Black Studies is expected to be on call night and day. He is a messenger, the courier who will be asked to carry student demands (or requests) to the college administration. He should be an individual who can translate their threatening rhetoric into commentary, dialogue, and verbal pressure that the college administration and faculty will not only listen to but also be willing to respond to. He must be accessible and should not be one who is a parasite on the program, or what students call "pimping on the program." At the same time he will be expected to demonstrate leadership on their behalf and become their spokesman both inside and outside of the institution. In some colleges, the black administrator is expected to take a posture as militant as that of the students. Both the black ambassador and the militant type of administrator will frequently seem antagonistic to faculty and high echelon administrators.

In terms of pure objective administration, if he does his job, he turns the students off. If, on the other hand, he is successful from the point of view of the students, he is rarely acceptable to the administration.

While it has been charged that many black administrators obtained their positions as a result of black student demands, this has not been the case in many places. Although 58 percent of our sample agree that they might have been hired because of student demands, 27.4 percent disagree and 12 percent have no opinion. The size of the disagreeing group is sufficiently large to support our theses that student demands are only one of the major factors in the selection and hiring of blacks. Competency, affirmative action, friends, and all the other influences which weigh in the selection process are certain to have been at work. Arthur Cohen still writes, however: "During the spring of 1969, students led a campaign for community control of Seattle Community College. The effort failed, but it resulted in the selection of a black president" (Cohen, 1971, p. 164). The selection of the president *was not* the result of student demands. The black president had been offered the presidency of the college and had accepted the offer more than a year prior to the student uprising. This was not publicized because the candidate had not terminated his employment with his previous employer. It was simply a coincidence that the agreed-upon announcement date occurred during the student uprising. We are sure of our facts, since one of us was that president. Cohen also implies that Seattle Central Community College is predominantly black, while less than 10 percent of the students and staff are black.

In many cases a black administrative assistant is expected to be an "expert" on blacks. White administrators attempt to pick his brain in order to find out about black students. They want to know how to work with, understand, and satisfy them. The black administrator who is used in this way, and most are, is expected to acquaint his superordinates with the black life style. He familiarizes his supervisors with techniques which will help him become sensitive to the black frame of reference: how to understand their humor, authors they read, heroes they mimic, taboos they respect, language they speak; how to anticipate their behavior and know what triggers their moods. Presidents and deans also want to know from this administrator how to keep black students quiet when they are angry and restive and how to stimulate or redirect their interest. White administrators are also curious about the students' dress; why they "strut black," move to music in the way that they do, and are as concerned about dress styles as they seem to be. The behavior of these students is not unusual. It is simply a different set of behaviors than those practiced by some white students. White students have their own particular and unique behaviors.

Many black administrators are hired as interpreters. This seems to us a bona fide role if the information they provide helps the institution to better understand the students and provide better services to them.

If the information is used in ways to more effectively oppress and control the students, the black administrator will not remain once the black students realize his role. The black administrator is not to be an informer; an informer tends not to last very long. If he reveals the secrets of the students, exposes the plans and strategies of the community, alerts the college administration to pending nonthreatening confrontation, and so forth, while playing the role of confidant to the students and the community, he is toying with disaster. Black students do, however, appear to appreciate the pure administrator, who admits he is a company man; they may disagree with him but at least they know where he stands. We do not mean a man who is a so-called Uncle Tom but rather a man who deals in facts, objectivity, and rules and who sees his job as one to administer regardless of the race of the students involved. He makes no commitment beyond the rules to either his superordinate or the students. He does not fear his bosses or their bosses, and he is not subservient to either the students or his supervisors. He is one of the well-respected black administrators. And contrary to what some may believe, this man's job seems more secure. Openly, students never praise him; privately, they relate that he is a leveling force for them, a force which attempts to keep their concerns in the proper perspective.

There are black administrators who have been hired without what would be considered the appropriate credentials. They have come from the Urban League, the YMCA, high school principalships, the ministry, Model Cities, and other social welfare programs, a few have come from municipal jobs. Most of these candidates are considered leaders in the black community. Leadership, of course, is defined by the institutions they join. For the most part, they are high-visibility blacks who have had some experience in relating to the white power structure. Some exert some leadership in the black community. They tend to be middle class, or at last think that way. Their children are in scouting and belong to the YMCA and other such organizations, while they themselves still have involvement with the alumni chapters of college fraternities and sororities and the black prestige social clubs such as the Links and Jack & Jill Incorporated. Many of these black administrators, we suspect, will never be permanent in the four-year college or the university; a few of them will and have been able to find a place for themselves in two-year colleges. Two-year schools will retain those who are effective and will provide some of them with tenure and other incentives to remain.

To put it bluntly, these black administrators are hired into predominantly white colleges and universities because they are "safe." A surprising number of them recognize this and do not hesitate to say so. Many of them feel, nonetheless, that they can and do make a contribution.

They are not likely to "rock the boat." Their careers were fairly successful before they joined the college. The great tragedy in the strategy of the institution which hires them is that it fails to make use of their talents. Many of these men and women are not only college trained but also have demonstrated their competence in the jobs they terminated. Most of their former positions were jobs which required them to work with a broad sampling of the public and to interact with people across the age, economic, political, educational, and social spectrum. Although many activist students may be hostile to them, their skills can assist both the institution and the activist students.

Blacks who are former radicals are heading special programs for the disadvantaged and for Black and Ethnic Studies. Some of them were students; others were leaders of militant groups outside of the college. In the recent past, they organized strikes and take-overs of administration buildings. They published underground newspapers, invaded classrooms, threatened faculty members and students, caused some damage to facilities, organized student groups, and conducted marches. Sometimes their influence was so pervasive and their following so great that they forced administrators and faculty members to resign. Repeatedly they authored the list of demands which were presented by student groups. They sat with the negotiators when the administrators agreed to meet with them. At one college two negotiators for the students turned out to be two passers-by who saw the students in revolt and stopped to watch. They were chosen because they "looked like militants" and to some degree were. The radicals know the rhetoric which will incite the students. They are masters at playing to the press and to television cameras. Although they do not now attract as much attention as they did in the late sixties, they can still call public attention to the situations, conditions, practices, inequities, charges of discrimination, and illicit affairs which exist inside the college. They can go to open hearings of the legislature and make charges that can get head-lines, although the charges may or may not be true. They can in-form their own legislators of illegal violations of the rights of black students in the college. Because America has demonstrated that it is such a racist society, the black-white issue is always an attention getter, community polarizer, and tax-levy and bond-issue defeater. In short, it is not difficult for the radical to find the bowels of an institution, and most institutions cannot risk a rupture in their academic plumbing.

One of the most effective strategies administrators have used to counteract the radical is to agree to Black Studies, separate dormitories, or a program for the disadvantaged and hire him to run the program.

The radical is often hired to keep him quiet. It is only later that he discovers that when he took the job he lost most of his power. First, he does not control the budget; the hiring of personnel has certification guidelines that he cannot change although they may be discretionary for the administrators of the institution; he is without the credentials to become permanent; when he com-promises he loses credibility with other activists. He sometimes finds that he enjoys only the association with an educational institution. If he goes out and purchases a home and other material objects which addict him to what some would call "a better life," he is hooked. He finds that he must protect his salary in order to keep his possessions. The higher salary, of course, may be paid with soft dollars. (Approximately 12 percent of our respondents have their positions so supported.) The radical finds himself in a dilemma or what blacks call "a trick bag." A respondent sums it up, "A house, car, and credit card have transformed many a loud and effective radical into a conforming member of the majority, enshrined with that noble epithet 'silent'."

There are, of course, some blacks who are full deans and who perform in the administrative capacity quite well. These are— or appear to be—outstanding individuals whose credentials cannot be questioned. One characteristic is observable in most of them. Those who are in four-year institutions were excellent students in college and later in graduate school. They received their Ph.D.'s from prestigious schools; those over forty have been active in higher education for some time. On the whole they have more experience at more levels of education than many of their white counterparts.

Black deans in two-year colleges may not hold the Ph.D. Most of them have come from public school positions. They usually have been excellent students and moved through the education chairs to the position of principal, director, and on up. We are not saying that they are not excellent administrators—many are. Both the two-year and the four-year men and women are—or tend to be—outstanding.

They were hired because they were competent.

A surprising number of black administrators are hired in public relations positions. Implicit in their duties if not clearly defined in their job descriptions is that they will primarily relate with the black public. This duty supercedes any of their other duties. They are in contact with the media, and other such sources to make sure that the institution enjoys a positive image in the black community both on and off campus. Rarely, however, are they the luncheon speaker at the Elks Club and other such organizations with exclusionary policies. They function primarily as liaison persons to the black community. Make no mistake about it, the black community is a complex plurality of ideas, values, ideologies, and life styles. It is filled with skeptics. A part of the job of this administrator is to convince the black public that the college is a friend of the community. He tries to dispel the bad image of his college that all but the middle-class blacks may hold (and even with many of them, the college has tenuous credibility). He works to turn outraged emotion and overreaction into constructive suggestion. He accompanies the white members of the administrative hierarchy (who will go) into the black community, protecting them from all of the imaginary assaults which hearsay and the headlines have convinced them to expect. Blacks call this "riding shotgun." He has his photograph taken standing next to specific administrators from time to time and may invite one or more of these administrators to a dance or some such affair in the black community. At these affairs, "Man, those white dudes come to a 'set' (dance, church, and so on) and act like spectators instead of participants" reported one respondent. Only the middle-class blacks, however, are likely to see them there. And some black maverick administrators help those in the black community to develop the system-beating determination to "promote the black agenda," to use the words of Charles Hurst of Malcolm X College. Back at the college they work with black staff members (administrators and faculty members) in what their superordinates hope will be an avenue for grievances. Sometimes this backfires when they assist black staff members in assuming a dominant role over, or achieving independence of, white supervision or activist influence. A part of this administrator's task is to refute the pathology and aberrations which have been the organizing principles in the study of black life.

This kind of black administrator is hired because he is a diplomat.

Black administrators have many other frustrations besides a lack of definition in duties and a lack of real authority. Some of these other frustrations are more subtle.

Blacks frequently note the reluctance of their immediate supervisors to put their promises in writing. They emphasize that these superordinates prefer to call them on the telephone or call them in for a conference. In many cases, no other person is present and no written record is made of the conversation. If he asks about putting the statements, orders, requirements, and promises in writing, the black is told that they have a gentlemen's agreement and that is all that is necessary. When it is suggested that the person who made the contract might leave to take another job, or die, or change his mind, the administrator may either agree to put it in writing and never quite get around to it or he will become indignant, thereby casting the person asking for the written commitment in the role of antagonist. At other times, the administrator will say that he is having one of his assistants draft the communique. Later checking with the assistant reveals that he has not been informed about the matter. Apparently these strategies are taken so that administrators can back away from certain positions and commitments they have taken if those positions and commitments prove to be unpopular.

Black administrators also find that it is extremely frustrating to have to go through a very rigorous screening process and then never have an opportunity to use the skills the institution claimed to have been seeking. It is as though they were hired under false pretenses. We found many black administrators working in areas completely remote from their titles, backgrounds, and training, while other blacks on campus held positions to which these blacks should have been assigned. There is considerable suspicion that some of these latter individuals have been placed in these positions and expected to fail, providing the administration with grounds for their dismissal. This seems like cynicism of the first magnitude, but we received this piece of information from a third echelon white administrator in a Chicago college. He had mistakenly been sent a questionnaire. He described a situation at his own institution: "They hired this black guy and they knew he would fail. They [the administration] needed an example of incompetence so they hired a guy, would not support him, and then took note only of his mistakes. They finally fired him. The scheme backfired though. The students supported the man, protested, and raised so much hell that the man was rehired in a tenured faculty position. Now, incompetent or not, he is untouchable. Had he not been hired with the wrong scheme in mind in the first place this would not have happened."

Why he was hired is a question that the black administrator never ceases to ask himself; and it is as much a problem for him as his lack of authority.

Some "assistants to" show considerable anger and hostility when they relate their experience with secretarial personnel. Few will deny that a competent secretary is a rare and priceless staff member. Too many of them, however, are neither exceptional nor invaluable. Many come from backgrounds which have shaped their behaviors and attitudes in ways which are antithetical to blacks; the submissive "assistant to" serves at the pleasure of these people. He can expect sloppy work, impudence, a lack of confidentiality, hostility, maternalism, and other contemptuous behavior and eccentricities that he is expected to tolerate. We are told that his errors may be transmitted to his superiors and their superiors, and that in some cases, he is to refrain from directly confronting the secretary or clerk but should talk to the person in charge of office personnel. The janitorial and cafeteria help also respond to him in much the same way. They are quick to inform him and others that their supervisors have informed them that he is not their boss and cannot tell them what to do. Many times the more moderate "assistant to" is discussed as the campus freak. This man or woman is considered weak—unable to change the behavior of these staff persons on his own and unassisted by his superordinates. Many of these staff persons are good and skillful workers. But, like many others in the society, they only do what they have to do, respect those who demand it, and demean and show insubordination to those who will accept it.

The militant "assistant to" does not encounter such behavior from classified personnel. They do not openly treat him with contempt, hostility, or inform on him; they would not dare. He will not only straighten them out from the outset, but also he will make his position known and felt to their supervisors and his own. This black administrator has more contempt for them than they could possibly have for his counterpart, the submissive black administrator. His work is done well and on time. Many of the secretarial staff as well as other classified personnel go beyond what is required to be helpful and pleasant to him. This man knows his rights and their limits and limitations as well as his own. The activist administrator is not a diplomat, smiler, and back patter. His brusque manner is likely to embarrass his less aggressive black colleagues, and because he has no respect for their timidity, he is contemptuous of them also. If the white secretarial personnel consider him arrogant, direct, and inconsiderate of the feelings of others, they conceal their attitudes and share them only with their more intimate associates. This administrator does not need other administrators to protect him, and they incur his wrath when they apologize for his behavior. He is his own man and he knows it. In some ways, he appears to be good for an office staff.

Another "assistant to" is equally as effective as the militant and more impressive than the moderate. Every inch a professional, he is neither submissive nor brusque; nonetheless, those around him know him, his capabilities, and know that he knows what he is doing and the options available to him to get things done well. The whole demeanor of the professional is such that one does not challenge him or his ability. If a job is not done as it should be done, he simply returns the task to the performer, checks to see if his instructions are understood, and leaves the task to be redone. He will continue to have the task completed until it is right. He is quiet, objective, and consistent. Since he is indifferent to any hostility which office and other classified help may hold toward him and since he will evaluate them in terms of what they do instead of trying to buy their good will, he has, in effect, the last word. This man is competent, punctual, exact, and pleasantly aloof. Unlike the erratic and explosive behavior that secretaries may encounter from the militant and the submissive demeanor of the moderate, the professional plays his own role—respected by not only the radical and the moderates, but also by the secretarial help who will initially try some of the behavior we suggested earlier. Sensing that he will not tolerate such performance, the clerical pool quickly changes its behavior. He, like the more militant, will not subject himself to the eccentricities of office personnel.

We are told by some respondents that their superiors ask them to ignore the eccentricities some classified staff display because they are veteran and loyal workers, because they are ill, because they are good friends to some political or influential persons, because good help is hard to find, because they are union members, and so on. Some respondents tell us that they are asked not to request tasks to be performed by certain staff members because they are uncooperative. We are further informed by blacks that some of these persons not only attempt to dictate to them, but also to their superiors. They tell us that they observe some secretaries make an office a smooth running operation and others who cause complete chaos. It is probably true that a secretary can make or break a project and keep conflict going in an office; the results of such behavior are well known. Yet, in spite of these general profiles of secretaries and clerical workers and the response of some black administrators to them, the overall response of black educators to these workers is quite positive.

Some of our respondents described to us how cafeteria workers and the janitorial staff caused problems with black students because these students played their transistors in the cafeteria or segregated themselves and congregated at one or more specific tables in the dining area. The following memoranda reflect the typical expectations laid at the feet of black administrators and the revelations of consequent investigation. The first memorandum is from a dean to his "assistant to."

> Pursuant to the matter I discussed with you briefly yesterday, I believe that some action must be taken. Our dining room supervisory personnel have complained that certain students monopolize certain tables in the dining hall, play their transistor radios very loudly, and carry on boisterous conversations, loud laughter, and horseplay all during the lunch hour. The cafeteria help complains that they cannot get to the tables to clean them off because of the crowd around them. We are told that other students are intimidated when they attempt to sit down at one of these tables. Our maintenance supervisor says that his crew cannot do their job because these tables are held up by the students long after the dining hour ends.
>
> Dr. Williams, we cannot have the work of the staff delayed because of the behavior of a few students. Most importantly, we cannot permit any of our students to be intimidated. We do have lounges and other student areas where these students can gather and enjoy themselves.
>
> Please give your attention to this matter and when it is settled, I would certainly like to know how it was resolved.

The following memorandum is the answer the "assistant to" supplied the dean about a week later.

Initially, I was confused with regard to your memo of Wednesday last. Since this was a student behavior matter, I thought that the Dean of Student Services would handle it, although we had talked about it a few days before. Nonetheless, I did look into the problem, and the following is my report.

I have spent the last two days (10:00 A.M. to 3:00 P.M.) investigating the situation. You were right. About 11:30 A.M. each morning black students do begin to gather around two tables on the west side of the dining hall; they do play their transistor radios rather loudly; they do carry on considerable loud conversations and horseplay. I did not see any gambling, but I did observe them playing cards all afternoon. It seems that Miss Nye and Mr. Volpe were right about the conditions in the dining hall.

I spoke to the students and initially they became quite hostile to me. They asked me if I was going to go over and say something to the group of white students two tables away with the two guitars who play and sing the loud country and western songs every day. They asked if I was going to speak to the members of the Honda Motorcycle Club whose table seemed to be off limits to all but their members. And they asked me if I intended to do something about that table on the south wall that that fraternity group dominates every day while they make their pledges carry out all sorts of assignments. And there were any number of other activities going on in that dining hall. I am surprised that Miss Nye and Mr. Volpe haven't mentioned this to you before. I did answer the black students' questions.

On the second day, I brought my camera and took pictures of all of these different groups, recorded the time they occupied the lunchroom, recorded what they did and so on. Then I went over to talk to each of them.

The blacks said that they did not know that they could not remain in the cafeteria all afternoon, that their radios were too loud, and not a single one in the group said or remembered a white being physically intimidated. They did indicate that they might intimidate persons psychologically. They said that all the cafeteria workers had to do was ask them and they would move aside so the dishes could be removed and the floor swept.

All of the groups but one were cooperative. The Honda Club group told me to "go shove it." They all, however, did ask why and I explained about the complaints.

When I went back today, all of the groups but the Honda Club were gone. The dining hall was practically empty. I am sure the income of that room will be affected, but at least we got rid of that loud noise, hoarding of tables, and intimidation of students. I am sure that Miss Nye and Mr. Volpe will see that we did everything we could to cooperate with them.

By this memorandum, then, my report is respectfully submitted.

P.S.   The pictures will be brought over today from the graphics department.

The route to decision is extremely cumbersome in colleges and universities. So complex is the process that many black administrators in charge of special programs demand to report directly to the president. This is a very common occurrence. The president already knows, and the black administrator soon learns, that little if anything can be accomplished through the typical decision-making apparatus of the college. Only special programs (Black Studies, remedial programs, and so forth) can avoid going through the "normal" college process, since these programs rarely have college-wide budget or professional support.

The thing wrong with this shortcut to a quick decision is that the black administrator who is able to circumvent the structure will often feel that his accomplishment is greater than it is. We have heard black administrators boast of their access to the president and their ability to go around the system. What they have failed to realize is that quasi structures which exist outside the system are temporary and alone. These blacks are destined for a sequence of temporary illusions. They are mere satellites around the system. Their budgets are tentative, and professional support for them is either tenuous or nonexistent. They fail to understand that the system, regardless of how cumbersome it may be, protects those who are in it, and eventually destroys or seriously curtails the activities of those outside. We fully understand that many programs would not exist if it were left solely to the discretion of the governing bodies (committee structure). Nonetheless, a program that has not been funded by federal or foundation money will not last if it does not proceed through the elaborate mechanism of the structure. What a black administrator may have mistakenly interpreted as his influence with the president and his ability to circumvent the governance mechanism may have been, in reality, the strategies of the president and the system that were supposed to be outfoxed. Since both the president and the governance body knew that most of the proposed programs of open admissions, Black Studies, programs for the disadvantaged, and so on, could not survive the institutional bureaucracy, a satellite was set up outside the bureaucracy.

The black administrator in these programs is saddled with a temporary program where the budget is controlled by the university, the legitimacy of the program is decided by those who are most hostile to it, and the man who runs it can neither protect the program nor himself. That same black administrator who commences with what he thinks is the cunning of a predator later finds himself among the prey.

Black administrators have slowly learned this. They are now asking for faculty appointments which lead to tenure for themselves and their staff members when they take on a program. They demand a department, not a program. They seek credentialed staff instead of those they chose in the past, although the former were sometimes better for the students. They send their friends into the senates and committees to listen and record what is said. They make sure that they know what decisions are made while the rules are suspended in the meeting, and so on. Still, the "special assistants to the president" exist. We asked one such designee, "What is your job?" He replied, "Anything necessary to make my program go." We then asked, "What does your title mean?" His response: "Not a damn thing!"

Substantive issues may never reach the "assistant to." White students rarely, if ever, confront the black administrator out of fear that he may charge them with racism. Black students may align themselves with him if they don't recognize that he does not have the power to make things happen within the institution. Faculty members rarely confront him for the same reasons. They know that most of the power is vested in themselves. The "assistant to" cannot pull rank and order things done. He quickly learns that authority is diffuse and a direct order unknown in a college. Moreover, the academic men he is serving boast of this absence of direction.

They emphasize the tradition and fact that their "bosses" are there for mere facilitation. Often he is not a member of the cabinet. And seldom, with the exception of prospect of or sequel to riots, does he get involved in the unmergeable functions of the college.

Barzun lists these unmergeable functions (1970, pp. 95–137):

> Alumni affairs; street policing; architectural plans; contracts for new construction; proposed gifts; government grants; fund-raising drives; dormitory rules; prospect or sequel of riots; extension of insurance and other fringe benefits; status of lawsuits; setting tuition fees; supervising standards of admission; studying effects of proposed federal and state legislation; appointing committees; issuing or revising guides and manuals; salary scale; income and budget estimates; announcements to the press; participation in conferences; proposed institutes; adding or phasing out divisions of instruction and research; allocating space and permitting alterations; planning major renovations; ensuring radiation safety; renewing labor contracts; relocating neighbors dispossessed by new buildings; holding scholars against raiding; mechanizing routine by computer; replacing and promoting administrators; preparing council-faculty-and-trustee meetings; revising current budget and preparing the next; meeting demands of government auditors; responding to proposals for exchanges and affiliations; awarding honorary degrees; organizing anniversaries, ceremonials, lectureships, and other public functions.

We did not find a single black administrator involved in institutional research. Although a black administrator may have access to mountains of data, he does not usually make decisions about any of it and is often excluded from the discussion of most of it. He has no authority, power, or constituency of his own.

Black administrators appear to need great orientation in the way authority is interpreted in predominantly white colleges and universities. White administrators appear to see their role as facilitators and serve to coordinate the functions within the college when others make the decisions, but blacks often feel that this is an inefficient use of time and talent. They feel if an individual is responsible for a decision, that decision should not be reached at the pleasure and convenience of those who do not have responsibility for the outcome of the decision. They do not suggest that others should not have significant input into any considerations affecting the institution or themselves, but rather that it should be understood that input is not a mandate. They do not believe that if a large representation of the academic community does not have its own way, that cadre of persons will withdraw en masse.

Perhaps the politics of surviving in a predominantly white educational institution should also be a part of the orientation for black administrators. Most indicate they did not receive any in-service training. It appears that more information was obtained from secretaries and other support personnel than from their designated supervisors. They were not told what committees or committee members were powerful or (in two-year colleges) what advisory groups exerted strong influence on the college. In a surprising number of institutions the black administrator did not receive the rules and regulations, policies, and state statutes until some situation occurred that required this information. In some of the new two-year colleges, there were no policies and procedures manuals; administrators would formulate policies as they went along. In other institutions the black administrator did not know the parameters of his responsibilities and, therefore, he did not always know when he was invading someone else's area of control.

Blacks have discovered that authority and power are nebulous concepts for administrators at all but the highest echelons, and even there it is hard to tell who can determine what. One does not know, for example, where a given directive might originate. A president or an executive vice-president in a four-year college or university who issues a directive may have several layers of assistants between himself and those for whom it is intended. Also, one does not always know that a spoken decision has come from the department chairman who verbalizes it for the faculty he represents. Many committees make far-reaching decisions affecting thousands of students, not having them checked by others in the college or by administrators who will defend them.

It is significant that the things administrators do in higher education are usually defined by professors. A number of them have described in some detail the task of administrators. Few administrators take the time to define and describe their own roles. Blacks who came from predominantly black colleges saw administrators use power and authority in their colleges. We are not saying that this was better; it was understood. We must also say, as have some of our predecessors, that final authority does not mean ultimate wisdom.

Chapter Five

• •
• •
• •

THE
BLACK FACULTY

• •
• •
• •

*"S*end a black student to an all-white college; *it is good for the student.* Send a white student to an all-black college; *it is good for the school."* This is the observation made by a junior college student when discussing the key assumptions of a workshop speaker. The statement is not only provocative but full of insight.

When John Munro left Harvard University to join the staff at Miles College, a small, predominantly black institution in the South, his actions made newspaper headlines, and national magazines carried the story. A staff member from Miles College later remarked that they were never allowed to forget how fortunate they were to have him and how much he would offer the college. There was no doubt about his competence and ability. But what struck this staff member at the time of the event was that neither the media nor any of his colleagues at Harvard who applauded his act mentioned the possibility that Miles College may have had something to offer Dr. Munro.

Black faculty members tell us that when they join the staffs of predominantly white colleges, many of their new colleagues treat them as though they have come only to be enriched, not to enrich the institution. They emphasize the implicit assumption that a black educator is something professionally different from his white counterpart. The consequence of this assumption is that they are treated differently and isolated both as persons and as scholars. "The world of the Negro scholar is indescribably lonely, and he must, somehow, pursue truth down the lonely path, while at the same time making certain that his conclusions are sanctioned by universal standards developed and maintained by those who frequently do not even recognize him" (Franklin, 1963).

This isolation and the consequent frustration and loneliness are reported by a large number of black educators who have left the marginal economics and (what some call) intellectual isolation of all-black colleges and others who have quit the public schools and other organizations and agencies to join predominantly white two-year and four-year institutions purported to have superior facilities for teaching and research.

Earlier we cited the Caplow-McGee study released in 1959 which barely recognizes that black scholars exist in higher education. In 1971, some twelve years after the Caplow-McGee study, Hodgkinson reports another major study in American higher education (1971, pp. 15–16) and makes no reference at all to the black scholar: "This is a book about change in American higher education. It attempts to state which changes have taken place, where they occurred, how they took place, and what they mean for the future of higher education."

We find it incredible that the increased presence of black scholars in predominantly white institutions is not viewed as a major change. Perhaps Hodgkinson should not be faulted for this oversight. It is highly possible that he is more victim than victimizer in his failure to report the nature and trend of the black presence in higher education, because he relied on U.S. Office of Education data and the results of questionnaire returns from twelve hundred thirty presidents of institutions of higher education.

It is difficult for writers who record the problems of black faculty members in higher education to refrain from dwelling upon the perennial survey of injustices, exposing the academic chauvinism and self-interest pragmatism of the academic community, analyzing the recoiling of intellectuals from the concept of affirmative action and implementations of equal employment opportunity, describing the extravagant claims made by academicians to maintain the status quo, permitting rhetoric to blur thought, overstating examples and ironies, and falling prey to black idolatry. Yet to simply introduce data leaves too many stories untold, conceals the circumstances of too many problems, and denies a particular group of educators a podium—one of the very few groups left in the United States who have not had one. Black faculty members have many opinions, and they have commented on everything from personal insults and institutional apathy to some of the strange behavior they have encountered with their black and white colleagues. Some, of course, comment on the satisfactions they enjoy.

It is important to know whether the new presence of black professionals in white institutions of higher education is creating a detrimental void in black ones. Several reporters have indicated that the expanded presence of black scholars in white institutions is creating a brain drain which threatens the continued existence of black institutions. They presuppose that the demand for black academic talent exceeds the supply to the extent that black academic talent in predominantly black institutions is steadily being syphoned off by larger and oftentimes more prestigious white institutions.

There is a locus of black academic talent in the predominantly black colleges and universities. This talent has traditionally been the moving force behind the educational achievement of black Americans, and we think it would border on tragedy to have it depleted and these institutions made impotent. Though the choice of higher educational institutions by blacks has widened to the extent that nearly 75 percent of all black students enrolled in institutions of higher education are today in predominantly white institutions, thousands still matriculate at the predominantly black institutions and, without them, would probably be denied access to higher educational opportunity (Kilson, 1973, p. 427). The black institutions, as other institutions, cannot function properly without professionally trained faculties and staffs, and they tend not to attract scholars from white and other racial and ethnic groups of sufficient quality and quantity to meet their needs. Moreover, because their student clientele is overwhelmingly black, it is both logical and sensible that their faculties and staffs be predominantly black.

Kent Mommsen claims (1972b, p. 8) that the outmigration of black Ph.D.'s from these black institutions amounts to a net loss of 12 percent with the greatest loss (21 percent of those) being persons between fifty-two and fifty-nine years of age. Supporting Mommsen's thesis, Kilson asserts (1973, pp. 428–429) that the future of black colleges is not bright because the shift in choice from black to white colleges by top-flight black students has caused a concomitant change in the recruitment patterns of white colleges. White colleges now seek and attract many of the better-trained black scholars because they offer superior salaries, conditions of service, and scholarly stimulus. Reporting the results of Mommsen's study, *Human Behavior* stated "the biggest buy on the academic market these days appears to be the black scholar with a Ph.D" ("Black Brain Drain," 1972, p. 39).

Our data do not affirm any of these claims without fundamental modifications. We do not find a strong outmigration of black scholars from black institutions. Of our respondents, only 12.8 percent from two-year institutions and 9.4 percent from four-year institutions indicated they left black institutions for their present positions. Only 6.1 percent of the respondents from two-year institutions held the Ph.D., it is not possible that the migratory group within these institutions was comprised totally of persons who held that degree. And it is not realistic to assume that the 201 persons comprising the migratory group in four-year institutions all held the Ph.D. The overwhelming majority of our respondents (87.3 percent in two-year institutions and 90.6 percent in four-year institutions) indicated that their career patterns did not include positions in black institutions. As a tangential but significant point more black women than men in both two-year and four-year colleges indicate that their career pattern included black institutions; 47 percent of the men in junior colleges and 55 percent of those in senior colleges have worked only in white institutions. Therefore, our data neither affirm nor support the notion of a brain drain based on the outmigration of black scholars from black institutions. To us, these assertions are akin to blockbusting in housing; the mere presence of blacks in environs formerly closed or off limits signals the beginning of all

sorts of unsubstantiated statements. Negative white reactions are
spawned by these assertions in housing communities; they are
similarly spawned in academic communities.

Consider the inflammatory nature of the language used to
describe the seeking of black professionals: "the biggest buy on the
academic market, the black doctor himself eagerly follows the
carrot extended by the elite schools" ("Black Brain Drain," 1972,
p. 39), "the most sought-after person in the labor market" (Staples,
1972, p. 43), "most black scholars have moved to white universities
in the North" (Staples, 1972, p. 45). We view these claims as
fraudulent and at best extravagent. Two questions stand out as
important upon closer examination: Is the black scholar the biggest
buy on the academic market? Is he the most sought-after person in
the labor market? Those who make up the black academic market
say yes and no. While seeking and hiring blacks at white institutions is the subject of much talk, movement beyond the talk is quite
limited. Some states have no black professionals working in two-
year institutions of higher education. Yet not a single state among
the fifty has no black population. The 1970 census indicates that
only one state has a black population of less than a thousand. And
while it is possible, we find it difficult to believe that all blacks
within those states where they are employed are unprepared or ill
suited to work in a single two-year institution of higher education.
In several other states, 80 percent of the institutions of higher education do not employ a single black professional. (See Chapter
Seven.) Does this portray a seller's market for blacks? Is one the
most sought-after scholar in academia when one is totally excluded
from the academic community in several states and virtually excluded in several others?

And what about the use of the adjective *elite?* What some
call common, run-of-the-mill white institutions suddenly become
elite when blacks begin to move toward and into them. Few agree
on what institutions of higher education in this country are elite.
Elite means "the choice part; a socially superior group." Though
institutions of higher education are difficult to rate and rank, the
vast majority do not rank in the superior category and those that
do do not employ the preponderance of black professionals.

A diminishing brain market for black institutions is so,

however. Mommsen calls attention to this and describes it (1972b, p. 8) as "another dimension of the brain drain—the highest proportion of respondents locating in white institutions for the first (26 percent) and present (31 percent) positions are among the youngest doctorates." Of our respondents in two-year institutions, 43.4 percent stated that their careers have embraced white institutions, 21 percent had been in integrated institutions, and 22.9 percent had been in other kinds of institutions and activities. Of respondents in four-year institutions, 52.3 percent had always been in white institutions, 17 percent had been in integrated institutions, and 21.3 percent had been in other kinds of institutions and activities. More than half the respondents from two-year and four-year institutions have been in higher education for three years or less. Almost 75 percent of the respondents in both categories of institutions have been in higher education six years or less. Of all our respondents, 80.8 percent in two-year colleges and 81.3 percent in four-year institutions have not been at their present institutions more than four years. It can be concluded that the preponderant number of blacks presently employed in predominantly white institutions are new both to higher education and to their institutions, and they have never worked as professionals in predominantly black institutions of higher education.

Age may be a major factor here. Blacks in higher education are young. Over half of them (55 percent) are forty or younger.

Numerically our Ph.D. respondent population is relatively small—593. Based upon an estimated total black doctorate population of three thousand, the 593 represent 19.8 percent of that population. If we adjust our figures to include nonrespondents from white institutions, the percentage increases to between 35 and 40 percent of the total black doctorate population; this leaves 60 to 65 percent black Ph.D.'s in black institutions, governmental agencies, business and industry, and social action agencies. Based upon James Bryant's prediction (1970) of a 20 percent increase by 1973 over his base figure of almost twenty-three hundred black holders of the Ph.D., our guess of three thousand is both inflated and optimistic and could be overstated. These facts show that surely no less than half of the black Ph.D.'s are in black educational institutions.

Black colleges and universities have long been the intellectual backbone of American blacks. They were not only the major educational developers of black people but the major employers of blacks attaining the doctorate degree. While the role of these institutions has shifted, the need for the continued presence and work of Ph.D.'s is beyond question. Thousands of black youths could still benefit from higher educational opportunity and are not likely to be recruited or accepted by white institutions with their forces of traditionalism, political conservatism, a pseudo liberalism, bureaucracy, and intellectual arrogance (Billingsley, 1970a, p. 131). Their hope for educational development is with the black institutions. The present concern should not be the increasing number of black students attending white institutions but the rapid enlargement of the black college student population, thereby expanding the black academic talent potential and pool for both categories of institutions. But the immediate problem for black institutions is how to attract the needed yearly percentage of blacks who graduate with the Ph.D. This problem can grow to critical proportions unless these institutions become more active in the black academic marketplace and compete more successfully with their white sister institutions. They do not, at the present time, appear to be suffering a severe outmigration of scholarly talent. But natural attrition, through retirement and death, will take its toll, and unless new talent is attracted voids are certain to occur. We believe what is described as the *black brain drain* is basically a one-dimensional phenomenon—white institutions are claiming most of the newly graduated black Ph.D.'s.

Our respondents, however, inform us that this one-dimensional phenomenon is rapidly taking on a new twist; black scholars are leaving white institutions for black ones, because white institutions fail to live up to their promises and harrassment is not uncommon. One Ph.D. respondent states his situation: "Failure to receive mail and having mail tampered with is a reality here for blacks. There are serious questions on the fair treatment of blacks when compared to their white counterpart(s). Salaries are good, on the plus side, but promotion and tenure is a no-no. Black professors with faculty status seem to be part of a cycling process. A maximum (quota) is maintained but no one stays the required five years, earliest date for tenure."

Other reasons our respondents give for leaving white institutions bear no negative connotations. These reasons seem to arise from a deep and growing concern to work for and with other blacks. Proponents of this view feel that limited black academic talent cannot be made available to black youth with required intensity if spread among the thousands of institutions across the country. They feel that this talent cannot impact society in a fundamental way if spread too thinly. Those who espouse these positions are not only moving to black institutions but are attempting to persuade others to join them.

Teaching, research, and service have long been heralded as the tripartite functions of the university. Research and service are heavily devalued in the two-year institution as a responsibility of the faculty; the teaching function is ranked the highest. In any institution of higher education, those who perform one or some combination of these functions are involved in the central functions of the institution. Those who do not are not considered to be centrally involved. Within four-year institutions, particularly universities, it is not uncommon to find administrators teaching and conducting research in addition to filling their administrative positions. If they do not, they are not usually fully accepted in the community of scholars and many times are derisively referred to as "just administrators." Few excuses are accepted for noninvolvement in research in major institutions and the reward system is tied to, if not based upon, what is described as the "productivity" of the person.

While teaching is purported to be one of the major functions of all colleges and universities, it is not the function which produces the greatest professional rewards. Yet, it is this function that black professionals perform most.

The majority of blacks in senior institutions teach in the departments of education and the social and behavioral sciences. English, languages, history, and philosophy appear to attract black scholars as well as administrative science, mathematics, and the physical sciences, but to a lesser degree. Contrary to what many believe, only 2 percent of our respondents reported teaching in a Black Studies curriculum. Very few individuals teach in the professional curricula: four in optometry and pharmacy, five in dentistry, twenty-five in law, and seventy-nine in medicine. Eighty-seven are in the allied health programs, and twenty-nine are in agriculture and home economics.

While their numbers in general are smaller, the percentage of women teaching in particular fields is greater than that of men—medicine, home economics, languages, English, social sciences, and education are examples. Our data indicate that in four-year colleges, 73 percent of our respondents teach in their fields of specialization although more women (75 percent) than men (72 percent) teach in their area of specialization. This is also true in junior colleges, where 87 percent of the women and 72 percent of the men teach in their fields of specialization.

The black educators who currently teach in predominantly white institutions have ranked their reasons for joining the institution. There was a complete consensus and in both two-year and four-year colleges, men as well as women gave the same ranking: (1) interest in students and in teaching, (2) an opportunity to work in an intellectual atmosphere, and (3) more money was offered. Such considerations as promotions and the prestige or social status professors and administrators hold were the last two of the nine possible choices. The opportunity to work with black students and black colleagues were ranked higher than either prestige or promotion as a reason for joining their institutions. This does not mean that their priorities will remain identical after they realize or understand the importance of the items rejected in the academic community and the blow to their idealism or commitment, however they view it.

When asked to rank the most critical needs at their institutions, black student counseling and a greater commitment to the resolution to social problems were ranked the highest, in that order. In addition to his regularly assigned duties the black professional has added or been thrust these. Of course, whether voluntary or assigned, he could hardly turn his back on black students particularly, since their experiences tend to be quite denigrating. Edgar Epp's report (1972, pp. 108–109) of the experience of one such student provides a poignant illustration, from which we have the following excerpts:

> Being black means to walk across the campus on my first day of class and not see one black student.
>
> Being black is tolerating "Nigra" for "'Negro" and favoring neither.
>
> Being black is to watch whites look upon my natural hair, my moustache, my African garments, my black music and literature, my black community language, and my other symbols of black pride as being deviant.
>
> Being black is to be a resource person for curious white folks, who after being answered are not willing to accept my expertise.
>
> Being black means to be in an ocean of white stimuli, to be angry consciously or unconsciously, to continuously struggle with oneself to deny hostile feeling, angry feeling. I might add there is no difference between the anger of a black rioter and that of a black Ph.D. but rather a difference in the way the difference [anger] comes out.
>
> Finally, being black means to be lonely, hyperalienated, depressed, displayed, ignored, and harrassed. Just the fact of being black is to be at the brink of revolt.

Many times the plight of the professional is just as severe as that of the black student. One can only speculate who is the counselor and who the counselee when the two come together to discuss and find answers to problems. The majority of our respondents who teach and work with black students, however, reported that they felt the need to give them special encouragement and emotional support.

A minority (less than 25 percent) of junior or senior college faculty members left their former jobs in order to get an increase in salary. More men than women did this in both two-year and four-year colleges; it occurred more in two-year than four-year colleges.

In our four-year college and university survey, 10 percent of the blacks taught only graduate students and 27 percent taught both graduate and undergraduates. More men (7.6 percent) than

women (6 percent) taught graduate students. The majority of men
and women teach only undergraduates. This fact alone seriously
challenges the opponents of affirmative action who say graduate
education will suffer when blacks and women are hired to teach in
the university if they are not "qualified," since the majority of the
blacks currently in the university are not permitted to teach graduate students. Among our 2174 respondents in four-year colleges
and universities, only 195 direct dissertations; of them, 24 are
women. Some 249 report that they can serve on dissertation committees; 38 of them women. We must conclude, therefore, the
direction of graduate study will remain for some time in the hands
of the white male ruling class of academe.

As might be expected, there are four times as many blacks
who hold the Ph.D. in senior institutions as there are in junior
colleges. According to sex, men hold the greater number of Ph.D.'s
by almost two to one.

In some areas of specialization, blacks experience severely
limited opportunities. Any one of several areas could be used to
illuminate this charge, but we have chosen athletics because of its
wide appeal and the undeniable fact that black students excel in
the area.

We found few black coaches in predominantly white two-
year or four-year schools. We did find several assistant coaches.
"White coaches are perceived as the most racially biased bloc on
campus," the U.S. Commission found in a study of the Wisconsin
State University system (*Chronicle of Higher Education,* p. 5).

Green and his associates of the Big Ten Athletic Conference
report (1972): "Of those coaching staffs which were found to have
black representation, the blacks were all assistant or freshmen
coaches. Many of these coaches stated that their roles and responsibilities were not clearly defined and that they were not given full
coaching responsibilities. This was complicated by the fact that
black assistant coaches typically did not have budget accessibility.
In addition these coaches felt that their major role was to recruit
black athletes, many of whom they had no control over once they
were officially enrolled in the university."

Green and his associates also reported the concerns of athletes who note that "Blacks who are typically hired for coaching

roles frequently end up performing menial tasks, serving as errand boys rather than coaches. At one Big Ten University, a black graduate assistant who was hired to coach at the freshman level was actually painting stadium benches."

Many black assistant coaches report that they see no future in the positions they hold, and black athletes indicate that their black coaches do not have concrete coaching functions.

It is ironic with the number of black athletes in higher education that so few black faculty members, counselors, and administrators are found on college staffs. One of our respondents postulated that this is so college officials and athletic department officials can exploit the students in the absence of witnesses. Since most of the students are receiving some type of financial assistance, in the past they have been blackmailed into keeping quiet. The exploitation of black athletes is well documented, and it is done with a cynicism all too evident (L. Johnson, 1972; Nowak, 1968). "The most glaring fallacy about intercollegiate athletic competition in the United States is the assumption that fairness is inherent. . . . College sports are not the haven of fair play and equal opportunity we have been led to believe. To black athletes, coaches, and officials, fairness and equal opportunity are myths. The patterns of racial discrimination, both overt and covert, institutional and individual, found in the larger society are reflected in and perpetuated by athletics in the United States" (Shapiro, 1970).

Whereas blacks hold very few positions in athletic departments they hold even fewer positions in physical education departments.

Our respondents do not feel that a great deal of the current and past research has much value. A full 78 percent (2516) of our respondents in both two-year and four-year institutions spend up to 15 percent of their time in research. Another 13.6 percent (439) spend between 16 and 30 percent in these efforts. The remaining 8 percent spend from 60 to 100 percent of their time in research. In sum, 92 percent of our respondents spend less than a third of their time doing research. Men spend about 3 percent more of their time than women do in senior colleges, about 2 percent more in two-year colleges. (What continues to strike us is the great similarity between black men and women in every area but salary and their actual numbers.) Blacks indicate overwhelmingly that while they see the need for research, teaching should have greater priority. They subscribe to and read the publications and encounter countless articles which they describe as "pointless," "witless," "irrelevant," and without enough academic or intellectual value to warrant the time, effort, and cost for their production and dissemination. Only about 12 percent in both two-year and four-year institutions do not subscribe to professional journals, while 75 percent in community colleges and 68.8 percent in four-year institutions subscribe to from one to four publications. The remaining 13.0 percent in two-year colleges and 19.3 percent in four-year institutions subscribe to five or more professional publications. Most black faculty members find it difficult to understand why academicians have built the reward system almost exclusively on one's bent to deal with the abstract and hypothetical rather than the real. What about real problems and solutions? Should not their worth be evaluated by the results of our efforts to work face-to-face with the problems, distill and translate the rhetoric, unravel and make known policies and traditions, serve as the interface between the institution and disparate groups, bring order out of chaos, and reduce dysfunctional conflict?

Research and scholarly writing require time and money. Those who have little time and money at their disposal tend not to do much research and scholarly writing. We suspect though, that just as the color of one's skin carries more weight than the quality of his character in white society, the length of the black scholar's bibliography is more of a factor in ascertaining his promotion and tenure in white academia than all of his other efforts combined. Tradition is fiercely guarded and changes slowly in academia; we know of no widespread move to significantly change the research and writing criteria as the basic arbiter for who moves ahead, who leaves, and who stays. In two-year and in some four-year institutions, however, teaching is the prized function. But good teaching too requires time and access to good research.

The overwhelming majority of black professionals are not producing written materials. Most of them subscribe to professional publications and hold membership in and attend professional meetings (17.5 percent do not attend professional meetings), but they tend not to present their ideas in written form. Eighty-eight percent of the respondents in two-year colleges and 80 percent in four-year institutions have not written a book; 93 percent in two-year colleges and 91 percent in four-year institutions have not edited a book; 79 percent in both categories of institutions have not reviewed a book; and 83 percent in two-year colleges and 66 percent in four-year institutions have not written a single article. Coauthoring was even less engaged in than solo authoring. Getting started writing is many times more difficult than actually writing, so we asked our respondents if they had received motivation to write from their colleagues through requests to coauthor; 68 percent in the two-year institutions and 53 percent in four-year institutions said no. Their colleagues tended not to ask them to coauthor, and when this did happen, the colleague was more apt to be white than black. It is notable that a surprisingly large number of white educators in colleges and universities have not published books. In one large midwestern state university, 70 percent of the non-minority faculty members have never published a book. Yet, the average department in the institution has 78 percent of its professional staff on tenure.

We know of many special uses made of the black professional; his ideas and opinions are regularly sought as information to be used in research and writing. He serves as liaison between researchers and subjects, provides frames of reference and perspectives for research activity, and himself is frequently the target of research. Many blacks no longer participate in research, or when they do, they ask exorbitant fees. We have already given some of the reasons for this growing rejection of research. Beyond that, the black scholar finds that he is seldom invited to be a full participant in the research activities conducted by his colleagues. Research support from the state, foundations, business and industry, the federal government, and his own institution is virtually nonexistent, though each of these entities invest hundreds of thousands of dollars each year in research activities. His consulting and service opportunities are greater and bear more fruit, but they too are limited.

Research is predicted to increase in importance in four-year institutions. The presidents of twelve hundred thirty institutions of higher education across the country indicate that by 1975 there will be over twenty thousand professors in 356 institutions whose sole activity is research. This trend supports the notion that there is a monolithic status system in American higher education, and that its basis is research that establishes a national reputation, both for the person and the institution (Hodgkinson, 1971, p. 17). Time, of course, will be the real test of the accuracy of these predictions, but they have implications for the black scholar today. Those who do not engage in research and scholarly writing are in a tenuous position and might not survive when examined and evaluated by their peers; promotion and tenure will be difficult, if not impossible to attain; and career patterns will probably be horizontal rather than vertical.

The percentage of our respondents who have already published is quite small; however, over half of those in the senior colleges and one-third of those in junior colleges are presently involved in activities leading to publication. This is true for men and women but for every six men, there are five women involved in such activity.

Promotion in two-year colleges appears quite different from that in four-year institutions. In two-year colleges, a faculty member may be promoted to department or division chairman or to some place in the administrative structure. Beyond these categories there are few other promotional options available. Most community colleges do not have a ranking system for faculty. In a sense, community college faculty members are promoted each year they receive an additional salary increase. Persons are placed in a particular category in order to assign them to a certain level on the salary scale. For example, faculty classifications may be instructor 1, 2, or 3. These classifications frequently indicate salary placement and seniority, and thus some people consider it a promotion to move from one category to the other. Although many two-year college faculties are attempting to mimic four-year college faculties in maintaining that they have the right to determine who gets promoted, this practice is not yet widespread.

Few blacks in community colleges become department or division chairmen. Black women appear to have been promoted as often as black men in two-year colleges. Four percent of the women believe that their chances for promotion are better than for whites; 61 percent believe that their chances for promotion are equal to whites. Contrary to other areas of higher education, in community colleges, women do get promoted often, and black women do hold department and division chairmanships. This is due in part because women dominate the field in certain disciplines such as nursing, some of the other health sciences, home economics, and a few other disciplines. It should be understood that a department is a subunit of a division in a two-year college. A department chairman in a two-year college is more like a head teacher in a high school than a department head in a college. Since most blacks are newcomers in the two-year college, they have not had sufficient time on the job to establish seniority and contend for promotion to certain positions. There are, of course, many exceptions where seniority is not a factor. In newly established colleges, for example, a person may be hired on the basis of his experiences and qualifications. If a department needs a special skill, if a new program is being developed and the only person available is a black, or if programs exist in which whites are unable, unwilling, or do not desire to participate, such as developmental programs, seniority is not a factor and blacks may very easily get an appointment. Many black faculty members are not interested in promotions beyond a good salary and good fringe benefits in the community college. They know that the department chairman's job is a thankless one; the individual is usually compensated only by a reduction in class load and a small differential in pay. He has no real power and he is caught between the two power-hungry groups in the college: the faculty and the administration.

Black professionals do not appear to be as concerned about prestige positions as their white counterparts when the position carries neither power nor substantial compensation. (This is not true of blacks in predominantly black colleges.) None of our respondents in white two-year institutions indicated that prestige was important to them either tangentially or specifically. They did indicate that the same opportunity should be available to them as others on the staff and the option of taking advantage of the opportunities is for their own deliberations. Some of them leave positions where the job carries great prestige but little money and poor fringe benefits.

Men hold a majority of the administrative positions and tend to cluster in higher pay brackets than women do. Men constitute 58.2 percent of the respondent population but hold 30.4 percent of the administrative positions; women constitute 41.8 percent of the respondent population but hold only 11.3 percent of the administrative positions. The percentage of women tends to exceed the percentage of men in each of the low-pay categories. Compared to 75 percent of the women, 48 percent of the men earn less than fourteen thousand. The rest earn fourteen thousand or more.

The age, professional preparation, number of years in higher education, and number of years in rank or position achieved by black women is not reflected in administrative positions and salary. In this respect the two-year institution seems almost as tradition-bound as the four-year institution. Women exceed men in the two-year institutions only in freedom from them—more women are single, separated, divorced, and widowed than men. This phenomenon may be more than coincidental.

Promotion in the four-year college and university is an elaborate procedure. For some, the promotion is monitored through every step and the candidate must have observed every rule and paid homage to almost every professor in the department. Others are promoted without challenge whether they have proved to be scholars and excellent teachers or not.

Van den Berghe insists (1970) that if the candidate belongs to a minority group he is at a distinct advantage: "Academics are so extraordinarily sensitive to any imputation of racism that a minority-group person can easily blackmail himself into a promotion. In fact, in most cases he will not even need to do so, because his WASP colleagues will gladly apply a double standard without any prompting on his part. Everybody wants a black face on his staff, and there are not enough to go around."

If this is true, members of minority groups do not know it. The statement is certainly inconsistent with our findings, which indicate an overwhelming majority of blacks clustered in the lower academic ranks. While we do not doubt that some blacks have bargained successfully for higher ranks, there is no evidence that their "WASP colleagues" have applied a double standard and promoted them either with or without an extortion attempt. All of the literature available on the recruitment and hiring of college and universiy staffs suggests that bargaining between an institution and a candidate is normal behavior for both parties; Van den Berghe himself describes this bargaining process in *Academic Gamesmanship*.

Jacques Barzun, too, has described this bargaining (1970, p. 37): "the dean is asked not for a fixed salary but for a bargaining range. Bargaining goes on not only about salary but also about teaching load, fringe benefits, and possibly special prerequisites, such as extra leaves, research assistance, laboratory space and equipment, or an allocation to the university library for the purchase of books at the incumbent's pleasure."

Caplow and McGee, too, wrote extensively (1965) about the bargaining process which takes place in colleges and universities.

As for Van den Berghe's charge of blackmail, we suggest that one cannot be blackmailed in the first place unless the extortionist knows something about him or some information he wishes to conceal, information which, if revealed, would seriously alter his image, expose his wrongdoing, or force an issue that he wants to keep suppressed. We concede that one can be blackmailed with threats against his own safety or the safety of his loved ones, but absolutely no evidence indicates that black educators have either used or contemplated such threats. Especially since only 8.1 percent of them in senior institutions are full professors. Since colleges and universities are purported to be an "open" system, the faculty and administrators of such a system cannot have anything to hide. Can they?

Our own data reveal that 56.9 percent of the blacks in higher education are still assistant professors and in other positions such as instructor and lecturer. From our sample, 208 respondents hold the professorship, and 347 hold the rank of associate professor. Notwithstanding, 54 percent of our respondents believe that their chances for promotion are equal to that of whites.

Contrary to pervading rumor (much of which is attributable to educators and to popular belief), a large number of incompetent black educators *are not* being hired into white institutions and promoted into positions where the institutions are forced to lower their standards in order to get them. We have not generally found that HEW forces institutions to hire blacks who are unqualified in order to meet some arbitrary quota set by the federal government. Our subjects resent the implication of certain authors and educators that when blacks demand equal opportunity they are asking that the institution lower its standards.

Misguided white liberals tend to respond more to pangs of conscience than rational judgment when faced with demands to redress grievances. Kilson alludes to this (1973, p. 435): "There are few white colleges and universities where white faculty and administrators have not allowed the established academic standards to be suspended in order to accommodate the militant (and violent) pressures of black students and faculty for an all-black, segregated status in the academic life of the institution."

Some of the spurious and often erroneous information about blacks begins because of situations like the one just described. Our experience, however, has been that the hurdles that guard the gates to white academia are usually too high for large numbers of blacks, competent or incompetent, to leap across and gain entrance. We have been told that all manner of devices have been used to keep blacks out rather than get them in. Search committees have been known to make a priori decisions about potential black candidates based solely on speculation about their present salary, rank, and institutional status; full credentials of a white candidate have been used against a simple vita of a black candidate as a basis for deciding which candidate should be offered the position; and as Staples indicates (1972, p. 45): "Many academic departments are engaged in running battles with the administration to increase the number of teaching positions they are allotted. Some use the demand for more black faculty as a leverage in this battle. They will fill all their available slots with white personnel and then begin their search for a black scholar. . . . When the administration does not come through with the position the black scholar is not hired."

Though there are many more examples of this kind of chicanery reported to us, these are sufficient to make the point that we know of no widesperad move within white academia to use extraordinary means to attract large numbers of blacks. Certain institutions make genuine efforts to recruit black scholars, but these institutions are the exception and not the rule. The barriers of exclusions have not been fully removed for blacks and, as our data show, blacks are not rushing in.

Rank, of course, is the objective of promotion. Professorial rank is uncommon in community colleges. Faculty members who seek it are primarily teachers with master's and doctor's degrees who teach in the transfer or college parallel programs and who attempt to behave in the university tradition (C. Monroe, 1972, p. 265). The question of how to determine rank always arises. If the master plumber teaching in the community college was first a plumber's apprentice, then a journeyman required to prove himself on the job as both a craftsman and a teacher, how can his rank be ascertained in comparison with the teacher who did his study in a specific subject matter field and received a master's or doctor's degree, who has done research but was neither taught to teach nor required to demonstrate that he could? The literature is voluminous and in agreement that a ranking system in a two-year college is not only undesirable and inequitable but also absurd. Such a system is not in harmony with the philosophy, structure, and operations of a community college.

Fortunately, most faculty members in two-year colleges do not pursue the issue of rank. In those colleges where it is used (in just a few state-controlled institutions in the East, Midwest, and Far West), it is meaningless. It has been instituted for some of the same reasons as the instructor classifications which we discussed earlier—for placement on the salary schedule, merit pay, and so forth. Collective negotiations have all but eliminated salary schedules based on rank. In the past, those who held the academic degrees were always at the top and dominated the higher lanes on the salary schedules. Two salary schedules were the consequent effect, a prestige factor for too few, and not worth the general loss in faculty morale and the inequity in salary and other benefits. Quite often the wrong people were rewarded. Those instructors who worked in the trades and the other vocational areas are more successful with their students than those who worked in liberal arts programs, if success is measured in terms of student retention, program completions, and most important, student placement.

In community colleges where there is a ranking system, the pattern is a familiar one for blacks—they are clustered in the lower ranks. Less than a quarter of our community college respondents indicated a rank. Most of them insisted that rank had no real meaning in their institutions, but if they deserved it and met the criteria according to the prescribed rules, then they would get it.

In four-year institutions, rank has real meaning and determines to a sizable extent the influence patterns within organizational hierarchies. Those who hold high professorial rank usually chair committees, participate in governing at the departmental, college, and institutional levels, are venerated by students, and ascertain better teaching schedules and consulting relationships. The difference runs deep between junior and senior faculty. Within some institutions and some departments, junior faculty do most if not all, of the teaching. Many times the classes of junior faculty are atrociously large and are scheduled at the least desirable times. Rank determines the pecking order in four-year institutions.

Relatively large numbers of black faculty members and administrators in white institutions is a recent phenomenon, so many have not been in their institutions long enough to have undergone the first evaluation for promotion. Therefore, to a large extent by academic custom and tradition, they cluster at the lower levels of academic rank and few are tenured.

Yet there is much about the black professional which is a stark contrast with his white counterpart. *Less than half* (42.5 percent) of our respondents hold full-time regularly appointed faculty positions. Of these, 46.8 percent (493 persons) of the people in community colleges and 40.4 percent (897 persons) of those in four-year colleges are full-time regularly appointed faculty members. Even more significant is the greater percentage of black women (60 percent) than men (46 percent) holding full-time faculty positions in both two-year and four-year colleges. Their actual numbers, however, are quite small. A number of things may account for this. Our data indicate that women earn lower salaries than men; women come for less. Whereas we do not have data in our possession to substantiate that white males prefer black women to black men as their colleagues, it is a perception widely held by both black men and women. There is also the emerging practice of hiring black women and thereby solving two affirmative action requirements—sex and minority group membership. When a single black is hired in both types of institutions, that person is usually a woman.

Another 10.7 percent (347 persons) of the total number of respondents reported that they serve in both administrative and faculty positions. Of these, 7.7 percent (eighty-one persons) are in two-year colleges and 12.2 percent (266 persons) are in senior colleges. Only eighteen persons (1.7 percent) reported working part-time in the junior college when the very nature of the institution is such that part-time staff members are entirely appropriate; the institution is noted for its short-term courses, its ability to develop almost ad hoc programs, and its ease of program and curricula establishment. We have since discovered, that due to the short-term duration of many of the programs, the lack of printed rosters of part-time staff, and the belief on the part of part-timers who did get a questionnaire that we would not be interested in their responses and that their responses to many of the questions would not apply, many of these persons did not return the questionnaires. We know that the majority of the staff of many community colleges are made up of such part-timers and that the number of blacks who are part-time faculty members is many times greater than the number who are full-time regularly appointed faculty members.

The seventy-six (3.5 percent) blacks who reported serving as part-time faculty in four-year institutions also do not reflect an adequate sample of part-time black faculty for some of the same reasons as noted above, particularly with regard to the appropriateness of their response to the questionnaire. Many of the part-timers who did return the survey instrument indicated this problem and also the necessity for them to omit many of the items listed. Only 2.9 percent of the part-time faculty in both types of institutions responded to our survey.

Counselors represent 8.3 percent of our respondents, more in the junior college (14.5 percent) than the senior college (5.2 percent). Although they may not have teaching responsibilities, counselors represent faculty in most two-year colleges and in many, though not all, four-year colleges and universities. What is significant to us is that less than half of the black professionals in both types of institutions are full-time, clearly defined, regularly appointed faculty members, the people who become permanent, gain tenure, affect curriculum, take part in governance, and work in those parts of the college or university which make significant impact on the education enterprise. Given these revelations of the percentage of full-time regularly appointed faculty members, it is understandable why so many of our respondents, especially those in the four-year colleges, hold only the master's degree (47.4 percent—1031 persons—of the black educators among our respondents in senior institutions). This has interesting and obvious long-range implications if the traditional credentials are used in the reward system and are applicable to black professionals. Two-thirds (66.3 percent, or 699) of our respondents in two-year colleges hold a master's degree. This, of course, is entirely appropriate. The percentage of women who hold this degree is greater in both types of institutions, though their numbers are smaller in both cases.

It is clear that while four-year colleges and universities have recruited and hired blacks, few of them work as full-time faculty members.

Closely related to securing a faculty position in a college is enjoying the rewards of the position. Tenure is one such professional reward. Hodgkinson informs us that the sixties were particularly good to and for academicians because "tenure was awarded more often and to younger men, as institutions bargained desperately to get and keep the most able young scholars. On many campuses, the instructor rank nearly died out completely—the initial appointment was at the assistant professor level. . . . Most notable is that during the sixties it became possible for a teacher to become a full professor, with tenure, by the time he was forty" (Hodgkinson, 1971, p. 15–16).

The "boom era" is over in higher education, and reduction and retrenchment are apparent. Private institutions, even those with handsome endowments, are having difficulty with their budgets. Citizen reaction to years of campus unrest, coupled with the natural conservatism of legislatures with rural and suburban domination, make it virtually impossible for presidents of public colleges and universities to find within those bodies ears receptive to their pleas for expanded budgets. Tenure too is caught up in the retrenchment mania and we suspect blacks will have difficulty getting it.

Only one black in five holds tenure in senior institutions,

one in three holds it in the community college. And when we compare men to women, we find that about a third of each have tenure in both types of institutions. The similarities are equally as close in tenure-accruing positions. A tenure-accruing position is not a tenured position and may never become one, however. Each regularly appointed faculty member is technically in a tenure-accruing position. This holds true to a lesser degree for administrators in two-year colleges and in many four-year colleges and universities, particularly if the administrator also holds faculty rank.

A further caution, though the number who hold tenure may seem significant for the length of time blacks have been in higher education in predominantly white institutions, the actual number of persons who reported being tenured was four hundred thirty out of 2174 in the senior colleges and three hundred forty out of 1054 in two-year colleges. With tenure under attack during the earlier years of this decade, there is little reason to believe that the representation of blacks as tenured professionals will increase greatly.

Our data reveal that almost 50 percent of the blacks in senior institutions are not only nontenured but are in nontenure-accruing positions. The 968 persons who fall into this category is more than twice the number who are tenured and one and one-third larger than the number of tenure-accruing respondents. Ninety-one persons in senior colleges did not respond to this item on tenure.

In two-year colleges, 32.3 percent (340) hold tenure, 33.7 percent (355) have tenure-accruing positions, and 30.3 percent (319) are nontenured. Thirty-six gave no response. We do know that if those persons in tenure-accruing positions remain at their two-year institutions they will be awarded tenure once their probationary period has ended.

Tenure is one of the much sought-after benefits awarded in colleges and universities. Those who gain it in two-year colleges need only to "serve time," as one student has put it. While this is also true in some senior institutions, in many of them the candidate for tenure must do research, publish, and teach, along with serving time. And teaching may often be the least important function with regard to getting tenure.

Chapter Six

•••••••••••••••••••••
•••••••••••••••••••••••
•••••••••••••••••••••••

THE BLACK WOMAN IN HIGHER EDUCATION

•••••••••••••••••••••
••••••••••••••••••••••
•••••••••••••••••••••••

*M*uch of what we know about black women in higher education has come from their autobiographies, letters, and papers.* These sources are often well respected but are frequently poorly documented. They contain the obvious biases inherent in such works. There is, however, a rich and varied body of knowledge about black women in higher education. The records of these women are widely scattered and "lie buried unread, infrequently noticed, and even more seldom interpreted. Their

---

* See the Mary Church Terrell Papers in the Library of Congress; the Mary McLeod Bethune Papers at Amistad Research Center, Dillard University, among the Rosenwald Fund Papers at Fisk University, in the Monroe Work collection of newspaper clippings at Tuskegee Institute, and at Bethune-Cookman College; and the Charlotte Hawkins Brown Papers at the Schlesinger Library, Radcliffe College. See also Lerner (1972b, pp. xxix–xxxii); Duster (1970); Holt (1964); Peare (1951); Emma Gelders Sterne, *Mary McLeod Bethune* (1959); S. Brown (1923); Coppin (1913); Smith (1893); Taylor (1886); and Stewart (1932).

names and their achievements are known to only a few specialists"
(Lerner, 1972b). The academic community, without even a
rationale or intellectual defense, has permitted the educational
involvement and contributions of black females in higher education
to go almost wholly unexplored.

Black women in higher education have not been a priority
issue in predominantly white colleges. We do know, however, that
prior to the turbulence of the late 1960s, black females participated
in higher education primarily by teaching and administration in
all-black colleges. Many agree that while the college president has
been the unchallenged authority in the black college, the black
woman was the backbone of it. Historically, it was she, armed with
a master's degree or less, who helped to mold the young blacks of
a nation who "made it." In contrast to many white females who
were discriminated against by white male academicians and administrators and were excluded from working as professionals in white
colleges and universities, black women did not encounter as much
resistance in all-black colleges. They did encounter some objections;
nonetheless, they were hired not only as faculty members but also
as administrators. They were promoted and awarded tenure and
the other benefits which accrue to those serving in the academic
community. One reason for their inclusion is that black males
appear to be more willing to accept the leadership and contributions
of females than white males.

A second reason is that many more college-trained black
women than college-trained black men were available. Their numbers have continued to increase over the number of black men
during the last three decades (Noble, 1965, p. 28; Epstein, 1972,
pp. 914–915). This gap in academic attainment between black
men and women only closes with the postmaster's degree level of
college training (Noble, 1965; Epstein, 1972; Ploski, 1967).

A third reason why black women have been teachers and
administrators in all-black colleges was that black men, even college-
trained ones, could often earn a better living for themselves and
their families by working in civil service occupations, as waiters, as
bellhops, and at other such jobs, than they could earn as professors
in small, poorly financed, ill-equipped, and nonaccredited all-black

colleges (Holmes, 1934, p. 158). The colleges themselves could be described as high-risk.

A fourth reason is that antinepotism rules were not applied as stringently in the black college as in the white college. In some institutions a white female could not—and still cannot—teach on the same college staff as her husband, but it was, and still is, common to find husband-and-wife teams on the same campus of an all-black college. This double standard operated within the same state. The husband-and-wife team has not become a common practice, although it does occur, on predominantly white campuses.

A fifth reason is that parents were forced to accept the idea that discrimination and its dehumanizing disparities would restrain but not be fatal to the black male; not being certain about the female, they were determined to "educate the girls out of the white folk's kitchen" (Noble, 1956, p. 30). Teaching was the most acceptable and accessible vehicle for doing this. The early founders of black colleges were convinced that the race needed teachers and encouraged black women to go into teaching.

Perhaps a final reason, although these are not all the reasons, is that professional black women who do marry have successfully combined careers with family life (Noble, 1965, p. 40; Epstein, 1972, p. 925).

Compared to white female administrators who, until fairly recently, were confined primarily to leadership roles in all-women colleges, black women, such as Mary McLeod Bethune, Lucy Laney, and Ruth M. Harris, headed coeducational institutions. Deanships and other administrative positions have been held by black women for decades in all-black colleges; they still hold a significant number of department chairmanships. They are not confined solely to such jobs as housemothers, deans of women, and other such positions which are more disciplinary than guidance-oriented, more custodial than professional.

Black women also had significant input into the curriculum of all-black colleges. Studies have documented their early observations (Holmes, 1934, pp. 187–189) that much of the content in the materials available to them was ill suited for the needs of the students in their institutions. As a consequence, they rejected the notion that a mere transfer of content from book to student was easy, desirable, feasible, or relevant. Much of the curricula in all-black colleges previously was often little more than a carbon copy of those used in predominantly white colleges, but the struggle to imitate the curriculum of white colleges was generally unsuccessful (Noble, 1965, p. 24). The most effective curricula and techniques for providing instruction to high-risk students at the college level were conceptualized, designed, developed, and introduced in the black colleges. Black women working in language arts and in mathematics were the primary progenitors. Now in predominantly white colleges working with the so-called low-achievers (disadvantaged, ghetto, minority-group, nonmotivated) strategy and curricula designated as "new," "innovative," and "novel" are considered neither original nor unique by black educators (over forty years old) who know that a significant number of these strategies were conceptualized and made operative by black women long ago. One woman, a long-time worker in a black college, relates, "We have already abandoned some of the models for working with low-achievers that white colleges are just beginning to pick up. There is little doubt that we were better at it." Another comments, "Because of open admissions, the same programs white educators previously condemned in black colleges are now being adopted in their own institutions." While black women may not have received professional credit for their contributions to the development of programs for high-risk and other underdeveloped students, many of them *are* recognized for their expertise in them. A number of black women have been hired to teach the so-called disadvantaged in predominantly white colleges and to work as consultants to higher education institutions and to the federal government; they are used as experts in dealing with high-risk students in every program from Headstart to Upward Bound to college-level compensatories.

Decades ago, as black women worked with young black students from rural areas of the South and from elsewhere, they developed and perfected the models and methods of working with such students. Their contributions can be examined (Woodson, 1915; Bullock, 1967; Phelps-Stokes Fund, 1932; A. Wright, 1933; Jones, 1937; *Twenty-two Years' Work*, 1893). Ruth M. Harris, the late president of Stowe Teachers College in St. Louis, Missouri, developed what she called the English Workshop more than a quarter of a century ago. Dr. Harris and her associates designed the workshop to aid freshmen who came to college and were not academically prepared to effectively do "college-level" work in the language arts and mathematics. Freshmen who had such difficulties were required to take the workshop. Contrary to current policies and practices of some colleges which prevent remedial students from taking courses in the regular curriculum until their academic deficiencies have been successfully cleared up, students at Stowe pursued a regular college program simultaneously with participation in the workshop. Tutorial service, flexible schedules, immediate exit after completion of the workshop, peer assistance, individualized instruction, contracting, and a number of other strategies which are currently designated as innovative in predominantly white colleges were techniques and services used in the English Workshop. The jargon has changed but the methods have simply been recycled. The workshop experience was an integral part of the college program for the student who needed all or part of the skills. Students were required to improve only the skills with which they demonstrated a deficiency.

The English Workshop was not a "special program," funded on "soft funds" and implemented by part-time, uncertified, non-tenured, and junior staff members; it was not designed for ghetto students, the disadvantaged, and other students currently designated with such euphemisms. All of the students were black; many of them were not disadvantaged, unless skin color validates deprivation. (One of us successfully completed that workshop twenty-six years ago.) Harris's nontraditional approach to higher education is testimony to both her insight and foresight. Almost any black college has such a program run by women.

Black women have contributed to higher education in other ways. For many years they were among the sole trainers of black teachers. Their efforts to train nurses in the many unaccredited nursing schools are still talked about among blacks in the medical field (F. B. Williams, 1904, p. 96). Many believe that their pioneering work in social work was the forerunner of current field work in the social services. The rudiments of our modern counseling concepts have their prototypes, if not their origins, in the black college and under many models suggested by black women.

In the early years the extreme problems of black students coming to college without counseling made some kind of student services absolutely imperative. It was common for a black student to leave for college with only the clothes he was wearing and two dollars in his possession. The student found himself thrust into a new and unfamiliar environment among strangers, without telephone resources, the postage to write home, or transportation other than his feet. He communicated with his home by word of mouth. He came to college not knowing what to expect or who could or would give him assistance. He came unsophisticated, afraid, with a good mind only partially developed, and almost always unskilled. Without home, family, friends, and a milieu familiar to him, he was understandably confused and many times lonely.

Student services in black colleges evolved out of this frame of reference. Few formal structures for student services were provided—few trained counselors, no office of student personnel, and so on. Counseling depended on the dedication and ingenuity of the black teacher, most frequently the female teacher. Students needed somebody to talk to. Teachers brought the students together in groups to discuss their personal and educational problems, provided them with individual attention, and oriented them to their new and often frightening environment. They secured jobs for the students, often sending them to work in the dining rooms and dormitories of nearby white colleges; they also sent the young men to work in the construction of the college physical facilities in exchange for tuition, board, and other essentials. They taught the young students how to use their leisure in the absence of money and recreational facilities. Black fraternities and sororities such as the Guide Right program of Kappa Alpha Psi Fraternity, grew to some extent out of these efforts. In spite of such efforts, some students quit college and returned home or went elsewhere. The teachers would follow them back to the rural farms, sawmills, loading docks, cotton fields, and the kitchens of the wealthy and would convince some of them to return to college.

Black women "begged, cajoled, urged, and pleaded for funds" (Lerner, 1972b, p. 125) to help finance students and teachers. Mary McLeod Bethune begged for funds to help her staff. In a letter to one of her benefactors, George R. Arthur, she wrote: "I would like to have you consider the traveling scholarship for some of the heads of our departments, so that we might have this representation and be able to make contacts with different educational organizations and investigate schools so as to keep abreast with the best methods. . . . We shall use to the best of our knowledge any opportunity that may come to us through your foundation in making more thorough those who work in the commercial, musical, and vocational departments."*

Other women worked as speakers, collecting nickles and dimes as honoraria while working as laundresses to support themselves as they continued to raise funds for their schools.

Hence we have the pioneering efforts at counseling, guidance, recruitment, and financial aid as it was carried on in the early black college. These activities were carried on by persons who were untrained as guidance personnel and who were not fully paid for their efforts. One of the motivations for their activities might have been their own survival. In cases where the funding of the college was dependent upon the number of students enrolled, it became necessary for the college personnel to take such actions.

The field of library science was and still is dominated by black women in the predominantly black college. And the concept of work-study was as common in the black college as the motto of the institution.

Many black women who formerly worked in all-black colleges now realize that they made the same serious academic mistake that black scholars as a whole have made and continue to make; they failed to write down many of their experiences and their activities. Too frequently others who have written about black women seem preoccupied with the problems and adversities in their homes, their bedroom behavior, their dominance or submissiveness, their position and role in the family, and how they treat their mates. Their roles in higher education do not appear to attract scholarly investigation. The good which they have done in the area of higher education

* From the Mary McLeod Bethune File, Julius Rosenwald Fund Papers, Fisk University, Nashville, Tenn.

finds the same fate as in Caesar's eulogy. These contributions which they were able to develop, they may not be able to bequeath.

Academicians have not done a single definitive study on black women educators in predominantly white colleges and universities.

Victimized by such scholarly neglect, black women are discussed and written about only in the context of the feminist and black movements and in affirmative action activities (Lerner, 1972a; Rickman, 1972; Smythe, 1972). A search of the literature reveals that writers only allude in passing to black female educators in colleges and universities. The women's activist organizations in academia, with their voluminous research, their spate of publications, and their hundreds of cases against colleges and universities charging discrimination, have not isolated and dealt with the problems of black women in higher education. Black women find themselves under the broad categories *women* or *minority women*. And just as the term *minority group* conceals the situation of a specific minority group, so the category *women* hides what is happening to a specific group of women.

An investigator discovers that he is plowing new ground when he attempts to find how black females fare in the struggle for equity in predominantly white colleges and universities. Most studies in higher education do not mention black women as academic professionals at all. For some reason the researchers who go in and count female heads fail to report the race differential or what kind of jobs, ranks, and so on that specific minority women hold, if any. Neither women nor men who claim to be concerned about this problem seem to consider such variables. White female researchers and activists who insist that they are fighting for equity for all women in higher education are evading the issue. The problem of women in higher education is not monolithic. It varies substantially between the majority group and the minority group and between two-year and four-year colleges. While white women may suffer only sex discrimination, black women encounter both sex and race discrimination. Black women cannot be preoccupied with such things as the disproportionately higher class load, the ceiling on the number and scope of promotions and rank awarded women, and the lack of opportunities for women to do research and other activities in higher education until they can win entry into the colleges and universities in order to generate interest in these concerns.

Black and white women are differentially dispersed among colleges and universities; proportional differences in the reward each group receives might be expected. Black women are concerned because they not only earn less salary, hold lower academic ranks, get promoted less frequently, teach in small, less prestigious colleges than black and white men, but also they encounter the same inequities in comparison to white women. Black career women constitute a larger proportion of the black professional community than women in the white professional world (Epstein, 1973, p. 916) but not as faculty members and administrators in predominantly white colleges and universities. The representation of black women in these institutions has been so miniscule in the past that their numbers have gone unreported and unanalyzed. Now, however, 41.7 percent of our black respondents in two-year colleges and 29.1 percent in four-year colleges are female. The percentages may appear high, but the actual numbers are small.

Most of the black women with whom we have had communication consider Caucasian men and women in academe the same enemy. They believe that once the discrimination and many of the inequities in higher education against white women have been negotiated, the white women will kiss and make up and then join and advocate the same system which denied them entry for so long, just as Jewish males in the academic community are now doing. "Black women see no reason to believe that a society in which white females hold positions of power would be any fairer than a system dominated by white males" ("Blacks vs. Feminists," 1973, p. 64). The example set by Jewish males is their point of reference. With increasing frequency one hears black women voice considerable concern about the attitude of Jewish males in academia. Hugh Lane (1973) calls on male Jewish intellectuals to join the effort to bring more women into higher education. He notes that "it is high time for the educated Jewish male to join the vanguard of those actively fighting for full rights for all."

Black women are assumed to be included in the thrust for equal employment opportunity for women in higher education. Not as many black women have been hired in predominantly white colleges and universities as white females, however. We have heard from 440 in two-year colleges and 633 in four-year colleges. A close examination of this number reveals that black women are under-represented in both community colleges and senior institutions. Considering that we contacted 2,289 institutions and heard from 1,764, it can be seen that 1,073 black females do not represent one person per institution. Our data are convincing that black females are at the bottom of the higher education heap.

Black women do hold administrative positions in some com-munity colleges. Although 50 percent of the women who hold such positions indicated that they held line positions in two-year schools, only five (1.1 percent) were deans, the highest line position held by a black woman in a predominantly white college or university. Three (0.7 percent) were associate deans and three were assistant deans. The remainder of the women respondents hold positions represented by staff rather than line designations, although they apparently misinterpreted the designation. Of the 1111 two-year colleges in the United States, only one black woman ever headed an institution, and that college was not predominantly white. We did not find a black female serving as a dean or manager of business, dean of vocational education, or in other positions which are con-sidered line responsibilities.

Most black women serve as assistants to assistants. Assistant and associate deans, special assistants to provosts, administrative assistants, coordinators, directors, and human relations specialists are common administrative title designations which indicate that these women serve only in supportive capacities. Both the titles and the jobs they hold are without definition and description. Those women who are the chairmen of divisions or departments have the best defined tasks. In some colleges these latter two positions are considered as faculty; and in still others they represent both faculty and administration. Eight of the black women are division chairmen and five are vice-chairmen.

In two-year colleges the women administrators make very few major decisions. Those minor determinations which they have are often not backed by their superordinates. One of their con-sistent complaints is that while they get the kind and amount of information needed to do their jobs, they do not have an opportunity to make significant decisions. They do not control any facet of the institution. They are lacking in power and authority appropriate to even the staff positions and fancy titles they do hold.

While black women administrators may be involved in the identification and recruitment of college personnel (primarily other blacks), they have little, if any, influence in the selection, hiring, and termination of personnel. Except as division and department chairmen they do not have the responsibility for recommending salary increases, promotions, rank, or tenure. They are rarely involved in long-range planning.

As might be expected, the majority of black female administrators are in urban institutions with large enrollments of black students. They are among many of those who were recruited as a result of black student demands of the late sixties and the first two years of the present decade; 599 or 58.4 percent believe that they were hired because they were black. A very few believe that they were hired in response to affirmative action plans. A few (9 women) believe that they were hired because they were women. Most had not been at their respective institutions long enough to have come up through the ranks. Some of these women were hired because the administration of the institution was committed to equality of employment opportunity irrespective of race and sex.

Some women indicated that, after being hired, they were placed in charge of trivia; their talents and abilities were not used except in management of remedial programs, as liaison persons with minority students, and as administrators in other soft-monied programs. A surprisingly large number of the women who wrote comments felt that they were not only the token black but also the token black female. More men than women get extra summer work.

Black women who are department and division chairmen are also tenured, while those who are in some category of the deanship may not be. Deans who have come through the ranks as faculty members and are promoted into the administrative ranks maintain their tenure as former faculty members; deans who did not proceed this way may not. Black females in community college administration see their jobs as dead-end positions; their chances for promotion to line positions are believed to be very slight.

The pessimism of the black female administrator is understandable. It appears that she is an endangered species. She has fallen prey to a number of reversals and change: extreme budget cuts; a withdrawal of foundation support; a deescalation of student demands since 1971; white females making demands for a larger share of the rewards of higher education; black men hired in preference to black or white women in administration; the impermanence of many of their positions and the apparent reluctance of the appropriate federal agency to enforce affirmative action plans. These factors lead one to the inevitable conclusion that the black female in community college administration and in four-year colleges will become almost extinct in a very short time.

No Afro-American woman holds the presidency of a predominantly white institution. In four-year colleges as in two-year colleges, the few who are in administration are usually in staff positions. They serve in positions denoted by the same collection of overdescriptive and poorly defined titles as denoted in community colleges. Of the 633 black women in four-year colleges in our sample, four black women (0.6 percent) hold deanships. Six black women (0.9 percent) are associate deans and twenty-two (3.5 percent) are assistant deans. Senior institutions have placed more black women in department chairmanships than community colleges have. Fourteen (2.2 percent) black women hold these positions, but only one (0.2 percent) black woman holds a vice-chairmanship. Few black women hold decision-making positions in senior colleges and universities. A few of them get on the central administrative staff but are excluded from the executive suites.

In four-year institutions, as in two-year colleges, black women serve as identifiers and recruiters of other blacks (both students and potential staff members), although they have little influence on the selection, hiring, termination, setting of salaries, or providing other fringe benefits of candidates. Most indicate that they are overpaid clerks, convention coordinators, counselors for black students, and public relations persons to the black community. One respondent indicates, "Is is strange, but to the white administration we blacks do not seem to have expertise in dealing with any problems except those of other blacks. I resent having to accompany these men every time they are required for some reason to meet with minority students."

Black females in four-year institutions are ad hoc administrators. Projects which some of them coordinated in the late sixties and early seventies are being dismantled, as they are in the community colleges. Their recruitment and selection follows the same pattern as in two-year colleges. A few of them (14 percent) worked formerly in all-black colleges; others came to higher education after spending time in secondary schools and then earning the doctoral degree. A few others (13.6 percent) have come into the temporary ranks of higher education to operate such programs as Upward Bound and other projects where the Ph.D. or Ed.D. was not a requirement. Many of our subjects indicate that they know these programs will be phased out along with the positions they hold. Some black women are not attracted to programs such as Upward Bound because they recognize the temporary posture of such programs. Women who hold the doctorate (16 percent of our female respondents) do not want to exist on the periphery of the college, so they seek better positions.

Black women without doctorates encounter even worse difficulties. They are not only shut out of the predominantly white colleges but also out of predominantly black ones, which are also seeking faculty and administrators with the doctorate and are turning more and more to whites and foreigners. Women who hold faculty tenure but are in administrative jobs may find themselves reassigned to the classroom. Others may find themselves in that unemployment wasteland, the academic job market. The best qualified and most fortunate will seek and obtain the most prized and sustained power base position in higher education—a tenured member of the faculty in a prestigious college or university.

In two-year colleges, 60 percent of the black women are full-time faculty members and 13.2 percent are full-time counselors. Unlike counselors in many four-year colleges, those in two-year colleges are also considered full-time faculty. Both groups become tenured members of the faculty after a stipulated probation period. Once placed on a salary schedule they get annual increments until they reach the maximum which the schedule will allow. The discrepancy between salaries of black and white women occurs in the initial placement on the schedule.

Black women who teach in the transfer or college parallel divisions of two-year colleges rarely teach the fine arts or the natural sciences. Only five black women in our sample were in the fine arts; twelve were in the natural sciences; two were in economics. The behavioral sciences, social sciences, education, English, and remedial education are the five areas in which their numbers are by far the largest. Participation in political science is growing, and 15.1 percent are directly involved in Black Studies. In vocational and technical education, black females teach mostly in the allied health fields and in business. Six black females were teaching physical education, which is understandable, as physical education is another area perceived by black women (and black men) as having in its ranks some of the most bigoted people in education.

The majority of black women faculty, like their white sisters, have come from the public secondary schools. They are well educated; most have done postmaster's work. Because they have followed a pattern of remaining in the profession after marrying and while rearing a family, they tend to be more experienced than white females who often quit the profession after marriage and return after their children have been reared. More specifically, black women in education have almost always combined their careers with family except in the cases where married teachers were not permitted to teach. Fifty-nine percent of our female respondents are married and another 18 percent are separated or divorced.

The women are likely to be prepared and required to teach in several subject-matter areas in the college parallel and the community service programs. Those who teach in vocational and technical disciplines tend to confine their instruction to their fields of specialization. The size, location of the school (rural, suburban, urban), the breadth of the curriculum, the union status of the college, and other factors can determine the teaching responsibilities, however. The instructional staff in very small rural colleges is often required to teach heavier loads than the teachers in large, urban, unionized colleges.

Some black female teachers in urban two-year colleges report that they are asked to teach evening courses because some nonblack teachers insist that they are afraid to come into urban communities and other so-called high crime areas after dark. Black women challenge this argument. They point out that most of them do not live any nearer to the immediate area of the college than white females do; they further note that blacks are the primary victims of crime.

Inner-city residents are also impatient with such complaints; one voices it in a community involvement session: "I'm a little sick of these teachers complaining. They don't live in this community; they ain't involved here. We don't never see them in church, at any of our community meetings, at a wedding, at the hospital, or at a funeral. They don't shop around here, put their clothes in the cleaners, or anything like that. They ain't got no investment around here. It's all get and no give. They ain't scared to come and get their paycheck. That goes for black and white alike."

When a two-year college has only one black professional staff member, that person is often a female. The reason for this has social implications. More explicitly, most community colleges are located in small, sometimes rural, frequently suburban, and often conservative communities. Community colleges reflect the values and practices of their locales. Less social resistance to black women than to black men exists in many such locations. Administrators, male faculty, realtors, merchants, and many others in the education and business community (especially small communities) accept black women much more readily than black men. Black males appear to be extremely threatening; they are still considered the universal studs. Although empirical data refute this stereotype, it is still a widely held belief. Both researchers and black women allude to the perceived threat of the black male. Cynthia Epstein writes (1973), "Although it is difficult, if not impossible, to document the sense of threat with which white male professionals react to the thought of black men as colleagues, it is clear that black men and women perceive this as a barrier to them. It was a common feeling among the black women in this study that this perceived threat was not as great for them. Being a woman reduced the effect of the racial taboo."

This perception is most pronounced in older black women.

In the same study, Epstein reported (1973): "Some older women felt that they had been accepted in their professional work because being a Negro woman was not as bad as being a Negro man. About a third said they believed Negro men were 'a threat' to white men or alluded to that belief as if it were well known to all, and that a black woman constituted less of a threat."

In conversations we have had around the country, blacks corroborate the reports cited above. When asked what insecurities they perceived in their white colleagues, three types of responses emerged. The first had to do with professional benefits and job protection (promotion, tenure, and so forth). The second most prevalently perceived insecurity was the threat of the presence of black males, which was characteristic of both males and females, although more among men. And finally, there were insecurities which could be defined as personal, relating to marital problems, personal conflicts having to do with prejudice and other racial attitudes. There is also the stereotype that black women are more dependable and more responsible than black males. Realtors may not hesitate to rent or sell to a black female but may refuse a black male. If a black woman is hired on a college staff, members of the staff and of the community may have little concern about the potential contact between white men and black women.

One woman in a Florida institution explained it in this way: "With me, the white vagina is safe. Because the males look upon me as just a woman, their manhood is not threatened. Because I am fairly attractive, I am looked upon as a kind of exotic toy that they can take to lunch and try to make a hit if no one else is around. Taking me to lunch is supposed to demonstrate their liberalism. But when a big black buck takes one of these white girls to lunch, it nearly drives these guys up a tree. Guys who have never spoken to him find a reason to go by the table to speak to him. Most of all, though, the white vagina is not threatened with me around. What the men don't know is that the white women are aware of their fragile ego and insecurity about their manhood. So most of them do as they please in spite of what the men think. The women really laugh at them. Everything from the way they comb their hair over their bald spot to the way they drive their cars. To answer your question more directly, although I would like to think that I was hired because of my competence, I am convinced they wanted a woman instead of a man because of the reasons I have given."

In answering the question, "Do you perceive attempts to minimize your contact with whites of the opposite sex on or off the job?" 16 percent of our respondents in two-year institutions and 13 percent in four-year institutions said yes.

The only other variable we found was that a single black woman may be hired at a lower salary than a single black male.

In senior colleges, black females carry heavy teaching responsibilities for undergraduate students, teach heavier loads, and carry more teaching hours than do their male counterparts. We found seven (1.1 percent) black women who directed dissertations and fourteen (2.3 percent) who served on dissertation committees. Only eighteen women spent as much as 50 percent of their time in research; 80 percent of the women have not published. Of those black women who have published, fifty-eight have written one book; seventeen have written two; ten have written three books and so on to two women who have written nine books. Twenty-five percent of the women have written journal articles. They seem to have neither the time nor the support to engage in research and publication activities to any significant degree. Yet, it is precisely these activities which colleges use as criteria to reward educators. In community colleges there is a more equitable distribution of the work load, and black women can be involved in more types of activities.

In senior institutions a black woman will not be promoted to a higher rank as quickly as her white and black male counterparts, regardless of her preparation and production. Particularly in four-year colleges, we found unique differentials in loads, salaries, and promotions, which would support the findings of Helen Astin and Alan Bayer (1972). In addition, we found that many of the other charges of excessive chauvinism which women's rights organizations make against the male-dominated academic community to be true.

The black woman in the academic community is finding new types of discrimination. Because of the past discrimination against blacks generally, and black men in particular, institutions are now discriminating against black women so that they can add more black men to their staffs. More succinctly, pursuit of the black male in higher education is an idea whose time has come. Whereas black women themselves have pushed for this, and many liberal whites and militant blacks both inside and outside of the institution have pressured for this, the selection of black men over women with the same qualifications is, nonetheless, discriminatory. It cannot be denied that some black women with better credentials than black male candidates find themselves passed over. And as more white women remain in higher education for longer periods of time and new ones pressure for equal opportunity, the black woman's chances are further diminished.

Black women educators talk about "the great count," a consideration in the recruitment, selection, hiring, remuneration, and promotion of black women. "They count heads, count variables, count the secretaries, count criteria—I hate that damn word—and count most of us out," states LaVerta Allen, a black, and the former assistant to the president at Laney College in Oakland, California. She continued: "The *Man* never stops 'running games' on us. I was told, off the record, I was a threat to the men and that was the reason why I couldn't get a higher job than I now have. When you consider that all of the administrators in the place were white, it was really revealing. The job I was holding was what the students at Berkeley call 'an assistant niggership'."

However comparable their backgrounds, work activities, achievements, and institutional work settings to those of their male colleagues, even when they make the same choices and proceed through the same hierarchy they neither secure commensurate treatment nor remuneration. One can only conclude that sex discrimination is rampant against black women.

While we have said she is preferred under certain circumstances, her recruitment has as much to do with the prevailing attitudes, values, and stereotypes of the community where she goes as her competency. This does not mean she will enjoy the same rewards as the other members of the staff she joins.

There are many bizarre cases to report. On the campus of one large university, one woman has not been promoted in fourteen years, in spite of the fact that her work has been favorably evaluated during this entire time. In one multicampus junior college district located in a city on the Mississippi River, a black female instructor at one of the suburban campuses was required to teach twenty-two contact hours and develop seven class preparations, while the published number of contact hours for teachers was fifteen, slightly higher for laboratory courses and slightly lower for English composition courses. When the teacher protested to the division chairman, she was ignored. When she approached the dean, he took her grievance "under advisement." And when she was finally forced to go to her campus president, a former public school man and former coach, she was reminded that she was earning more money than she had ever earned as a high school teacher and she should be satisfied. Moreover, she was informed that if she were not satisfied, she could seek a transfer into another college in the district and he would support it. She did—and he did.

At a small college in rural Oklahoma, the lone black faculty member is a woman. In this particular college, faculty members live on campus. While all of the white faculty members live in what has been designated as faculty quarters, the black faculty member, who has a husband and child, is required to live in student housing with the students. When questioned about this segregation of a faculty member, the administration replied that her housing is the newest and the best on campus.

Another young woman, a counselor, was instructed not to counsel students when she was dressed in pantsuits. The president of a midwestern college requested that a young black woman not wear her Afro wig on the campus. (The president himself wore a wig). A student personnel administrator who, when we saw him, had on a lavender suit with all of his accessories the same color, indicated to his black counselors (two women) that their dress was too "mod" and that they should adjust their attire in such a way as to reflect positively on the institution.

It must be said that black women who are treated most unfairly are those working in small colleges with small enrollments of black students; those who appear to be weak and fail to speak up for themselves; those who are at the mercy of administrators who are themselves without credentials and drive to compete; and those where the administration aids and abets the discriminatory practices of the faculty, staff, and community.

In large colleges and universities, black women have been treated unfairly in some cases because they have not always known or understood what the system was doing to them. Some women were given joint appointments who felt that because they had expertise in two areas they had a good situation. They later discovered, when salary and promotion time came, that neither of the departments where they held a partial appointment claimed them. They discovered that the term *adjunct professor* and other such high-sounding titles were institutional jargon used to indicate a limited relationship and that the person who holds the title is temporary and not a continuing member of the college community. They discovered that the criteria for rank and promotion were difficult to determine and were applied differently to them than to men—black or white. Some found that to get fair treatment they had to talk like militants, demand like prima donnas, never permit the slightest deviation from the rules to go unchallenged, question each directive, be more competent than the men, and refuse to let their successes and talents be subsumed under the rubric "our staff." They learned that political contact was important; a larger percentage of black women than men belong to teacher unions. Black women indicate that their white colleagues, especially males, seem more concerned about what they wear, drive, the incomes of their husbands, and other such material trivia than they are about their scholarship, training, and effectiveness, or lack of it. They point out that their administrators will not say when something is wrong. Rather than face up to the problem or issue, administrators generally begin to act peculiarly, avoiding eye contact when they encounter these women (or avoiding them altogether) and "a lot of other stupid and assinine things that a pouting child would do," cites one woman. This is not to imply that all administrators behave this way or that black administrators do not behave in all or some of these ways.

The examples we have given are only a few of the hundreds of individual problems encountered by black women in predominantly white colleges. Yet in spite of the discrimination, she appears to have done better than the black male in many ways. She has long been allowed to protest while black males (and white females) could not.

The typical black female educator is disinterested in the women's liberation movement, however (Chisholm, 1970, pp. 3–4; N. Giovanni, 1971; LaRue, 1970; Morrison, 1971). Joyce Ladner has advanced the notion that "black women are now serving as role models for white women who are beginning to question such things as the institution of marriage, the concept of illegitimacy, and the general moral code traditionally associated with this society. It is interesting to note that much of the behavior characterized as deviant when practiced in [parts of] the black community is now being sanctioned by the majority groups and thus becoming 'legitimate' " (Adams, 1972).

Some of the behavior we now see manifested in white women in the women's liberation movement is past history to black women, because of their unique position as the best educated of the sexes in the black community, their somewhat higher level of economic solvency in that community (Moore, 1969), and because they have been more effective liaisons between the races at all levels as a worker, confidant, and sex object. The black woman has been able to do what both the white female and the black male, until fairly recently, could not do. Historically she has been strong and has been considered the cohesive force which held the black family together. White sociologists in particular have labeled her and the black culture matriarchal and dominating. Black females counter by suggesting that black female independence is not as debilitating as white male domination. They are extremely sensitive and hostile to the charge that they are dominating.

Black females in the academic community indicate that they are still cast in the stereotypic roles which some black males jokingly call the "sapphire syndrome." The role is a caricature, picturing the black woman as a loud, strong, independent individual, with the verbal and physical ability to protect and dominate those around her.* Because social scientists, using selected samples, have given

---

* Sapphire was one of the characters in the radio show *Amos 'n Andy*. Some considered her amusing there, but it is not advisable for whites to speak of the "Sapphire syndrome" around black women.

creditability to this portrait, black women suggest that their colleagues accuse them of the purported castration of the black male. Frances M. Beal rejects this charge of emasculation: "The black woman in America can justly be described as the slave of a slave." Others say that she is the victim's victim. Beal does agree that black males have been brutalized; she notes, however, that "it is a gross distortion of fact to state that black women oppressed black men" (Beal, 1970, p. 343). Nonetheless, the image persists even in academic circles. Castration is always dehumanizing, but black women appear to know this, and they continue to challenge the charge that they are responsible in the case of black men.

We recently observed this at a conference. After the woman speaker terminated her address, she responded to a question from a male member of the audience who brought up the charge of the castration of the black male by the black female: "I have not seen or heard of a black woman discriminating against a black man because of his color. I have never seen one refuse him a job, picture him as an idiot in the media, or refuse him entry into a college as a student or teacher because he was black. We [black women] have never sat in the legislatures of this country and exercised the democratic process to exclude black men from full participation as citizens. No sir, we did not castrate these men. You did. We were the wives and mothers, sisters and daughters, mistresses and maids of the black men that a society castrated. I, for one, refuse to be the scapegoat for the sins and guilts of you and your fathers. I say you because racism is recycling. And you are equally as responsible because you do nothing about it."

We believe that social scientists have done a serious disservice in stereotyping the image of black women. Beginning with E. Franklin Frazier (1949) and later St. Clair Drake and Horace Cayton (1962) the portrait has been painted of the black woman as a matriarch and dominant character in the black community, most especially in the family. Other sociologists have further perpetuated the myth of female dominance in the black community to the extent that the society believes the stereotype.

It cannot be denied that black women have demonstrated considerable independence. Black women were not educated for adornment, but for utilitarian purposes. They not only expected to work but also planned their education for continuous employment throughout their lives. Going to college to capture a husband was incidental rather than a priority. Most of these women knew that they would have to work regardless of their marital status. Only a few of them have made careers as housewives. During slavery the black woman's condition of servitude dictated self-sufficiency; later, the economics of the black family mandated it; and subsequently, her social role made her the equal, if not the academic superior, to the black male.

Black men do not appear to respond to the independence of black women in the same way Caucasian males respond to white females who attempt to exercise their independence. Perhaps black males do not have the same options. Some of them may certainly prefer to have black women behave in the dependent way that white females seem to behave.

Most black men in the academic community treat women as equals. They have not attempted to convince black females who are independent and who make their own way that they are less ladylike. Anyone who is familiar with middle-class black women would hardly describe them as unladylike. Nonetheless, because black women do not wring their hands when they encounter adversity and because they have had to fight their own battles, support their families, and develop unique kinds of coping skills, their behavior has often been described as aggressive. Many of the women with whom we have had communication in higher education agree that they are, indeed, aggressive; one asked, "What would you have had us do—or become? We have had to be aggressive. We have not enjoyed nor do we want to enjoy being totally dependent on any person—man or woman."

The white female, on the other hand, seems to have been taught dependence. The society in general, and white males in particular, place her on a pedestal and proclaim that she is too fragile to work. "A woman's place is in the home" ("I don't need a competitor, I want a wife and homemaker"); she is incapable of making decisions ("a woman is too emotional to think rationally"); she should not be forthright and competitive ("if there is anything I can't stand, it is an aggressive woman"); she is not to question the judgment of the head of the house ("don't worry your pretty little head about it"); she is to make her husband look good, encourage him, inflate his ego, make his home beautiful, bear and rear his children, support his ideas, and do everything possible to make *him* a success ("behind every successful man, there is a woman"); she is not to present her own ideas or to contradict him either in the family or, especially, in public ("shut up and look pretty"). Black women note that their white sisters are more like accessories than partners. "The women who submit to the stereotypic roles outlined for them tend to atrophy as persons," states a black counselor from a Miami, Florida, college.

Black women who have been accused of "ruling the roost," "wearing the pants," and other such trite expressions reported to describe their behavior suggest that their independence is described as dominance and reject this characterization. Black women are dismayed when their white colleagues imply (but never say) that they are dominant. They insist that their issue with higher education is not perceptions of their familial, work, or societal posture, be it dominant or submissive. They are fighting rather for equal opportunity to be employed by a college or university if they hold the appropriate credentials. Once hired, if and when they are hired, they have the right to enjoy professional behavior from their colleagues. They maintain that there is no rationale for social submission of their personal independence and intellectual integrity to the conformity of the girl next door, den mothers, Miss America, and Momism.

Chapter Seven

●●●●●●●●●●●●●●●●●●●●●●●●
●●●●●●●●●●●●●●●●●●●●●●●●
●●●●●●●●●●●●●●●●●●●●●●●●

PROGRESS
AND PLIGHT

●●●●●●●●●●●●●●●●●●●●●●●●
●●●●●●●●●●●●●●●●●●●●●●●●
●●●●●●●●●●●●●●●●●●●●●●●●

One cannot deny that more black men and women are visible in colleges and universities. It appears that the turbulence and unrest of the sixties have launched open admissions, Black Studies, and especially the recruitment, selection, and hiring of black Americans in predominantly white institutions. But if one judges by the continuing vitriolic dialogue of women, blacks, and others who have been previously excluded from professional positions in colleges and universities, by the plummeting support of some liberal organizations, by the attitude of indifference to minorities by the federal government, or by the tone and content of conversations, it is clear that disillusionment is the prevailing mood. While the recent visibility of black educators may give both the layman and the nonminority professional a firm impression that the representation of blacks in colleges and universities has increased significantly, we again pose the question: Has significant progress been made in the recruitment, selection, and hiring of blacks and in assigning them to positions of responsibility and authority commensurate with their education and training?

We have presented several facts in the preceding chapters

upon which to base our conclusions. Some of these facts stand out enough to merit repetition and elaboration.

Almost half (416 or 48 percent) of the two-year colleges which we sampled do not have a black faculty member or administrator. The number of two-year colleges has grown at an unprecedented rate over the past two decades. Over two hundred were established between 1966 and 1970 (Kelley and Wilbur, 1970, p. 14). The number of faculty members has increased by thirty-eight thousand from 1968 to 1972. The most recent of these institutions did not have the restraints of long-standing tradition. The Ph.D. was not necessary or demanded for employment; publications and research were not required. The spokesmen for these institutions maintained that they were *teaching* colleges. During the peak of their most dramatic growth (1965–1972), they had the philosophical mandate, the social and political climate, and the resources with which to hire minorities. A large pool of black educators with a master's degree were available. New community colleges could start from scratch in hiring professional staffs. Moreover, many community colleges were located near large minority populations, from which many people had great need for educational services. When two-year colleges contained the opportunity, the need, and the philosophy, it is difficult to identify *legitimate* reasons why these colleges did not hire more black professional men and women.

Perhaps reasons can be found with the governing body of the institution. Boards of trustees represent the same populations and are representative of the same types of community people as public school boards of education. In some communities the college is under the local board of education. While the members of the two-year college governing body may be legally representing the entire community, they actually do not represent many of the specific groups of the total community.

> On the whole, boards of trustees are not the peers of the parents they claim to represent. Most of them are white (95 percent), male (85 percent), over forty years of age (88 percent), did not graduate from a junior college (98 percent), Protestant (77 percent), consider higher education a privilege,

not a right (68 percent) earn more than $15,000 annually (70 percent) [Harnett, 1969].

To tell it "like it is," community college boards are, for the most part, fifty-year-old conservative WASP male managers earning more than $25,000 annually, who listen to "the people" speak in his golfing foursome at the local country club and over the tinkle of martini glasses at "sophisticated" cocktail parties. . . . Other board members come from less sophisticated settings. The male members of the board often have membership in, and listen to "the people" from a cadre comprised of organizations such as the Rotary and Kiwanis. These groups have come to represent what some call middle America. Some trustees belong to organizations which require that their membership be "male, white, over twenty-one years of age . . . and believe in God." In short, the Benevolent Protective Order of Elks is hardly an open-door institution. For a trustee to simultaneously hold membership in two groups with such contradictory philosophies as those of the Elks and the community college must be incomprehensible to many; especially those in the population who are minority group members. The same observation would be true for female members belonging to the Junior League or the Daughters of the American Revolution on the one hand and the community college board on the other. The variant social levels characterizing these groups are irrelevant. Their organizations have one thing in common: As a matter of policy they are discriminatory [Moore, 1973, pp. 173–174].

Given this description and profile and the historical knowledge of the behavior of public school boards of education with regard to integration of black students and educational personnel since the 1954 Supreme Court decision of *Brown* v. *Board of Education,* it is not surprising that many boards of trustees not only have not developed policies of equal employment but also have failed to mandate that their adminstrators carry out such policies even when they have been established. Yet, administrators represent the one group in higher education which can be terminated when they fail to carry out board policy. Many of them do not hold tenure and are not represented by collective bargaining; this is especially true of the president. Administrators will do what vigilant and alert boards direct. When an administrator fails to execute a specific policy of the board and that governing body does not hold him accountable, that administrator has tacit approval of his action or lack of action.

We find that many boards of trustees aid and abet the breaking of laws when they approve the establishment of some apprenticeship programs. These programs not only break federal laws by supporting discriminatory policies and practices in both the training of minority students and in the certification of black faculty, but they also contradict the philosophy of community colleges. These illegal practices have long been observable in public schools.

Two-year colleges represent a public school syndrome in other ways. Some of them grew out of public school vocational and adult programs, and some are still under the control of public school districts and are responsible to and directed by the district executive officers—superintendents (Shane, 1973). A large number of former superintendents currently serve as junior college presidents. Superintendents do not appear to have a reputation for endorsing and implementing equal hiring and placement practices, judging by the last two decades of court litigation with regard to student and faculty integration. Many school superintendents have ignored or challenged Supreme Court decisions. When these administrators move to the community college, they establish some of the identical policies and practices which they used as public school administrators. An example of these policies and practices is the "buddy system," often used in the public schools to keep recognition and promotion within the system. The exclusion of black educators is another example.

Just as former public school administrators make up much of the leadership of two-year colleges, so many former public high school teachers make up the faculty (McConnel, 1970, p. 223; Medsker, 1960, p. 172; Medsker and Tillery, 1971, p. 89). There is no evidence that white teachers who previously worked in predominantly white high schools accepted and promoted the inclusion of blacks as their colleagues. In certain areas of communities and in certain schools within those communities, the absence of blacks on the high school teaching staffs has not been interpreted or intended to be accidental. When public school administrators and secondary school teachers moved to the community college, they appear to have transported many existing public school policies and practices, including the exclusion of blacks.

Two-year colleges did not respond to the synthesis of moods and issues of the sixties and the inaugural years of the seventies. Except for urban areas, black student protest did not proliferate in community colleges as it did in senior institutions so these colleges were not pressured much to hire blacks (R. Wilcox, 1968; Lombardi, 1969; Monroe, 1972, p. 222). Vocational institutions and vocational and technical divisions of community colleges in rural and some urban settings even had a counter force to black student protest—most of the students enrolled in these schools were white, first-generation college students, the sons and daughters of blue-collar workers, service workers, and that group of workers labeled "hard hats" (Kriegel, 1972, p. 51; Cross, 1968). The teachers of these students, except for those with degrees in the more technical fields, have also come from a white working class background (McConnel, 1970, p. 222). Both the teachers and the students, and especially the students, have shown considerable resentment to the attention given minority students and appeared to be the only persons in the academic communities who were consistent in their willingness to stand up to minority students and resist their demands. We know of two colleges in communities where the male citizens of the area were willing to offer their guns to the college administration to put down any uprising from black students. Some boards of trustees, adminstrators, and faculty members have used the mood and attitude of these kinds of communities to justify their refusal to recruit, select and hire nonwhite staff members.

In still another vein, two-year colleges have not received large federal grants such as those awarded to senior institutions. They have consequently avoided much of the affirmative action activity encountered by senior institutions. Also there are a significant number of women who work in community colleges and thus two-year colleges have not been under the severe political and legal pressures of the feminist movement nor has the underrepresentation of black women in these schools been widely publicized.

Only four two-year and five four-year predominantly white institutions have blacks as their chief administrators. One of the reasons offered for not hiring blacks in some of these institutions is that the communities where the colleges are located have small black populations. If this explanation is accepted as a legitimate one, the criterion for hiring personnel appears to be based on the black population of the community. How can proponents of such an argument explain the inconsistency of no black staff members in two-year colleges with black student enrollments of over 50 percent located in communities with a total black population of 50 percent and more? And what about community colleges in large urban areas where the majority of the district population is black but the college staff is 95 percent nonblack?

Perhaps a black president could not fit into some white communities. This consideration seems realistic to us. It cannot be denied that the race of "an administrator should be an inadmissable criterion for his selection to supervise an educational venture. That is an ideal. The fact is, the race of the . . . administrator is an unmistakable variable. The observer who is willing to venture beyond the many obvious and specific exceptions will readily see the pervasiveness of the race variable. All things being equal (credentials, experience, training, and so on), a white face gets its possessor in the door many times when a black face will not. Even when all things are not equal, on the whole, a white face is a more effective calling card than a black face, both inside and outside of the institution" (Moore, 1970, p. 143).

It can be said that "on the whole, a black *administrator,* regardless of his level of competence, in a rural area where there are virtually no other minority group members, cannot expect to get enthusiastic support from such a community. It is probable that he would not have the support of his coworkers beyond lip service. . . . he would probably not be supported in many middle-class communities where he would be peripheral and add only a touch of color to the community. . . . he can expect polite acceptance or, even worse, toleration from his academic peers. There are many other insular communities, suburban and urban, composed of specific ethnic, national, religious, and special-interest groups where a black would not be welcome. In fact, some of these subcultures would be hostile toward him. . . . such communities are polarized and they are becoming more solidified. Only a few people migrate to them. . . . people who are of the same ethnic, national, religious, philosophical, and political persuasion. Only a few blacks live in or near such communities. In these areas the whites choose each other. The blacks do not have a choice" (Moore, 1970, p. 145).

No black directs, controls, or implements an apprenticeship program in a predominantly white two-year college; the number of blacks who serve as faculty members in these programs is too small to analyze. Most of the teachers in the apprenticeship trades in two-year colleges come from the field. Since there are very, very few blacks working as journeymen in the field in most of the trades, their representation as teachers are even fewer. People in charge of apprenticeship programs have discriminated against not only qualified blacks, refusing to allow them entry into programs as professionals, but also they have not permitted the untrained to become prepared. Blacks are trained and get work in the trades in the South; however, when they migrate north, east, and west, they find themselves unable to get into unions and to become certified because of a lack of reciprocity between states or because their original training was not under union supervision. And if we judge by their representation as faculty members and administrators in two-year colleges in the South, blacks must also have difficulty gaining entry even in southern states.

If blacks do migrate from the South and cannot find training or jobs, many of them turn to teaching as an alternative. They find, however, that educational institutions with vocational and technical programs are closed shops as are business, industries, and unions. These blacks run into many barriers. The vocational or apprenticeship advisory committees in two-year colleges are made up of businessmen, dealers, suppliers, and union members. These committees are also composed of members from agencies and institutions which employ community college graduates and influence the hiring of faculty members. National and especially state and local joint apprenticeship committees control the apprenticeship system by determining the students who will be admitted, the schools which will handle specific trades or programs, the curriculum to be taught, the time allotted and so on. Blacks have been excluded from these committees and also from certification and licensing boards. It is thus rare to find a black who is in a position to even monitor the recruitment, selection and hiring of black personnel.

Labor unions have considerable influence on and control over programs carried on in community colleges. In one West Coast two-year college a teacher received a direct order to permit the student to his class and to provide him instruction in a trade, and he refused, indicating that the union had not given him permission. The student in question owned his own business and was not seeking to become an apprentice. College administration did nothing to resolve the problem. It took citizen action directly with the board of trustees. The student maintained that he was a taxpayer who thus even helped to finance the college. The teacher, fired for refusal to provide instruction to a student, appeared to be more loyal to (or afraid of) the union than concerned with losing his job. The union threatened to withdraw the program from the college, but when the board did not weaken, the union withdrew the threat. The teacher was still out of a job.

In a similar case, a community college president refused to hire a credentialed black teacher who met all of the job specifications because that teacher had not been okayed by the union. His explanation too was that the union threatened to withdraw the program and set up the program elsewhere. In this case, one member of the board was a union member and two other members of the board had dealings with the unions. The president's action stood even though that union in no way supported the school financially and most of the graduates of the program were not placed in the same community.

A number of white teachers who work in vocational programs of community colleges also maintain their membership in unions. They sit on the faculty committees which choose new faculty members for their particular discipline, program, and trade. From this vantage point, they are able to monitor in some cases, and restrict in others, the persons who apply for teaching positions.

Of the total full-time faculty members in community colleges, less than 3.5 percent are black. According to the 1972 *Junior College Directory,* there are 123,334 faculty members in two-year colleges. The estimated percentage of those that are blacks includes predominantly white and black colleges. Although Goodrich and his associates received responses from 191 fewer chief administrators than we did when he gathered data for inclusion in the 1971 *Junior College Directory,* the comparisons between the two sets of data are fairly similar. Goodrich and his colleagues (1972–1973, p. 30) found that 3.2 percent of the full-time faculty and 5 percent of the full-time administrators in two-year colleges were black. We were able to identify a total of two thousand blacks (slightly less than 2 percent) in two-year colleges working as faculty members and administrators; 1054 of them were our respondents.

These percentages are of particular note since one-third of the black students in higher education attend community colleges (Janssen, 1972, p. 2), and this number is expected to grow to the point that the majority of black students will be in two-year colleges (Medsker and Tillery, 1971, p. 78). In fact, 30 percent of all minority (including black) students in higher education are in community colleges (Gleazer, 1973, p. 27).

While the number of hirings may be decreasing in public schools and in senior colleges, the number of hirings in community colleges continues to increase, since the number of colleges continues to increase. (The number of two-year colleges increased by seventy-three over 1971.) The opportunity to hire blacks without the built-in resistance of a veteran faculty was a distinct opportunity which two-year college administrators apparently did not take advantage of. If college officials had taken advantage of these optimum conditions to hire blacks during the decade of the sixties, affirmative action and other legal procedures initiated by minorities would not be necessary to get compliance with nondiscrimination laws in the seventies.

Blacks were available, if the job applications submitted to the placement service during the 1972 and 1973 American Association of Community and Junior Colleges conventions are any indication. Two graduate students attending these conferences tallied the number of blacks seeking jobs. The job applicants were new graduates, persons moving from four-year to two-year schools, persons seeking to leave predominantly black schools to join community college staffs, persons who anticipated the awarding of their degrees the following spring and summer, persons who were working in government and seeking to change jobs, and a number of secondary school teachers, counselors, and administrators seeking to join the community college. In 1972 in Dallas, Texas, the students collected the names of 834 persons. The folowing year, the students collected the names of 623 persons. About a third of the first group (291) from 1972 were repeaters in 1973. The majority of these persons, 533 from the first group and 414 from the second group, were not delegates to the conference but were among the thousands of job seekers who come to establish contacts for current and future employment possibilities. We would estimate that about three to four times as many blacks are seeking employment in two-year colleges as are currently teaching in them.

There are entire states within which not a single two-year college has black representation on the professional staff. In Montana, South Dakota, Utah, and American Samoa, 100 percent of the colleges reported and none had a single black on the staff. All of the colleges in North Dakota, Rhode Island, and West Virginia did not respond, but none that responded had hired any black professionals. Of the colleges in Arkansas, Hawaii, Maine, Minnesota, Nebraska, New Mexico, and Wisconsin, 80 percent did not report having a black faculty member or administrator. And 50 percent or more of the colleges in the states of Alaska, Colorado, Connecticut, Delaware, District of Columbia, Indiana, Idaho, Iowa, Kansas, Kentucky, Louisiana, Missouri, Nevada, New Hampshire, Oklahoma, Oregon, and Tennessee reported no black staff members. (See Table 2 for a detailed analysis of data collected from all the states and territories.)

Our sources of these data were the college presidents. Data on four-year colleges indicate that they do significantly better. (See Table 3.)

To summarize some of the data from Tables 2 and 3, 50 percent or more of the two-year colleges in thirty-one (62 percent) of the states and territories and 50 percent of the four-year colleges in seven (16 percent) of the states and territories do not have black professionals.

Much of this ceases to be surprising when one continues to unravel the hiring practices, goals and priorities in two-year colleges. Edmund J. Gleazer, president of the American Association of Junior and Community Colleges, found in his nationwide study

Table 2.

PERCENTAGES OF PREDOMINANTLY WHITE TWO-YEAR COLLEGES
WITHOUT BLACK PROFESSIONAL STAFF

(Predominantly black colleges were excluded from this study.)

State	Number of Colleges	Number of Colleges Responding	Number of Colleges Responding Without Blacks	Percentage of Colleges Responding Without Blacks
Alabama	20	14	3	21
Alaska	8	7	4	57
Arizona	13	11	5	45
Arkansas	8	5	4	80
California	98	90	19	21
Colorado	16	15	10	67
Connecticut	22	14	7	50
Delaware	4	2	1	50
District of Columbia	3	2	1	50
Florida	22	21	2	10
Georgia	23	14	3	21
Hawaii	6	6	5	83
Idaho	4	4	3	75
Illinois	53	39	17	44
Indiana	4	2	1	50
Iowa	25	24	19	79
Kansas	25	23	13	57
Kentucky	23	19	14	74
Louisiana	8	3	2	67
Maine	6	6	5	83
Maryland	21	17	5	29
Massachusetts	33	25	12	48
Michigan	36	28	12	43
Minnesota	23	23	20	87
Mississippi	14	12	2	17
Missouri	22	17	11	65
Montana	3	3	3	100
Nebraska	13	12	11	93
Nevada	3	2	1	50
New Hampshire	4	4	2	50
New Jersey	22	16	3	19
New Mexico	9	6	5	83
New York	61	45	14	31
North Carolina	65	41	10	24
North Dakota	5	3	3	100
Ohio	38	42	19	45
Oklahoma	18	17	10	59
Oregon	16	16	11	69
Pennsylvania	49	35	17	49
Rhode Island	3	2	2	100
South Carolina	22	18	3	17
South Dakota	2	2	2	100
Tennesee	15	10	5	50
Texas	54	32	11	34
Utah	5	5	5	100
Vermont	5	3	3	100
Virginia	27	17	5	29

Table 2. (cont.)

Washington	27	24	9	38
West Virginia	7	3	3	100
Wisconsin	50	45	38	84
Wyoming	7	6	6	100
American Samoa	1	1	1	100
Canal Zone	1	1	0	0

Sources: 1972 *Junior College Directory; Predominantly Negro Colleges and Universities in Transition* (Bureau of Publications, Teachers College, Columbia University). (The number of predominantly black colleges was subtracted from the total number of colleges to arrive at the number of predominantly white colleges.)

of community colleges (1973, p. 27): "Almost without exception there is a call for more black . . . faculty and administrative personnel. However, students, faculty, and presidents are not inclined, as judged in their responses to institutional goals, to rank among the top institutional goals that of attracting a representative number of minority faculty members. *Faculty and students, though, assign more importance to this purpose than do presidents.* [Italics added.]"

Only 1 percent of the Ph.D.'s in America are black (Bryant, 1970, p. 7), and only 100 of the four-year colleges of America are predominantly black. It is significant that in 1972 the 100 black colleges still hire more of the available black Ph.D.'s than the approximately 2000 colleges which are predominantly white. The percentage of black Ph.D.'s falls far short of black representation in the total American population (11 percent). In 1940 there were only three hundred thirty blacks in the country who held the Ph.D. (Ballard, 1973, p. 27). Thirty-seven thousand people received a Ph.D. between 1964 and 1968 (Bryant, 1970, p. 7). This figure is twelve times more than all of the blacks, living and dead, who have earned the Ph.D. The highest estimate of black Americans who hold the doctorate is less than three thousand, which is less than 0.0002 percent of total black population. Yet those few blacks who are academically prepared do not seem to have an equal opportunity for employment.

Why does such fear and opposition accompany the issue of hiring black professionals in higher education? The underrepresentation of blacks with the terminal degree leads to the inevitable conclusion that their numbers are too small to have a significant

Table 3.

PERCENTAGES OF PREDOMINANTLY WHITE FOUR-YEAR COLLEGES
WITHOUT BLACK PROFESSIONAL STAFF
(Predominantly black colleges were excluded from this study.)

State	Number of Colleges in the State	Number of Colleges Responding	Number of Colleges Responding Without Blacks	Percentage of Colleges Responding Without Blacks
Alabama	18	12	1	8
Alaska	2	2	0	0
Arizona	4	2	0	0
Arkansas	13	9	2	22
California	85	57	12	21
Colorado	16	14	4	29
Connecticut	20	17	3	18
Delaware	1	1	0	0
District of Columbia	7	7	0	0
Florida	15	15	5	33
Georgia	22	15	2	13
Hawaii	4	4	3	75
Idaho	5	5	1	20
Illinois	51	34	5	14
Indiana	40	33	7	21
Iowa	29	27	13	48
Kansas	25	17	8	47
Kentucky	20	19	7	37
Louisiana	16	5	0	0
Maine	16	13	9	69
Maryland	22	17	8	47
Massachusetts	62	39	6	15
Michigan	36	25	4	16
Minnesota	25	24	6	25
Mississippi	9	6	1	17
Missouri	41	27	10	31
Montana	9	8	1	13
Nebraska	15	11	6	55
Nevada	2	2	0	0
New Hampshire	10	10	7	70
New Jersey	25	18	1	6
New Mexico	9	8	3	38
New York	110	80	12	15
North Carolina	34	30	10	33
North Dakota	8	6	3	50
Ohio	53	42	8	19
Oklahoma	17	12	4	33
Oregon	20	20	6	30
Pennsylvania	88	20	6	30
Rhode Island	9	6	1	17
South Carolina	15	12	5	42
South Dakota	13	11	10	91
Tennessee	29	25	14	56
Texas	47	30	8	27
Utah	6	5	2	40
Vermont	12	11	6	55
Virginia	26	21	8	38

Table 3. (cont.)

Washington	16	12	2	17
West Virginia	15	14	4	29
Wisconsin	31	22	5	23
Wyoming	1	1	0	0

Predominantly Negro Colleges and Universities in Transition (Bureau of Publications, Teachers College, Columbia University). (The number of predominantly black colleges was subtracted from the total number of colleges to arrive at the number of predominantly white colleges.)

impact and influence on the senior institutions of the nation. Even if the established professoriate of this country withdrew their opposition to affirmative action, if blacks received preferential treatment in hiring, and if each black who holds the Ph.D. were hired in a predominantly white senior institution, each institution would average less than three blacks. The negative behavior, anxiety, and opposition of the existing ruling class of higher education (notably males) is obviously unwarranted. The jobs of those who are already employed are not in jeopardy from blacks. And for those seeking employment, the competition from blacks is so small as to be negligible.

Of our respondents, one black in five in senior colleges and universities and one in three of those in two-year colleges hold tenure. (See Chapter Five for more details.) A person hired into an institution of higher education is not necessarily awarded tenure. The strategies to award or to avoid awarding tenure have been chronicled in academic department publications, in the policy statements of institutions, in a number of reports of studies, and elsewhere. At the least a half dozen volumes have been published on tenure in the last year. Tenure has been a subject of conferences, a problem for commissions, a target for legislatures, a demand of collective bargaining, and a whipping boy for boards of trustees. Tenure from the perspective of blacks in colleges and universities, is just one more domain and reward system that the higher education power system (the faculty members) and the academic executives (the administration) have withheld from black Americans.

We can cite cases, as can many of our colleagues in higher education, where tenure has been awarded upon the hiring of persons who would not be judged worthy of such a safeguard; we can point to other examples where it has been withheld from out-

standing persons. We have seen tenure abused by those who discriminate according to race and sex; we have seen it awarded in the
absence of evaluation, and we have seen it withheld after well-
documented evaluation. It is not surprising, therefore, that the
whole concept of tenure is under severe criticism and attack.

**Only 8.1 percent of the black faculty members in pre-
dominantly white senior institutions hold the rank of professor.**
(See Chapter Five.)

**In both the two-year and four-year college systems, it is
common practice for an institution to hire only one black professional staff member.** Out of 459 (53 percent) two-year colleges
and 619 (69 percent) four-year colleges and universities that reported black professionals, eighty-nine respondents in two-year
and seventy-three in four-year institutions wrote, "I am the only
black," or "I am the *token black*," or "this question does not apply
since I am the only black," and so on. In a number of other two-
year colleges we could only identify a single black professional, more
blacks could have been at the college. It has become a tragic joke
among blacks as they greet each other at conventions and elsewhere
when the greeter says, "I'm him." Or when one asks about the
black faculty, he is told, "*I am* the black faculty." The colleges
which have a representative black faculty seem to continue adding
black people while those without black faculty members or with
only one seem slow to add them.

While we are aware of some specific exceptions, on the
basis of the data which we have, we conclude that colleges *do*
discriminate against minorities. We simply do not believe that the
extreme disparity between the 5 percent of minority educators
(blacks, Chicanos, Native Americans) and the 95 percent Cau-
casians who work in community colleges (Gleazer, 1973, p. 27)
has been accomplished by chance. We conclude, as do many of
our respondents, that more administrators and faculty members of
the majority group are either racist or support racist practices in
colleges than those who are nonracist or resist racist practices. We
also believe, as do many of our respondents, that the men demonstrate their racism more than the women.

Black professionals of all age ranges, of both sexes, in two-
year and four-year colleges, in all ranks of the faculty, at every

level of administration, tenured and nontenured, full and part-time, in public and private institutions, of moderate and militant philosophies, perceive their predominantly white colleges and universities to be racist. Mommsen reported (1972a) that over 90 percent of the blacks in predominantly white colleges believed that their colleges were discriminatory; our respondents prefer the word *racist*. Our data indicate that 83.6 percent share this belief (85.9 percent in four-year institutions and 79.4 percent in community colleges). The higher education system in the United States is a system *of whites*, is controlled and operated *by whites*, and reserves its major rewards *for whites*. The years of stress (1968 to 1971) did not change the pattern.

During the preceding decade (1963–1973), during the crisis of student demands and counter demands (1968–1971), and while two-year college administrators insist on proclaiming that their institutions are designed to serve the entire community, more than 500 community colleges were established. Most of these colleges were built outside areas which could serve minority groups in the local communities.

Has significant progress been made in the recruitment, selection, and hiring of blacks and in assigning them to positions of responsibility and authority commensurate with their education and training?

Chapter Eight

●●●●●●●●●●●●●●●●●●●●●●
●●●●●●●●●●●●●●●●●●●●●●
●●●●●●●●●●●●●●●●●●●●●●

THE ROAD
AHEAD

●●●●●●●●●●●●●●●●●●●●●●
●●●●●●●●●●●●●●●●●●●●●●
●●●●●●●●●●●●●●●●●●●●●●

*T*here is a gigantic and almost universal tokenism in American higher education. With regard to black educators, our data indicate that this tokenism is present in both two-year and four-year colleges and universities; is geographically widespread; is practiced against men and women; is present in both prestigious and lesser known institutions; is evident in state-supported, private, municipal, parochial, and federally supported colleges; is observable in urban, suburban, and rural institutions; is evident in large and small colleges; and is clearly identified in both academic as well as vocational programs in institutions of higher education.

Educational institutions, "although public employers, have responded to equal employment opportunity regulations in token fashion. Despite various federal edicts, coercion by the courts, and pleadings of the minorities . . . the skill and erudition of college heads have been employed more often to evade rather than effectuate fair employment" (Houston, 1973). The present token selection of black professionals to work in colleges and universities is surpassed only by the past complete exclusion of them.

194

In 1936, while 80 percent of all black Ph.D.'s worked in three black colleges (Green, 1937, p. 35), only three black Ph.D.s worked in predominantly white colleges (Winston, 1971, p. 695). After a quarter of a century, still only two hundred black Ph.D.'s worked in predominantly white colleges; there were fourteen and one-half times as many predominantly white colleges and universities as there were black professionals working in them. Historical evidence demonstrates unequivocally that black educators cannot depend upon their white colleagues for assistance in changing this state of affairs (Winston, 1971, pp. 684–719). In recent years, a number of predominantly white professional organizations have had to amend their constitutions and by-laws in some cases and change their practices in others, in order to accommodate black membership. The necessity of such parliamentary actions indicates that scholars have been parties to and preoccupied with racist activities in their professional organizations and institutions just as individuals in other organizations and institutions have.

If the past is at all instructive and the mounting evidence of the present accurate, the future is predictable. Those black scholars who hope to bring about change in their own professional status and to increase the opportunities for other blacks who may wish to work in a predominantly white institution should do so without expecting much, if any, help, encouragement, or acceptance from white educators.

Progress in the recruitment, selection, and hiring of blacks has been made because of events, forces, and rewards outside of the colleges and universities. Affirmative action was initiated by the federal government; the academic community continues to resist it (Bunzel, 1972; Seabury, 1972a). Managers of the Julius Rosenwald Fund wrote to five hundred college and university presidents and requested them to make some effort to recruit and hire black faculty members. "Four-fifths of the colleges did not deign to reply to this outrageous request;" the other fifth refused (Ballard, 1973, p. 28). The stipulations of the various "money" acts (National Defense Education Act, for example) with their emphasis on the "disadvantaged" influenced higher education to seek blacks; the demands of white tenured faculty did not. The Ford, Danforth, and other private foundations first recruited blacks and provided them with financial assistance so that they might earn the Ph.D. (Bryant, 1970, p. 9); the educational institutions vended and provided hired hands, not leaders, for this endeavor. Even in research, external, nonacademic organizations such as the Ford Foundation appeared to be more concerned about appraising the black professionals in higher education than organizations of white professional educators. Black students demanded faculty members and administrators from their racial group; white faculty members and administrators did not seek black colleagues or work to integrate staffs. Most of the research on black educators in colleges and universities has been done by blacks, usually blacks in predominantly black institutions. One investigator found that over a fifteen-year period the overwhelming majority of master's and Ph.D. theses and dissertations on the subject of blacks accepted by American universities were done by blacks (Knox, 1947). The academic community resisted all of these efforts except those with dollars attached. A teacher from a Chicago college said, "Put some bread [money] in the pen and my colleagues are the first hogs to the trough" (Moore, 1971, p. 79).

Historically, colleges have been imbedded in racism—a fact so obvious, widespread, and well known as to need no documentation here. Many white scholars have spent their time, talents, and professional careers promoting the conventional wisdom of the class, social, and racial group of which they are a part (sociologists, psychologists, and educators in particular). For some of them, this has meant using their skills to prove that blacks were not only incompetent but also were incapable of becoming competent. For others it has meant using the findings of the first group to support the same conventional wisdom. Perhaps this is understandable; "those forces which we all understand to be self-interests motivate us to pursue certain practical ends and actuate us in the pursuit of our intellectual endeavors as well" (Tillman and Tillman, 1972, p. 52). Contemporary academicians can find precedent for any antiblack views from the racist scholarship of their predecessors (Winston, 1971). DuBois observed more than a qaurter of a century ago (1935, pp. 726–727) that white scholarship, "when it regarded black men, became deaf, dumb, and blind." When one looks at the exclusion of nationally and internationally known black scholars from predominantly white colleges, the evidence is overwhelming that merit alone is not enough for a black to secure a faculty position in a white college.* Over thirty years ago, E. L. Lyons, Dean of the University of Minnesota Medical School, summarized the conflict between racism and merit in academic life (Karpman, 1943, p. 252; Nabrit, 1946, pp. 121–125). "At least until 1940, no amount of distinction in research was sufficient for a Negro scholar to be offered the superior research advantages of white institutions" (Winston, 1971, p. 703). In 1940, one still could not identify a half dozen blacks in predominantly white colleges.

Just as merit alone was not sufficient to guarantee equality of opportunity in the past, it is not the sole criterion in the present. If positive action is to be taken to change the situation, specific steps must be taken. For some colleges lawsuits will be needed to force them to obey the laws. The charges of bias in hiring must be increased a thousandfold. Some blacks are beginning to organize the electorate to withhold support of bond issues and tax levies until they receive certain guarantees that black professionals (and their own college-aged youngsters) have an equal opportunity for employment and an education. More research is planned to demonstrate the extent to which colleges still discriminate and the lack of intellectual as well as professional integrity present in the academic community.

Other blacks are currently preparing strategies to confront their legislators, particularly the education committees, with charges that they aid in job discrimination in colleges and universities by voting federal funds for institutions which do not follow federal guidelines with regard to employment. Blacks are also volunteering testimony to special commissions looking into discriminatory practices of colleges and universities.

Others are planning publicity campaigns to demonstrate the inequities. As one young faculty member recently observed, "Any

* Rayford W. Logan, Percy Julian, Ernest E. Just, Charles H. Turner, E. Franklin Frazier, Ralph Bunche, Charles Drew, W.E.B. DuBois, and Sterling Brown are a few of the outstanding nationally and internationally known scholars who were never sought by white colleges and universities, although their work has been used by the entire academic community and has been judged outstanding even by those considered racists in the academic community.

good newspaper reporter looking for a series of unique and sensational stories has but to dig into the practices of educational institutions and into the behavior of the people who manage and maintain them to see how often the law is ignored; that funds are mismanaged; that discrimination is rampant; that the rights of individuals are violated; and that the members of the academic community work hard not only to keep minority persons, especially blacks, at a disadvantage, but also to conceal their activities as active participants in the process."

The black scholar is asked to play an increasingly central role in exposing these situations and helping to plan these strategies. He is expected in some cases, and is asked in others, to permit his function as a scholar to transcend that of the traditional scholar in an academic community. The various constituents in the black community, including the intelligentsia, now ask the black scholar to broaden his commitments and involvement beyond his academic discipline to include the social arena and to assume many more roles than should really be asked or expected of a person. In this total process, he must also win the respect and support of his white colleagues. Our respondents indicate that they perceive the reaction of their white colleagues to them to be at best indifference and at worst, toleration.

Betty Pollard, a divisional chairman at Forest Park Community College, describes her perceptions of the reactions of white academicians to the black educator:

> They tolerate him at first because they often misjudge him; some are amused by him, scornful of his style, certain that while he possesses the academic credentials to demand their respect and cooperation, he has neither the grace, wit, nor knowledge to match their competence or to expose their incompetence. They do not consider him a peer. It is only recently that a few, in spite of their consternation and outright shock, have begun to comprehend that intelligence might indeed find refuge in the black scholar.
>
> Somehow white academicians are not perceptive enough to recognize that the black educator is a scholar of his time, an individual that is assaulted by it, who reacts to it in personal terms. White educators, on the other hand, are consumed and

guided only by precedent and do not appear to trust uniqueness, originality, or their own gut feelings. They do not have the merit of being less prompted by greed and the image of the academic legacy *that was* than by the accumulated mountain of abuses of racial and sex discrimination in academe *that is*. Close up, these men seem extremely parochial, diminished, and flawed. In the final analysis, they are human too—even if they aren't humane.

Image is one thing. Role is another. During the last decade the black scholar was overshadowed by the mood of the times and by some of those who could be described as antiintellectuals. The instant black experts, the television militant, the verbal exhibitionist, the coordinators of some special programs, and the white pseudo-liberal no longer demand and get as much attention. They served a limited purpose—they convinced black students of the important virtue of pride and of demanding representation and a hearing; and they developed some of the tactics for getting a response from an unresponsive academic bureaucracy. Some of them were also opportunists, extortionists, and parasites on programs designed to help black students and thus *used* the black students. They taught black students how to intimidate black and white faculty and administrators and how to mute their peers who refused to accept without question their goals. They imposed drama onto the educational enterprise. Imposed drama takes priority over elected drama; just as action takes precedence over tradition. It is unanticipated conflict which has contempt for past practices; it is brash, arbitrary, and violates the expectations; it influences style and content, interrupts sequence, and creates dichotomy. In short, imposed drama is revolutionary. Some of the dramatists so visible in colleges and universities during the period of unrest in higher education institutions lacked creditability. They were, nonetheless, active participants.

The chronic sensationalism of some of these people (by no means all) obscured the real black scholar. The sensationalists rose in turbulent times and meandered through phases of the black past and present—highlighting and rehighlighting the outrages, violations, and defeats of black people. Finding a response, they sought, won, and maintained their positions, with a type of fanaticism we had not previously seen in education. While many of them did make minor contours in the higher education system and in some ways higher education will never be the same again, the influence of the antiintellectuals has ended. The turfs which they held on campus are gone. The graffiti of protest has been painted over. The decibels are lowered; no one listens to them anymore. Perhaps it was their lack of scholarly thought, systematic planning, and organized principle which contributed to their downfall. In many ways they were like a monsoon which comes and passes and leaves no sign of rain.

The true black scholars may now have their turn; they have no choice but to commit themselves to a better educational environment and experience for many facets of the academic community. What are some of the roles which they might play in some of the diverse areas of higher education as they look to the future? It is evident that black scholars will have to review and correct the prevailing generalities concerning themselves in higher education and in the society. Only they have been willing to question the validity and social consequences of the sweeping conclusions made about them and their racial group by their white colleagues. The black academicians are the only scholars who appear to have the personal interest and commitment to gather and analyze the hard data to refute the damaging stereotypes about themselves and their group. It is the black scholar who must set the historical and sociological record straight, who must also interpret the black frame of reference instead of leaving the interpretation of black men solely to white men such as Daniel P. Moynihan (1965), Christopher Jencks and David Riesman (1969), Frank Riesman (1962), Arthur Jensen (1969), and others who have described blacks only in terms of the wretchedness of their families, the inferiority of their colleges, the problems in their public schools, and their purported low genetic inheritance. It becomes, therefore, the task of black scholars to monitor these men who represent the community of scholars, to redirect them, if necessary, and to deny them the continued pursuit of the pathology they seek. A number of blacks appear to recognize that when they assume this responsibility, the research methodology must be sound in terms of universal and unquestioned standards which have been created and sustained by many of those who often neither accept nor recognize them. The research must stand on its own merit. Black researchers also seem to agree, however, that they should not hesitate to evolve new methodologies. One thing almost all blacks note: both private foundations and the federal government fund white men to study black men but seldom fund black men to study white men or other black men.

Beyond significant research, black scholars are increasingly concerned about excellence in teaching. Instruction must go beyond the simple mastery of discipline content. All students should be taught to examine the academic conduit through which scholarly contributions have established, transmitted, and preserved the social, economic, and academic norms of a racist society.

Black scholars cannot afford a vested interest in mediocrity, whether perpetrated by themselves or their white colleagues, especially as this relates to black students. It is they who must advise them (students) against much of the antiintellectualism so prevalent among many Afro-American youths. They cannot hesitate to say to black students that regardless of their quest for liberation, for revolutionary change, and for input into those things which affect their lives, black students will have to be well prepared to be of any real value to the black movement or to any other movement. The students must learn that everything worthy of learning cannot be directly related to the "black experience;" while they may choose the writing of Eldridge Cleaver and Franz Fanon over Ernest Hemingway and William Faulkner, if they cannot read, they cannot understand Cleaver and Fanon. In spite of the uniqueness of black slang, the creativity of the black dialogue, and the acceptance and adoption of this informal communication by others, black students must ultimately compete in standard English, at least when they write and often when they speak. We are not suggesting which form of English is best; we are simply noting the reality. The heroes of young blacks (Cleaver, Fanon, and others) also have these language skills; they write books. Black antiintellectuals and white intellectual romantics who say to black students that alternative schools and street academies are best for them, that the society should be deschooled, that the Ph.D. is irrelevant, or that luck and personality, not education, make one a success in life are the same people who choose and use the education system which rewarded them and which they condemn. Their own children, for the most part, *are not* experimenting with what they prescribe for black students. Faculty members who condemn the Ph.D. as worthless are often the persons who already have them. Some of them are full professors who have jobs for life, good salaries, fine homes, European travel, money to send their children to college; they are entrenched in the system they claim to reject. Some of them have sat and continue to sit on the committees which have made the Ph.D., research, and publication the criteria for hiring. They are also among the first to say that blacks and women are unqualified and incompetent when confronted with a concept such as affirmative action. We do not know of a single college president, dean, or full professor who was hired and who later became successful without an education, regardless of his personality, luck, and social background.

Black professors may agree with students and other critics of education that much within the college experience may be bad, may need overhauling, and may need to be eliminated, but they must also impress upon students that when they learn, they can keep that which is worth keeping and discard or reject that which is of no value. Students must be told to respect teachers enough to allow them to teach, not because they deserve respect, but because the students are the losers when teachers fail to teach. The black scholar must be sure to alert the students to the professor who awards unearned grades, does not challenge students, has low expectations, wastes time in rap sessions, does not give important feedback on student work, and dismisses classes too often. This type of professor not only disrespects but also cheats his students. He may be black or white. It is common belief that the only way a black student can be cheated without making him complain is to free him from academic demands, and thus cheat him out of his education. Black educators must somehow convince black students that their demands alone are not sufficient criteria upon which to base an education enterprise. Those educators who acquiesce and support the sometimes ridiculous demands of black students, either because a different and opposing position would be unpopular or because they are afraid, do the students a disservice. Students should be supported when their grievances and motivations are sound; they should be told when their demands appear unsound.

Black educators must assist students in seeing that it is a

contradiction for some of their popular leaders to tell them that they must become politically astute and then tell them to mock and demean the very scholarship and cognitive involvement with subject matter which can develop that astuteness. Black students need to know more than their history; they need to hear more than rhetoric; and they need more breadth and depth than their own ethnocentrism. But they must be encouraged to keep the pressure on.

We believe that black scholars must also be in the vanguard of those who demonstrate to their white colleagues that black colleges play a viable role in American education. Predominantly white institutions have much to gain from black scholars. These scholars represent a unique paradox in higher education. Most of them have come from black institutions that are considered below academic standards. Up to 97 percent of the students which they have taught at various times have been described as not being "college level;" the facilities which they have used have been substandard; 70 percent of their black colleagues have never pubished; more than half of their colleagues hold the master's degree or less; most of the colleges where they taught were unaccredited; the programs they taught were ill-financed; the boards which governed the colleges were racist, and the administrators who administered them were tyrannical (McGrath, 1965). Yet, more than 90 percent of all blacks who have earned a baccalaureate degree were taught by these teachers, their predecessors, and their contemporaries. While more than 97 percent of all blacks who hold the Ph.D. got the degree not only from predominantly white colleges and universities but also from the most prestigious ones, they were taught as undergraduates in black colleges and by black teachers. In the presence of this data, the academic community may well ask: What were their secrets?

One theme seems to run through all of the commentary on black educators. They all seem willing to experiment with social change. Almost all of them suggest that the intellectual enterprise can be a rational source of social decision. Each appears to view his role as a dual one—that of scientific investigator and that of provider of intellectual input into the social process. Only more counseling service to all students ranked higher than commitment to social problems (race relations, urban problems, social class) with the black educators who were our respondents. Black scholars consistently maintain that detachment and neutrality in scholarship is an illusion. Dispassionate analysis made by passionate men can never be completely neutral.

Some black scholars who want to assist others to enter the academic community indicate that they must also identify certain subtle hypocrisies present in that community. We have observed, for example, that search committees, administrators, and department chairmen seeking applicants for vacant positions have an additional line added to their letters, sometimes as a postscript. Sometimes it is written in by hand; sometimes it is printed directly on the stationery. This line reads: *We are an equal opportunity employer.* We took twenty-six of these letters from separate educational institutions (fourteen from community colleges and twelve from senior institutions) and checked the number of blacks employed on the campus. Ten of the fourteen two-year colleges did not have a black staff member; four of the colleges within that ten were located in predominantly black communities. Of the four community colleges that had blacks, one institution had only one, another had two, another had three, and one had seven. Of the twelve four-year colleges we selected, six had four blacks on their staffs, all in education; two had one black, and six had no blacks. Like banks which claim to be equal opportunity lenders and building contractors that claim to be equal opportunity builders, colleges are more concerned about image than about practice.

There is a general belief that—as one search committee member of a Big Ten University has put it—"Any person who has to advertise for a job or has to hire a commercial agency to get him a job can't be very good." More than a dozen persons serving on search committees confided to us that while their committees did place such ads as a recent "policy," they doubted whether any serious consideration would be given to the names of applicants submitted in this way. Only in cases where the person had a national reputation and his name was submitted by another person did the search committees give the names any attention. More specifically, search committees place ads more as a strategy to demonstrate that they are meeting affirmative action guidelines than as a means of identifying potential candidates. Another committee member confessed, "These ads keep the 'Feds' off our back. The fact remains, the process for seeking professors and administrators has not changed. And because most of those in the higher education marketplace know this, such advertisements attract few applicants. This can vary of course, depending upon the size of the institution, where it is, its prestige, and so on. Nonetheless, only the naive or the uninformed would expect to get consideration for a college or university position by responding to a newspaper or journal ad. Two-year college people use this technique much less than senior college personnel, although the *Junior College Journal* does carry a few such advertisements.

One also observes a wider application of this when he sees the pages of advertisements, indicating job vacancies in colleges and universities throughout the nation, listed in the *Chronicle of Higher Education* each week. The common element in all of these ads is a statement that the college placing it is an "Equal Opportunity Employer" or "An Affirmative Action Employer." They may be. We found, however, that only 36 persons (10 in two-year colleges and 26 in senior institutions) or a total 1.1 percent of our respondents found out about their positions through journal advertisements. And all of them secured their positions before the "Equal Opportunity Employer" advertisements began to appear in academic publications in significant numbers (about 1969).

The academic community is filled with discrimination and racism. Some argue that it does not consciously produce it. Others contradict this argument strenuously. Nonetheless, whether it produces it or not, it does distill it, use it, and provide it in the purest form (research is one such form) for the many in a society who do consciously discriminate. Although we can identify few cases of overt discrimination in many colleges, blacks perceive it as always being there; like relative humidity, it is present, penetrating, oppressive, encompassing, and pervasive.

Some of our findings may be considered startling. But we know that many exposes are transitory both in terms of the concerns they generate and the needed changes they surface. History has guided us to be aware of the limited impact and the lack of sustained interest of both the public and those responsible for implementing the demonstrated changes needed. It is easy to become almost psychotic when one looks at the state and status of black Americans in colleges and universities. But we are no more concerned than our respondents. For them, the paranoia sometimes becomes truth, truth reality, and reality behavior. They maintain that their white colleagues yield too little and protest too much. It is tragic that the negative conditions and wrongdoings which may be uncovered by any study and which the public should want revealed may be presented to that public on the six o'clock news and forgotten by the nine o'clock movie.

BIBLIOGRAPHY

ADAMS, C. Review of *Tomorrow's Tomorrow: The Black Woman,* by Joyce Ladner. *American Journal of Sociology,* 1972, *78* (2), 456–458.

ALTMAN, R. A., and SNYDER, P. O. *The Minor Student on the Campus. Expectations and Possibilities.* Denver: Center for Research and Development in Higher Education, University of California, Berkeley, and Western Interstate Commission for Higher Education, November 1970.

American Association of Colleges' Statement, November 8, 1971.

American Council on Education Fifty-Fifth Annual Meeting, entitled "Women in Higher Education." Miami Beach, Fla., October 6, 1972.

ANDERSON, J. "The Agonies of Black Militancy." *Dissent,* February 1971, *18* (1).

"A Radical Rebuff." *Newsweek,* January 15, 1973.

ASTIN, H. S., and BAYER, A. E. "Sex Discrimination in Academe." *Educational Record,* Spring 1972, 101–118.

ATWOOD, R. B., SMITH, H. S., and VAUGHAN, C. O. "Negro Teachers in Northern Colleges and Universities in the United States." *Journal of Negro Education,* 1949, *18* (4).

BALLARD, A. B. "Academia's Record of Benign Neglect." *Change,* March 1973, *5* (2).

BANFIELD, E. *The Unheavenly City.* Boston: Little-Brown, 1969.

BARATZ, J. C. "Neo-Knownothingism: New Restraints on Research in the Black Community." *Urban and Social Change Review,* Spring 1972, *5,* 76–79.

BARZUN, J. *The American University.* New York: Harper and Row, 1970.

BEAL, F. M. "Double Jeopardy: To Be Black and Female." In *Sisterhood Is Powerful,* edited by Robin Morgan. New York: Random House, 1970.

BEAN, R. B. "Some Racial Peculiarities of the Negro Brain." *American Journal of Anatomy,* September 1906, *5.*

BELL, D. "On Meritocracy and Equality." *The Public Interest,* Fall 1972.

BELLIS, A. G. "Negroes are Few on College Faculties." *Southern Education Report,* 1968, *4* (1).

BERNARD, J. *Marriage and Family Among Negroes.* Englewood Cliffs, N.J.: Prentice Hall, 1966.

BILLINGSLEY, A. "The Black Presence in American Higher Education." In *What Black Americans are Saying,* edited by Nathan Wright, Jr. New York: Hawthorn Books, 1970a.

BILLINGSLEY, A. "Black Families and White Social Science." *Journal of Social Issues,* 1970b, *26* (3).

BILLINGSLEY, A. *Black Families in White America.* Englewood Cliffs, N.J.: Prentice Hall, 1966.

BILLINGSLEY, A., and GIOVANNI, J. M. *Children of the Storm: Black Children and American Child Welfare.* New York: Harcourt Brace, 1972.

BIRENBAUM, W. A. "White Power and American Higher Education." In *The Minority Student on the Campus: Expectations and Possibilities,* edited by R. A. Altman and P. O. Snyder. Boulder, Colo.: Western Interstate Commission for Higher Education, 1971.

"Black Brain Drain." *Human Behavior,* March/April 1972 (2).

"Blacks vs. Feminists." *Time Magazine,* March 26, 1973.

BLAU, E. "Black Professor Seeks to Aid Fisk." *New York Times,* February 11, 1973.

BOLMAN, F. D. "The Administrator as Leader and Statesman." In *Stress and Campus Response: Current Issues in Higher Education,* edited by G. K. Smith. San Francisco: Jossey-Bass, 1968.

BOND, H. M. "The Negro Scholar and Professional in America." In *American Negro Reference Book,* edited by John P. Davis.

Englewood Cliffs, N.J.: Prentice-Hall, 1966.

BOYD, W. M., II. *Access and Power for Blacks in Higher Education.* New York: Educational Policy Center, 1972.

BROWN, D. G. *The Market for College Teachers: An Economic Analysis of Career Patterns Among Southeastern Social Scientists.* Chapel Hill, N.C.: University of North Carolina, 1965.

BROWN, S. L. "Alice Freeman Palmer Memorial Institute." *Opportunity,* August 1923, *1* (8), 246–268.

BRYANT, J. W. *A Survey of Black American Doctorates.* New York: Ford Foundation, Special Projects in Education, 1970.

BUDIG, G. A. "Wanted: Academic Straights." *Phi Delta Kappan,* June 1972, *53* (10).

BULLOCK, H. A. *A History of Negro Education in the South, from 1619 to the Present.* Cambridge, Mass.: Harvard University Press, 1967.

BUNZEL, J. H. "Black Studies at San Francisco State." *The Public Interest,* Fall 1968, (13).

BUNZEL, J. H. "The Politics of Quotas." *Change,* October 1972.

CAMPBELL, L. "The Difference." In *What Black Educators are Saying,* edited by Nathan Wright, Jr. New York: Hawthorn Books, 1970.

CAPLOW, T. and MC GEE, R. J. *The Academic Marketplace.* Garden City, N.Y.: Anchor Books, Doubleday, 1965.

Careers of Ph.D.'s Academic vs. Non-Academic, A Second Report on Followups of Doctoral Cohorts, 1935–1960. Washington, D.C.: National Academy of Science, 1968.

CHALMERS, E. L. "Achieving Equity for Women in Higher Education Graduate Enrollment and Faculty Status." *Journal of Higher Education,* October 1972.

CHAMBERLAIN, J. "Every One Under the Gun." *Boston Herald Traveler,* November 12, 1972.

CHISHOLM, S. "Racism and Anti-Feminism." *Black Scholar,* 1970, *1.* *Chronicle of Higher Education,* May 30, 1972.

CLARK, K. B. *Dark Ghetto: Dilemmas of Social Power.* New York: Harper and Row, 1965.

CLARK, K. B. *Racism in American Education.* New York: Harper and Row, 1970.

COHEN, A. *Dateline '79: Heretical Concepts for the Community College.* Beverly Hills, Caif.: Glencoe Press, 1969.

COHEN, A. *The Constant Variable.* San Francisco: Jossey-Bass, 1971.

COLEMAN, J. *Equality of Educational Opportunity.* Washington, D.C.: U. S. Government Printing Office, 1966.

COLES, R. *Children of Crisis: A Study of Courage and Fear.* Boston: Little-Brown, 1967.

Commission on Higher Educational Opportunity in the South. *The Negro and Higher Education in the South.* Atlanta, Ga.: Southern Regional Education Board, August 1967.

Comparative Guide to American Colleges. (5th ed.) New York: Harper and Row, 1972.

CONYERS, J. E. "Negro Doctorates in Sociology: A Social Portrait." *Phylon,* 1968, *29,* 209–223.

COPPIN, F. J. *Reminiscences of School Life, and Hints on Teaching.* Philadelphia: African Methodist Episcopal Book Concern, 1913.

CORCORAN, T. B. "The Coming Slums of Higher Education." *Change,* September 1972.

CROSS, K. P. "Higher Education's Newest Student." *Junior College Journal,* 1968, *36.*

CROSS, K. P. *Beyond the Open Door.* San Francisco: Jossey-Bass, 1971.

CRUSE, H. *The Crisis of the Negro Intellectual.* New York: William Morrow, 1967.

DRAKE, S. and CAYTON, H. *Black Metropolis.* rev. ed. New York: Harper and Row, 1962.

DRAKE, S. "The Black University in the American Social Order." *Daedalus,* Summer, 1971, 833–897.

DU BOIS, W. E. B. *Black Reconstruction.* New York: Harcourt Brace, 1935.

DU BOIS, W. E. B. *The Souls of Black Folks.* Greenwich, Conn.: Fawcett Publications, 1961.

DUNGAN, R. A. "Higher Education: The Effort to Adjust." *Daedalus,* Winter 1970, *99* (1).

DUNNING, W. A. *Reconstruction: Political and Economic.* New York: Harper and Row, 1907.

DUSTER, A. (Ed.) *Crusade for Justice, the Autobiography of Ida B. Wells.* Chicago and London: University of Chicago Press, 1970.

EGERTON, J. "The White Sea of Higher Education." In *The Minority Student on the Campus: Expectations and Possibilities,* edited by R. A. Altman and P. O. Snyder. Boulder, Colo.: Western Interstate Commission on Higher Education, 1971.

EGERTON, J. "What Progress in Faculty Desegregation." *Chronicle of Higher Education,* May 20, 1968, *2* (18), 1–6.

EPPS, E. "Higher Education and Black Americans: Implications for the Future." In *Black Students in White Schools.* Worthington, Ohio: Charles A. Jones, 1972.

EPSTEIN, C. F. "Positive Effects of the Multiple Negative: Explaining the Success of Black Professional Women." *American Journal of Sociology,* January 1973, *78* (4).

EPSTEIN, C. F. "Successful Black Professional Women." *American Journal of Sociology,* 1972, *78* (4).

"Faculty Backlash." *Newsweek,* December 4, 1972, 127–128.

FIELDS, C. M. "The Government's Guidelines on Sex Bias Greeted with Optimism and Relief on Many University Campuses." *Chronicle of Higher Education,* October 25, 1972a, *2* (5), 1–5.

FIELDS, C. M. "Senate Approves College Aid Bill; Forbids Sex Bias." *Chronicle of Higher Education,* March 6, 1972b, *6* (22).

FIELDS, C. M. "Women's Rank, Pay and Tenure Status Found Behind Similarly Qualified Men's." *Chronicle of Higher Education,* May 15, 1972c, *6* (32).

Fisk University, Nashville, Tenn. Julius Rosenwald Fund Papers, Mary McLeod Bethune file.

FISKE, E. B. "Jewish Studies: A New Favorite on Campus." *New York Times,* January 14, 1973.

FLINT, J. M. "Behind a Black School Aide's Suicide: A Conflict in Basic Values." *New York Times,* March 19, 1972.

FRANKLIN, J. H. "The Dilemma of the American Negro Scholar." In *Soon One Morning,* edited by Herbert Hill. New York: Alfred A. Knopf, 1963.

FRASER, C. G. "Black Sociologists are Seeking Black Perspectives on Realities." *New York Times,* July 22, 1972.

FRAZIER, E. F. *Black Bourgeoisie: The Rise of a New Middle-Class in the U. S.* New York: Collier Books, 1962a.

FRAZIER, E. F. "The Failure of the Negro Intellectual." *Negro Digest,* February 1962b, *2.*

FRAZIER, E. F. *The Free Negro Family.* Nashville, Tenn.: Fisk University Press, 1932a.

FRAZIER, E. F. *The Negro Family in Chicago.* Chicago: University of Chicago Press, 1932b.

FRAZIER, E. F. *The Negro Family in the United States.* Chicago: University of Chicago Press, 1948.

FRAZIER, E. F. *The Negro in the United States.* New York: Macmillan, 1949.

GIOVANNI, N. "Conversation with Ida Lewis." *Essence,* 1971, *2.*

GLEAZER, E. J. *Project Focus: A Forecast Study of Community Colleges.* New York: McGraw-Hill, 1973.

GOLDSTEIN, R. *Black Life and Culture in the United States.* New York: Thomas Y. Crowell, 1971.

GOODMAN, W. "The Return to the Quota System." *New York Times Magazine,* September 10, 1972.

GOODRICH, A. L., LEZOTTE, L. W., and WELCH, J. "Minorities in Two-Year Colleges: A Survey." *Junior College Journal,* December/January 1972–1973.

GORDAN, E. W. and WILKERSON, D. A. *Compensatory Education for the Disadvantaged: Programs and Practices, Preschool Through College.* New York: College Entrance Examination Board, 1966.

GREEN, H. W. "Sixty Years of Doctorates Conferred Upon Negroes." *Journal of Negro Education,* January 1937, 6.

GREEN, R. L., MCMILLAN, J. H., and GUNNING, T. S. *The Status of Blacks in the Big Ten Athletic Conference: Issues and Concerns.* East Lansing, Mich.: Michigan State University Press, March 1972.

GREENE, H. W. *Holders of Doctorates Among American Negroes.* Boston: Meador, 1946.

GRIER, W. and COBBS, P. *Black Rage.* New York: Bantam Books, 1968.

HARE, N. "What Black Studies Mean to a Black Scholar." *College and University Business,* May 1970.

HARNETT, R. T. *College and University Trustees: Their Backgrounds, Roles, and Educational Attitudes.* Princeton, N.J.: Educational Testing Service, 1969.

HART, A. B. *The Southern South.* New York: Appleton-Century-Croft, 1912.

HENDERSON, V. "Negro Colleges Face the Future." *Daedalus,* Summer 1971, 630–648.

HEXTER, J. H. "Publish or Perish—A Defense." *The Public Interest,* Fall 1969, (17).

HILL, R. B. *The Strengths of Black Families.* New York: Emerson Hall, 1972.

HODGKINSON, H. L. *Institutions in Transition.* New York: McGraw-Hill, 1971.

HOFSTADER, R. *Social Darwinism in American Thought.* Boston: Beacon Press, 1955.

HOLMES, D. O. W. *The Evolution of the Negro College.* New York: Bureau of Publications, Columbia University Teachers College, 1934.

HOLT, R. *Mary McLeod Bethune.* New York: Doubleday, 1964.

HOUSTON, J. "Citizen's Report: College Hiring Bias is Charged." *Chicago Tribune,* May 3, 1973.

"Inside HEW: Women Protest Sex Discrimination." *Science,* October 1971, *174.*

JACKSON, G. G. "Black Youth as Peer Counselors." *Personnel and Guidance,* December 1972, *51.*

JACOBSON, R. L. "Retain Tenure But Ration It, Panel Advises." *Chronicle of Higher Education,* January 22, 1973, *7* (16), 1–5.

JANSSEN, P. A. "Higher Education and the Black American: Phase Two." *Chronicle of Higher Education,* May 30, 1972, *6* (34).

JEFFERS, C. *Living Poor: A Participant Observer Study of Choices and Priorities.* Ann Arbor, Mich.: Ann Arbor Publishers, 1967.

JENCKS, C., and RIESMAN, D. *The Academic Revolution.* Garden City, N.Y.: Anchor Books, Doubleday, 1969.

JENSEN, A. R. "How Much Can We Boost IQ and Scholastic Achievement?" *Harvard Educational Review,* Winter 1969, *39* (1).

JOHNSON, J. J. "The Black Psychologist: Pawn or Professional." In *What Black Educators Are Saying,* edited by Nathan Wright, Jr. New York: Hawthorn Books, 1970.

JOHNSON, L. T. B. *The Interaction of Soul, Mind and Body: A Study of the Role Compatibility, Role Conflict, and Role Resolution of Black Student Athletes on a Predominantly White University Campus.* Unpublished master's thesis, Purdue University, 1972.

JOHNSON, T. "The Black College as System." *Daedalus,* Summer 1971.

JONES, G. E. *The Jeanes Teacher in the United States.* Chapel Hill, N.C.: University of North Carolina Press, 1937.

Junior College Directory. Washington, D.C: American Association of Junior and Community Colleges, 1972.

KARPMAN, B. "Ernest Everett Just." *Journal of Nervous and Mental Disease,* February 1943.

KEAST, W. R. and MACY, J. W. *Faculty Tenure: A Report and Recommendations by the Commission on Academic Tenure in Higher Education.* San Francisco: Jossey-Bass, 1973, p. 7.

KEETON, M. *Shared Authority on Campus.* Washington, D.C.: American Association of Higher Education, 1971.

KELLEY, W. and WILBUR, L. *Teaching in the Community Junior College.* New York: Appleton-Century-Crofts, 1970.

KERR, C. *The Uses of the University.* Cambridge, Mass.: Harvard University Press, 1964.

KERR, C. "Governance and Functions." *Daedalus,* Winter, 1970.

KEYES, R. "Intentions vs. Reality." In *The Minority Student on the Campus: Expectations and Possibilities,* edited by R. A. Altman and P. O. Snyder. Boulder, Colo.: Western Interstate Commission for Higher Education, 1971.

KILSON, M. "The New Black Intellectuals." *Dissent,* July/August 1969, *16* (4).

KILSON, M. "Whither Black Higher Education." *School Review,* May 1973, *81* (3).

KONHEIM, B. G. "Report of the Council Committee on Discrimination." *AAUP Bulletin,* Summer 1972.

KNOX, E. O. "The Negro as a Subject of University Research in 1946." *Journal of Negro Education,* Spring 1947, *16,* 180–189.

KRIEGEL, L. "When Blue-Collar Students Go To College." *Saturday Review,* July 22, 1972, *45* (30).

LADNER, J. *Tomorrow's Tomorrow: The Black Woman.* Garden City, N.Y.: Doubleday, 1971.

LANE, H. "New Students in the New World of Postsecondary Education." Lecture presented at the Twenty-eighth National Conference on Higher Education. Chicago, March 13, 1973.

LA RUE, L. "The Black Woman and Women's Liberation." *Black Scholar,* 1970, *1.*

LAWTON, S. B. "Minority Administrators in Berkeley: A Progress Report." *Urban Education,* January 1972, 321–329.

LEMELLE, T. J. and LEMELLE, W. J. *The Black College.* New York: Frederick A. Praeger, 1969.

LERNER, G. "Black Liberation—Women's Liberation: A Study in Ambivalence and Tension." A paper presented to the Fifty-fifth Annual Meeting of The American Council on Education. Miami Beach, Fla., October 6, 1972a.

LERNER, G. (Ed.) *Black Women in White America.* New York: Pantheon Books, 1972b.

LIEBERMAN, M. "Professors Unite." *Harper's,* October 1971, 61–70.

LOMBARDI, J. *Student Activism in the Junior College: An Administrator's View.* Washington, D.C.: American Association of Junior Colleges, 1969.

LURIA, Z. and LURIA, S. E. "The Role of the University: Ivory Tower Service Station, or Frontier Post?" *Daedalus,* Winter, 1970.

MC CARTHY, B. and MICHAUD, P. "Companions: An Adjunct to Counseling." *Personnel and Guidance Journal,* 1971, (49), 839–841.

MC CONNEL, T. R. "Faculty Resources for Universal Higher Education." In *Trends in Postsecondary Education*. Washington, D.C.: U. S. Government Printing Office, October 1970.

MC GRATH, E. J. *The Predominantly Negro Colleges and Universities in Transition*. New York: Columbia University Teachers College, 1965.

MEDSKER, L. L. *The Junior College: Progress and Prospect*. New York: McGraw-Hill, 1960.

MEDSKER, L. L. and TILLERY, D. *Breaking the Access Barrier: A Profile of Two-Year Colleges*. New York: McGraw-Hill, 1971.

"Minority Hiring Practices in California State University System Discriminates Against White Men, B'nai B'rith Charges." *Chronicle of Higher Education*, September 25, 1972.

MOMMSEN, K. G. "Black American Doctorates: An Indirect Test of the 'Low Access' Hypothesis." A paper presented to the Annual Meeting of the Southwestern Sociological Association. San Antonio, Tex., March 1972a.

MOMMSEN, K. G. "Career Patterns of Black American Doctorates." Unpublished doctoral dissertation, Florida State University, 1970.

MOMMSEN, K. G. "Professionalism and the Racial Context of Career Patterns Among Black American Doctorates: A Note on the 'Brain Drain' Hypothesis." *Journal of Negro Education*, Fall 1972b.

MONROE, C. R. *Profile of the Community College*. San Francisco: Jossey-Bass, 1972.

MONROE, S. "A Guest in a Strange House: A Black at Harvard." *Saturday Review of Education*, January 1973, *50* (1).

MOOG, F. "A Dragon Called Tenure." *Change*, November 1972.

MOORE, W., JR. *Against the Odds: The High-Risk Student in the Community College*. San Francisco: Jossey-Bass, 1970.

MOORE, W., JR. *Blind Man on a Freeway: The Community College Administrator*. San Francisco: Jossey-Bass, 1971.

MOORE, W., JR. "The Community College Board of Trustees: A Question of Competency." *Journal of Higher Education*, March 1973, *44* (3).

MOORE, W., JR. *The Vertical Ghetto: Everyday Life in a Housing Project*. New York: Random House, 1969.

MORRIS, E. W. "The Contemporary Negro College and the Brain Drain." *Journal of Negro Education*, Fall 1972, *41* (4).

MORRISON, T. "What the Black Woman Thinks About Women's Liberation." *New York Times Magazine*, August 22, 1971.

MOSS, J. A. "Negro Teachers in Predominantly White Colleges." *Journal of Negro Education*, 1958, 27 (4).

MOSS, J. A. and MERCER, N. A. "A Study of the Potential Supply of Negro Teachers for the Colleges of New York State." Unpublished report to the New York State Commission Against Discrimination, 1961.

MOYNIHAN, D. P. *The Negro Family: A Case for National Action.* Washington, D.C.: U. S. Department of Labor, 1965.

MYRDAL, G. *An American Dilemma.* New York: Harper and Row, 1944.

NABRIT, M. S. "Ernest E. Just." *Phylon,* Second Quarter 1946 (7).

NEWMAN, F. *Report on Higher Education.* Washington, D.C.: U. S. Government Printing Office, 1971.

NEWMAN, F. *Report of the Committee on Senate Policy.* Academic Senate, University of California, Berkeley, 1970.

Newsweek. Letters to the Editor. December 25, 1972, 5.

NKRUMAH, K. *The Autobiography of Kwame Nkrumah.* Edinburgh: Thomas Nelson, 1959.

NOBLE, J. L. *The Negro College Woman's Education.* New York: Bureau of Publications, Columbia University, 1956.

NOWAK, W. S. *Black Athlete Under Tender: An Investigation of the Sociological Background of the Negro Football Player at a Midwest University.* Unpublished senior honor's thesis, University of Illinois, Urbana, 1968.

OLSON, C. T. "The U. S. Challenges Discrimination Against Women." *Junior College Journal,* July 1972.

PEARE, C. O. *Mary McLeod Bethune.* New York: Vanguard Press, 1951.

PEARL, A. "The More We Change the More We Get." *Change,* September, 1970.

PERRINS, R. "Computing Minorities." *Change,* September 1972.

Phelps-Stokes Fund. *Twenty-Year Report, 1911–1931.* New York, 1932.

PLOSKI, H. *The Negro Almanac.* New York: Bellwether, 1967.

POINSETT, A. "The Brain Drain at Negro Colleges." *Ebony,* October 1970, 74–84.

POINSETT, A. "The Politics of Benign Neglect." *Ebony,* February 1973.

POTTINGER, J. S. "The Drive Toward Equality." *Change,* October 1972.

PYLE, R. and SNYDER, F. "Students as Para-Professional Counselors at

Community Colleges." *Journal of College Student Personnel,* 1971 (12), 259–262.

RAAB, E. "Quotas by Any Other Name." *Commentary,* January 1972, *53* (1).

RAFKY, D. M. "The Black Professor and Academic Freedom." *Negro Education Review,* July 1971a.

RAFKY, D. M. "The Black Scholar in the Academic Marketplace." *Change,* October 1971b.

RAFKY, D. M. "The Black Scholar in the Academic Marketplace." *Teachers College Record,* 1972.

Report of the Committee on Senate Policy. Academic Senate, University of California, Berkeley, 1970.

Report of the President's Commission on Campus Unrest. New York: Avon Books, 1971.

RICKMAN, G. "Affirmative Action Programs: Their Relationship to Feminism and Racially Based Movements." Paper presented to the Fifty-fifth Annual Meeting of the American Council on Education, Miami Beach, Fla., October 6, 1972.

RIESMAN, F. *The Culturally Deprived Child.* New York: Harper and Row, 1962.

RIST, R. C. "Black Staff, Black Studies, and White Universities." *Journal of Higher Education,* November 1970, *41* (8).

ROCHE, G. C. "On Campus: An Iceberg of Government Intervention." *U. S. News and World Report,* January 1, 1973, *24* (1).

ROSE, H. M. "An Appraisal of the Negro Educator's Situation in the Academic Marketplace." *Journal of Negro Education,* 1966, *35* (1).

ROSE, H. M. "The Market for Negro Educators in Colleges and Universities Outside the South." *Journal of Negro Education,* 1961, *30* (4).

ROUECHE, J. E. *Salvage, Redirection, or Custody?* Washington, D.C.: American Association of Junior Colleges, 1968.

ROYKO, M. "Mickey Mouse Needn't Apply." *Chicago Daily News,* December 8, 1972.

RUSH, S. and CLARK, C. *How to Get Along With Black People.* New York: The Third Press, Joseph Okpaku Publishing Company, 1972.

Salaries in Higher Education, 1956–66. National Education Association Research Report 1966R-2, February 1966.

SEABURY, P. "HEW and the Universities." *Commentary,* February 1972a, 38–44.

SEABURY, P. "The Idea of Merit." *Commentary,* December 1972b.

SEMAS, P. W. "Sex and Sexism Pose Special Problems for Psychologists, Women Say." *Chronicle of Higher Education,* September 25, 1972, *7* (1), 1–7.

SHANE, J. A. "Administrative Organizational Structures and Community College Comprehensiveness." *Journal of Higher Education,* March 1973, *44* (3).

SHAPIRO, B. J. *The Black Athlete at Michigan State University.* Unpublished master's thesis, Michigan State University, East Lansing, Michigan, 1970.

SHEARER, L. "Negro Problem: Women Rule the Roost." *Parade Magazine, St. Louis Post-Dispatch,* August 20, 1967.

SHILS, E. "Color, the Universal Intellectual Community, and the Afro-Asian Intellectual." *Daedalus,* Spring 1967.

SIEVERT, W. "Ethnic Studies: Vanishing or Not?" *Saturday Review of Education,* January 13, 1973, *1* (1).

SIEVERT, W. "NCAA Concerned About Legality of Its Exclusion of Women." *Chronicle of Higher Education,* January 17, 1972, *6* (15), 1–4.

SLATER, P. *The Pursuit of Loneliness: American Culture at the Breaking Point.* Boston: Beacon Press, 1970.

SMITH, A. *An Autobiography of Mrs. Amanda Smith, the Colored Evangelist.* Chicago: Meyer and Brothers, 1893.

SMYTHE, M. M. "Feminism and Black Liberation: Common Experience and Pitfalls." Paper presented at the Fifty-fifth Annual Meeting of the American Council on Education, Miami Beach, Fla., October 6, 1972.

Special Report of the U. S. Commissioner of Education /87/. Moorland Collection, Howard University Library, Washington, D.C.

STAPLES, R. E. "The Black Scholar in Academe." *Change,* November 1972.

STEWART, M. W. *Meditations from the Pen of Mrs. Maria Stewart, Negro.* Washington, D.C.: Garrison and Knopp, 1932.

"Summer School for Administrators." *Change,* October 1972.

TAYLOR, I. E. "Negro Teachers in White Colleges." *School and Society,* 1947, *65,* 1691.

TAYLOR, M. W. *Amanda Smith, or the Life and Mission of a Slave Girl.* Cincinnati, Ohio: Crouston and Stowe, 1886.

THOMPSON, D. C. "The Teacher in the Negro College: A Sociological Analysis." Unpublished doctoral dissertation, Department of Sociology, Columbia University, 1956.

THOMPSON, D. C. *The Negro Leadership Class.* Englewood Cliffs, N.J.: Prentice Hall, 1963.

THOMPSON, W. *The Eighth Generation: Cultures and Personalities of New Orleans Negroes.* New York: Harper and Row, 1960.

TILLMAN, J. A., JR., and TILLMAN, M. N. "Black Intellectuals, White Liberals and Race Relations: An Analytic Overview." *Phylon,* Spring 1972, *33.*

Time Magazine, August 7, 1972a, 46–47.

Time Magazine, October 16, 1972b.

Trends in Educational Attainment of Women. Washington, D.C.: U. S. Department of Labor, 1969.

TROW, M. "Reflections on the Transition from Mass Education to Universal Higher Education." *Daedalus,* Winter 1970.

TURNER, D. T. "The Afro-American College in American Higher Education." Paper presented at the Faculty Conference, Benedict College, S. C., August 1968.

Twenty-two Years' Work of the Hampton, Virginia Normal and Agricultural Institute. Hampton, Va.: Hampton Institute, 1893.

"University Women's Rights: Whose Feet are Dragging?" *Science,* January 1972, *175.*

U. S. Department of Labor. *Handbook on Women Workers.* Women's Bureau Bulletin No. 294, 1969.

VAN DEN BERGHE, P. *Academic Gamesmanship.* New York: Abelard Schuman, 1970.

VAN DYNE, L. "Pressures to Limit Tenure Pose Hard Questions for Universities." *Chronicle of Higher Education,* January 29, 1973, 7 (17).

VRIEND, T. "High-Performing Inner-City Adolescents Assist Low-Performing Peers in Counseling Groups." *Personnel and Guidance Journal,* 1969, (47), 897–904.

WARD, S. H. and BRAUN, J. "Self-Esteem and Racial Preference in Black Children." *Journal of Orthopsychiatry,* 1972.

WARNATH, C. F. *New Myths and Old Realities.* San Francisco: Jossey-Bass, 1971.

WATTS, L. G. *The Middle Income Negro Families Face Urban Renewal.* Waltham, Mass.: Brandeis University, 1964.

WILCOX, P. R. "Education for Black Humanism: A Way of Approaching It." In *What Black Educators are Saying,* edited by Nathan Wright, Jr. New York: Hawthorn Books, 1970.

WILCOX, P. R. "The School and the Community." *CAP/School Semi-*

nar Papers. Trenton, N.J.: Community Action Training Institute, 1968.

WILEY, B. L. "A Different Breed of Administrator." *Phi Delta Kappan,* May 1971, *52* (9).

WILLIAMS, F. B. "A Northern Negro's Autobiography." *The Independent,* July 14, 1904, *57* (2902).

WILLIAMS, F. H. "The Black Crisis on the Campus." Jacob Ziskind Lecture, Smith College, Mass., April 18, 1969.

WILSON, L. *The Academic Man: Sociology of a Profession.* London: Oxford University Press, 1942.

WILSON, P. "IQ: The Racial Gap." *Psychology Today,* September 1972.

WINSTON, M. R. "Through the Back Door: Academic Racism and the Negro Scholar in Historical Perspective." *Daedalus,* Summer 1971, *100* (3), 678–719.

WISPE, L., AWKARD, J., HOFFMAN, M., ASH, P., HICKS, L. H., and PORTER, S. "The Negro Psychologists in America." *American Psychologist,* February 1969, 142–150.

WOODSON, C. G. *The Education of the Negro Prior to 1861.* New York: G. P. Putnam, 1915.

WRIGHT, A. D. *The Negro Rural School Fund (Anna Jeanes Foundation) 1907–1933.* Washington, D.C., 1933.

WRIGHT, N., JR. "Serving Black Students: For What?" *Journal of Afro-American Issues,* Fall 1972, *1* (2).

INDEX

A

Academic rank of black faculty, 4, 31, 147, 149-150, 192

Accreditation and blacks in professional organizations, 49

ADAMS, G., 174

Administrators, black: as "assistant to," 31, 99-129, 163, 171; authoritarianism of, 102-106; authority of, 125-129; backgrounds of, 115-119; black faculty as, 144-146; and black students, 107-108, 113; characteristics of, 99-106; frustrations of, 119-125; heading white institutions, 106, 182-184; isolation of, 30-31; number of, 5; women as, 163-167. *See also* Educators, black

Affirmative action, 72-98; history of, 73-74; opponents of, 74-85; Order No. 4 for, 80; results of, 195-196, 204-205. *See also* Discrimination

Africans, relationships of to black educators, 22-24

ALLEN, L., 171

ALTMAN, R. A., 110

American Association of University Professors, 41, 49, 58, 76, 80

ANDERSON, J., 96

Antiintellectualism, role of in education of blacks, 199-201

Apprenticeship programs, blacks underrepresented in, 184-185

ARTHUR, G. A., 160

Assistants, black: administrators as, 31, 99-129; as interpreters, 114-115; women as, 163, 171

ASTIN, H. S., 85, 170

Athletics, black coaches for, 140-141

ATWOOD, R. B., 13n

Authoritarianism of black presidents, 102-106

AWKARD, J., 57

B

BALLARD, A. B., 189, 195

BANFIELD, E., 14

BARATZ, J. C., 18-19

BARZUN, J., 50, 86, 147

BAYER, A. E., 85, 170

BEAL, F. M., 175

BELL, D., 85

BELLIS, A. G., 13n

BERNARD, J., 18

BETHUNE, M. MC L., 154n, 156, 160

221

Teaching: as criterion for employ-
ment, 86-87; as function of
black faculty, 137-141
Tenure: of black educators, 70-71;
of black faculty, 31, 152-153,
191-192
TERRELL, M. C., 154*n*
Texas, University of, 111
THOMPSON, C., 63
THOMPSON, D. C., 13*n*, 18, 49
THOMPSON, W., 18*n*
TILLERY, D., 181, 186
TILLMAN, J. A., JR., 196
TILLMAN, M. N., 196
TROW, M., 102, 112
Trustees, boards of, discrimination
by at two-year colleges, 179-181
TURNER, C. H., 197*n*
TURNER, D. T., 19
Two-year colleges: black educators
underrepresented in, 4-7, 29-
30, 179-182, 184-189, 192-
193; black studies in, 109-
110; black women promoted
in, 145; doctorates held in,
46; public school syndrome of,
179-183; ranking system in,
144, 149-150; recruitment of
nontraditional faculty by, 68;
teachers in from public
schools, 56

U

Unions, influence of on two-year
colleges, 185

V

VAN DEN BERGHE, P., 82, 86, 146-147
VAN DYNE, L., 70

VAUGHAN, C. O., 13*n*
VRIEND, T., 60

W

WARD, S. H., 17*n*
WARNATH, C. F., 60, 62
WATTS, L. G., 18
WILBUR, L., 179
WILCOX, P. R., 19, 21, 182
WILEY, B. L., 107-108
WILLIAMS, F. B., 158
WILLIAMS, F. H., 42
WILSON, L., 56
WILSON, P., 17*n*
WINSTON, M. R., 20, 42, 49, 63, 195,
196, 197
WISPE, L., 57
Women, black, 154-177; in administrative positions, 163-167;
career patterns of, 133, 167;
college trained, 53; compensation of, 145-146; curricular
developments by, 156-159; discrimination against, 170-173;
as faculty, 166-170; fields
teaching in, 138, 167; in full-
time positions, 150; promotions of in two-year colleges,
145; role of in black institutions, 155-161; roles of, 174-
177; student services developed by, 159-160; and white
women, compared, 161-163,
174-177
Women, discrimination against, 73,
84, 85-86, 92-94, 96-97
WOODSON, C. G., 63, 157
WRIGHT, A. D., 157
WRIGHT, N., JR., 112